Long regarded as "the forgotten people," the Chicanos, or Mexican-Americans, are finally emerging into the mainstream of our society. With new awareness of their roots, they are asserting their right to preservation of their rich cultural heritage, as well as to sociopolitical equality. This book is a representation of modern Chicano expression, which must be recognized as an important strand in the thread of American literary tradition.

WE ARE CHICANOS:

An Anthology of
Mexican-American Literature

Edited by **Philip D. Ortego,**
Assistant to the President and
Professor of Urban Studies,
Metropolitan State College,
Denver, Colorado

WASHINGTON SQUARE PRESS
POCKET BOOKS · NEW YORK

To Ruth, dear Ruth

WE ARE CHICANOS:
An Anthology of Mexican-American Literature

WASHINGTON SQUARE PRESS edition published July, 1973

L

Published by
**POCKET BOOKS, a division of Simon & Schuster, Inc.,
630 Fifth Avenue, New York, N.Y.**

WASHINGTON SQUARE PRESS editions are distributed
in the U.S. by Simon & Schuster, Inc., 630 Fifth Avenue,
New York, N.Y. 10020 and in Canada by Simon & Schuster of Canada, Ltd., Richmond Hill, Ontario, Canada.

ACKNOWLEDGMENTS AND COPYRIGHT NOTICES

"The Art of Mexican-America," by Jacinto Quirarte from *The
Humble Way,* Second Quarter, 1970. Reprinted by permission
of Exxon Co., U. S. A.

"Aztec Angel," by Luis Omar Salinas from *Crazy Gypsy* (Fresno,
Calif.: Fresno State College, 1970). Copyright © 1970 by
Luis Omar Salinas. Reprinted by permission of the author.

"The Cell of Heavenly Justice," by Arthur L. Campa from *The
New Mexico Quarterly Review* (August 1934). Reprinted by
permission of the author.

"Chicano Is an Act of Defiance," by Tino Villanueva, originally appeared in *Hay Otra Voz Poems* (New York: Colección Mensaje, 1972). Reprinted by permission of the author.

"Chicano Youth and the Politics of Protest," by Mario T. García. Printed by permission of the author.

"Count La Cerda's Treasure," by Nina Otero from *Old Spain in Our Southwest* (New York: Harcourt Brace Jovanovich, 1936). Copyright 1936 by Harcourt Brace Jovanovich, copyright renewed © 1964 by Nina Otero. Reprinted by permission.

"Crazy Gypsy," by Luis Omar Salinas from *Crazy Gypsy* (Fresno, Calif.: Fresno State College, 1970). Copyright © 1970 by Luis Omar Salinas. Reprinted by permission of the author.

"Cultural Heritage of the Southwest," lecture by Sabine R. Ulibarri. Printed by permission.

The Day of the Swallows, by Estella Portillo from *El Grito* (Spring, 1971). Reprinted by permission of the author.

"Don Tomás," by Jovita Gonzáles from "Among My People," *Southwest Review,* Winter, No. 2 (Dallas: Southern Methodist University). Copyright 1932 by *Southwest Review.* Reprinted by permission of *Southwest Review.*

"El Paso," by Ricardo Sánchez from *Canto y Grito Mi Liberación* (El Paso: Mictla Publications, 1971). Copyright © 1972 by Ricardo Sánchez. Reprinted by permission of the author.

"Escape," by Margarita Virginia Sánchez from *Regeneración,* Vol. I, No. 5. Reprinted by permission of *Regeneración.*

"Everybody Knows Tobie," by Daniel Garza from *Descant,* Vol. VII, No. 3, Spring 1963. Copyright © 1963 by *Descant,* the Literary Journal of Texas Christian University. Reprinted by permission of *Descant.*

"The Eyes of a Child," by Tomás Rivera. Copyright © 1972 by Tomás Rivera. Reprinted by permission of the author.

"Gentlemen of Rio en Medio," by Juan A. A. Sedillo from *The New Mexico Quarterly* (August 1939).

"Hasta La Victoria Siempre," by Raymundo Pérez from *Free, Free at Last.* Copyright © 1970 by Raymundo Pérez. Reprinted by permission of the author.

"Homage to the Greek," by Rafael Jesús González from *Interim,* Vol. I, No. 10. Reprinted by permission of the author.

"Hunchback Madonna," by Fray Angélico Chávez from *New Mexico Triptych* (New Jersey: St. Anthony Guild Press, 1940). Copyright 1940, © 1959 by Fray Angélico Chávez. Reprinted by permission of the author.

"incongruity," by Jane Limón from *Odes of March,* Vol. I, March 1965. Reprinted by permission of *Odes of March.*

"An Interview with Julián Samora," from *The National Elementary Principal,* November, 1970 (Washington, D. C.: NAESP/NEA). Copyright © 1970 by National Association of Elementary School Principals, National Education Association. Reprinted by permission of NAESP/NEA.

"I, Too, America," by Leo Romero from *Thunderbird,* Vol. XX, No. 2, 1971 (Albuquerque: The Associated Students of the University of New Mexico). Reprinted by permission of *Thunderbird.*

"Kiss of Death," by Armando Rendón from *Chicano Manifesto* (New York: Macmillan Co., 1971). Copyright © 1971 by Armando B. Rendón. Reprinted by permission of the Macmillan Co.

"La Causa," by Abelardo Delgado from *25 Pieces of a Chicano Mind* (Barrio Publications, 1972). Copyright © 1970 by Abelardo Delgado. Reprinted by permission of the author.

"La Raza," by Abelardo Delgado from *25 Pieces of a Chicano Mind* (Barrio Publications, 1972). Copyright © 1970 by Abelardo Delgado. Reprinted by permission of the author.

"La Raza," by Margarita Virginia Sánchez from *Regeneración,* Vol. I, No. 5. Reprinted by permission of *Regeneración.*

"La Tierra," by Abelardo Delgado from *25 Pieces of a Chicano Mind* (Barrio Publications, 1972). Copyright © 1970 by Abelardo Delgado. Reprinted by permission of the author.

"The Legend of Gregorio Cortez," by Américo Paredes from *"With His Pistol in His Hand": A Border Ballad and Its Hero* (Austin: University of Texas Press, 1958). Reprinted by permission.

"A Letter from Jail," by Reies López Tijerina from "Letter from Sante Fe Jail," in *El Grito del Norte* (Fairview, New Mexico). Reprinted by permission of the author.

"Life of a Bracero When Cotton Is in Season," by Jaime Calvillo from *ARX,* Vol. III, July 1969 (Austin, Texas: ARX Foundation). Reprinted by permission of the ARX Foundation.

"Los Caudillos," by Raúl Salinas. Appeared in *La Raza,* Vol. I, No. 4. Reprinted by permission of the author.

"Lupe's Dream," by Raymond Barrio from *The Plum Plum Pickers* (New York: Harper & Row Publishers, Inc., 1971). Copyright © 1969, 1971 by Raymond Barrio. Reprinted by permission of Harper & Row Publishers, Inc.

"The Meaning of the Chicano Movement," by Lydia R. Aguirre.

Appeared in *Social Case Work*, 1971. Reprinted by permission of the author.

"Message from García," by Philip D. Ortego. Copyright © 1972 by Philip D. Ortego. Printed by permission of the author.

"My Certain Burn Toward Pale Ashes," by Tino Villanueva, originally appeared in *Hay Otra Voz Poems* (New York: Colección Mensaje, 1972). Reprinted by permission of the author.

"Nag's Head, Cape Hatteras," by Javier Honda from *Desert Gold: An Anthology of Texas Western College Verse*, Joan Phelan Quarm and Rafael Jesús González, eds. (Texas Western College Press, 1964). Reprinted by permission of the author.

"Of Bronze the Sacrifice," by Nephtalí De León. Copyright © 1972 by Nephtalí De León. Printed by permission of the author.

"Open," by Elvira Gómez, from *Odes of March*, Vol. I, March 1965. Reprinted by permission of *Odes of March*.

"The Other Pioneers," by Roberto Félix Salazar. Appeared in *LULAC* (League of United Latin American Citizens) *News*, July 1939. Reprinted by permission of LULAC.

"The Oyster of the Green Gaze," by Rafael Jesús González from *Experiment*, Vol. VIII, No. 1-2. Reprinted by permission of the author.

"Past Possessions," by Tomás Rivera. Copyright © 1972 by Tomás Rivera. Reprinted by permission of the author.

"Profile: Rubén Salazar," by José Andrés Chacón from *The Minority No One Knows* (Potomac, Md.: José Andrés Chacón & Associates). Copyright © 1972 by José Andrés Chacón. Reprinted by permission of the author.

"Saltillo Mountains," by José Antonio Navarro. Appeared in *LULAC* (League of United Latin American Citizens) *News*, September 1940. Reprinted by permission of LULAC.

"Soundless Words," by Tomás Rivera. Copyright © 1972 by Tomás Rivera. Reprinted by permission of the author.

"Speak Up, Chicano," by Armando M. Rodríguez from *American Education*, May 1968. Reprinted by permission of the author.

"Stepchildren of a Nation," by George I. Sánchez adapted from *The Forgotten People* (Albuquerque: University of New Mexico Press). Copyright © 1940 by George I. Sánchez. Reprinted by permission of the author.

"Stupid America," by Abelardo Delgado from *25 Pieces of a Chicano Mind* (Barrio Publications, 1972). Copyright © 1970 by Abelardo Delgado. Reprinted by permission of the author.

"Suffer Little Children," by Georgia Cobos. Appeared in *El Grito,* Summer 1969. Reprinted by permission of the author.

"Tales from San Elizario," by Josefina Escajeda from *Puro Mejicano,* Frank Dobie, editor (Austin: the University of Texas Press Society, 1935). Reprinted by permission of the Texas Folklore Society.

"to a child," by Ricardo Sánchez from *Obras* (Pembroke, N. C.: Quetzal-Vihio Press, 1971). Copyright © 1971 by Ricardo Sánchez. Reprinted by permission of the author.

"To an Old Woman," by Rafael Jesús González from *New Mexico Quarterly,* Vol. XXXI, No. 4. Reprinted by permission of the author.

"Toward a History of the Mexican-American," by Feliciano Rivera from *A Guideline for the Study of the Mexican-American People in the United States* (San Francisco: Fearone Press, 1969). Reprinted by permission of the author.

"A Trip Through the Mind Jail," by Raúl Salinas. Appeared in *Entrelineas,* Vol. I, No. 3. Reprinted by permission of the author.

"22 Miles," by José Angel Gutiérrez from *El Grito* (Spring 1968). Reprinted by permission of the author.

"vision," by Ricardo Sánchez from *Canto y Grito Mi Liberación* (El Paso: Mictla Publications, 1971). Copyright © 1972 by Ricardo Sánchez. Reprinted by permission of the author.

"When Love to Be?," by Tomás Rivera. Copyright © 1972 by Tomás Rivera. Reprinted by permission of the author.

CONTENTS

4 · VOICES AND THE MOVEMENT

Part II

THE CREATIVE SPIRIT

5 · POETRY

CONTENTS

6 · DRAMA

7 · FICTION

GLOSSARY

SUGGESTED FURTHER READING

Among the valiant (Héctor Melgoza)

PREFACE

Chicanos, Mejicanos, Hispanos, Mexican-Americans, Latin Americans—whatever they call themselves, they share in common the travails and miseries of isolation, alienation, neglect, and such a cultural oppression that a National Education Association survey as recent as 1966 labeled them "the invisible minority." In his book, published in 1940, Dr. George I. Sánchez called them "forgotten people." And though they have been part of the American scene since long before the arrival of the Anglo-American in the Southwest, they are treated and regarded, as Rubén Salazar put it, as "strangers in their own land."

This ethnic group constitutes the second largest minority in the United States, ranging in population from 8 to 10 million people, by conservative estimates, to upwards of 12 million people, depending on who is doing the counting. Linguistically, Spanish ranks next to English as the most used language in the United States. But despite these facts, Hispano-Americans in the United States—Chicanos, Puerto Ricans, Cubans, and other Spanish and Spanish-Americans—are, some of their spokesmen have suggested, "the best-kept secret in the United States."

Chicanos comprise more than 90 percent of this Spanish-speaking (Hispanic-American) population of the United States and, unlike their Puerto Rican and Cuban brethren, have a distinct and longer continental history which has been part and parcel of the American experience, despite its omission in the literary and historical descriptions of the United States. The history of the American Southwest is inextricably part of the historical fabric of the Chicano. Yet until recently the life and literature of the Southwest reflected only the Anglo-American pioneer tradition, the Chicano and his kin lost in the desert landscape.

This neglect of Chicanos has been the product of many attitudes, including national myopia, literary and linguistic chauvinism, jingoism, and ignorance, not to mention outright discrimination, prejudice, and racism. There is growing evidence, however, that this neglect is ending. Not because of any change of heart on the part of Anglo-America but because of Chicanos themselves who are insisting unequivocally on change right now!

Who are these people, these Chicanos who have suddenly vaulted into the national limelight? Demographically they are Americans of Mexican ancestry. Religiously they are predominantly Catholic. And politically they have been as disenfranchised as the blacks, although traditionally they have been identified as Democrats. Realizing that neither major political party in the United States has responded to their needs, Chicanos have more recently formed their own political party, "La Raza Unida," and have already made significant political gains where the Raza Unida has challenged the traditional political structure and machine. Ideologically Chicanos are uniting behind what they call the Chicano movement with its tenets of *chicanismo* and *carnalismo*. The former is a recognition of their socio-political and cultural emergence as a potent force for change in American society; the latter is the spirit of a brotherhood that binds them ineluctably one to the other, regardless of their position or station in life.

The Chicano is to the Mexican-American as the black is to the Afro-American: he represents a higher level of consciousness in the evolving quest for identity. And just as there are Americans of African ancestry who prefer to identify themselves as Negroes, so too there are Americans of Mexican ancestry who prefer to identify themselves as Hispanos. Like the blacks, Chicanos have come to grips with their racial identity and, like the blacks, articulate the concept of "brown is beautiful."

Many Chicanos see themselves as the mediating force in the black–white conflict. Although classified as whites, Chicanos regard themselves as members of the Third World. Unfortunately, however, since Chicanos are classified as white, some school systems have used them as a means of complying with integration mandates by mixing them with blacks. The result has been simply a continuation of the same kind of unequal education both groups received separately, only now it is under the legal aegis of "integration."

Invariably, the question arises as to the meaning of the word "Chicano." And while there are many suggestions, no one is really sure of the origin of the word. Some explanations ascribe the word to Nahuatl origin, suggesting that the Indians pronounced "Mexicano" as "Me-shi-ca-noh," and that in time the soft "shi" was replaced by the hard "chi." Other explanations suggest the word is a mixture of two words containing elements of each, such as "smog" resulting from the words "smoke" + "fog." Such words have been "Chihuahua" + "Mexicano"; "Chicago" + "Mexicano"; "chico" + "ano," etc. Despite the tenuous origin of the word "Chicano" it continues to gain ground in the identification of Americans of Mexican ancestry as it gains in usage. Mexican-Americans from all walks of life use the word interchangeably with the word "Mexican-American" to mean an American of Mexican ancestry.

While this anthology does not attempt a comprehensive survey of the development and backgrounds of Mexican-American literature, it does nevertheless provide a well-balanced selection from modern and contemporary Mexican-American writers whose literary attitudes bear importantly on contemporary Chicano writers. At once readers will comprehend the Hispanic literary consciousness of writers like Josefina Escajeda and Jovita González whose works reflect their existence as simply extensions of Mexican life. By juxtaposition writers like Armando Rendón, Raúl Salinas, and Mario T. García reflect a literary consciousness drawing from both the American and the Hispanic literary traditions, reflecting their existence as the point of contact in a cultural conflict that seeks to refashion them with the apparatus and mentality of American culture.

The introduction and commentaries preceding the various categories of this anthology are intended to provide the reader with the essential backdrop necessary for a fuller understanding of the selections included therein. The scope of the anthology is both thematic and generic rather than historical or chronological. A good many of the writers are young people, and a genuine effort was made to keep a balance between men and women authors, for the essence of Chicano liberation lies equally in the liberation of the Chicano woman——La Chicana!

We Are Chicanos: An Anthology of Mexican-American Literature is designed both as a text for classroom use and as a general introduction to the long neglected body of Mexican-American literature which needs desperately to be incorporated into the body of American literature if that body is to truly reflect the American experience.

There are many people to thank in the preparation of this work. To all of them *muchísimas gracias y que viva la raza!*

PHILIP D. ORTEGO

INTRODUCTION

Like Anglo-American literature, the roots of Mexican-American literature extend back into the history and culture of the diverse peoples who were their progenitors. Most Anglo-American literary historians begin their account of American literature with the arrival of the British in Virginia, usually citing John Smith's letters as the beginning of the American literary tradition. Occasionally an Anglo-American literary historian has given appropriate lip service to the Spanish enterprise in America by citing first the letters of Columbus to the King of Spain as the earliest efforts of a literary tradition which soon became British in every respect.

The unfortunate consequences, as Professor Thomas M. Pearce correctly pointed out as long ago as 1942, in his article "American Traditions and Our Histories of Literature" (in *American Literature,* November, 1942), is that "the English tradition, as it is carried on by the English language, has made few concessions to other elements in the literary history of this country." Few Americans today really understand the fullness of what American literature should have been: that is, a literary fabric not exclusively woven on the Atlantic frontier by the descendants of New England Puritans and Southern Cavaliers, but one woven in the American Southwest as well, and with marvelous Hispanic threads which reach back not only to the literary heritage of the European continent but also the very heart of the Graeco-Roman world.

Like the British roots in the new American soil, the Hispanic literary roots have yielded a vigorous and dynamic body of literature which unfortunately has been studied historically as part of a foreign enterprise rather than as part and parcel of our American heritage. The reason advanced has been that such works are not properly within the traditional Anglo-American definition of American literature. Linguistic chauvinism has been the principal reason for the exclusion of the Spanish-language literature of the United States from the corpus of American literature, although, as Professor Pearce concluded, "language does not seem to be a logical bar to recognition of non-English material as literature of the United States."

In the pluralistic cultural and linguistic context of contemporary American society we can no longer consent to accept unquestioningly arbitrary criteria about the parameters of American literature nor can we accept without comment the contention that American literature begins properly with the arrival of British colonials in America. The fact of the matter is that American literature actually begins with the formation of the United States as a political entity. Thus, the literary period from the founding of the first permanent British settlement at Jamestown, Virginia, in 1607 to the formation of the American Union, properly speaking, represents the British period of American literature. So, too, the literary period from the first permanent Spanish settlement at Saint Augustine, Florida, in 1565, to the dates of acquisition of Spanish and Mexican lands by the United States should, in fact, represent the Hispanic period of American literature. And properly speaking, Mexican-American literature begins in 1848, the date the United States acquired the Mexican land in the Southwest as a result of the Mexican-American War and the Treaty of Guadalupe-Hidalgo.

Instead of gaining fuller comprehension of the ethnic phenomenon of Mexican-Americans in the personal context of their literature, what we have seen has been the myriad educational, socio-political, and socio-economic accounts by Anglo investigators and researchers.

Like other minority groups, Mexican-Americans were,

and continue to be, inaccurately and superficially represented in literature, movies, TV, and other mass media. This has sometimes been due to prejudice, but also to those "well-meaning romanticists" who have seriously distorted the image of the Mexican-American for the sake of their art. Mexican-Americans have been characterized at both ends of a spectrum of human behavior (seldom in the middle) as untrustworthy, villainous, ruthless, tequila-drinking, philandering *machos,* or else as courteous, devout, and fatalistic peasants who are to be treated more as pets than people. More often than not, Mexicans have been cast as either bandits or lovable rogues; as hot-blooded, sexually animated creatures or passive, humble servants.

So deep is the lack of attention to the Mexican-American literary heritage that few of the 10 million Mexican-Americans themselves are aware of its existence as an organic body. For a people whose origins antedate the establishment of the United States by well over a century (and more, considering their Indian ancestry), this bespeaks a shameful and tragic negligence. And the shame and tragedy are compounded when Mexican-American youngsters learn about their Puritan forebears at the expense of their Hispanic forebears about whom they have as much right—if not more—to be proud.

Like black American writers, Mexican-American writers have been the victims of systematic discrimination and neglect based in large part on the mistaken notion that the American reading public would not be interested in the Mexican-American writer. Besides, how many wrote in English? Many—for the Mexican-American writer soon became bilingual and biliterate. However, over a hundred years of neglect have produced unfortunate literary consequences for Mexican-Americans and have left Anglo-Americans completely ignorant about the Mexican-American literary tradition.

Heretofore, Mexican-Americans have been a marginal people in a sort of no-man's-land, who, like Hamlet crawling between heaven and earth, have been caught between the polarizing forces of their cultural-linguistic Hispanic heritage and their political-linguistic American context. They have become frustrated and alienated by the struggle between the system which seeks to refashion them in its own image and the knowledge of who and what they really are. As a consequence, this cultural conflict has debilitated the Mexican-American. For as Francisco Ríos writes in "The Mexican in Fact, Fiction, and Folklore," in *El Grito: A Journal of Contemporary Mexican-American Thought* (Summer, 1969), Mexican-American youngsters "read of the cruelty of the Spaniard toward the Indians, of the Spaniard's greed for gold, of the infamous Spanish, always Spanish, Inquisition, of Mexican bandits, and of the massacre at the Alamo." They seldom if ever "learn that alongside the famous men at the Alamo there were other men, unknown and unsung heroes of American history, killed in the same battle and fighting on the Texas side; men like Juan Abamillo, Juan Badillo, Carlos Espalier, Gregorio Esparza, Antonio Fuentes, José María Guerrero, Toribio Losoya, Andrés Nava," and others.

Only recently have the Mexican-Americans received any kind of significant attention in this country. This is notwithstanding the fact that Mexican-Americans constitute the second largest minority group in the United States, and that outside of the speakers of English they constitute the single largest linguistic group in America. Most Mexican-Americans live in the five-state area of Texas, New Mexico, Colorado, Arizona, and California, with the largest single concentration in Los Angeles. But there are Mexican-Americans throughout most of the United States, from Washington to Florida, and from California to Maine. Almost two million Mexican-Americans are to be found in the Ohio Valley crescent from Madison, Wisconsin, to Erie, Pennsylvania.

In the greater sense of the word, Mexican-Americans have always been "Americans," more so than Anglo-Americans. For Mexican-Americans are not "transplanted" Americans; they were here before the Puritans, before the Dutch, before the Irish and the Italians, before the Poles, before the Hungarians. They were, as Carey McWilliams put it, in his book *North from Mexico,* very much a part of the landscape when the Anglo-American arrived. Yet despite this and their size in numbers, Mexican-Americans have been the most shamefully neglected minority in the United States. In the Southwest where approximately seven million of them live, they subsist on levels of survival well below national norms. But the reason for this, many Mexican-Americans argue, is that they are victims of the Treaty of Guadalupe-Hidalgo, a treaty which identified those who came with the conquered lands of the Southwest as a defeated people. And those who came afterwards in the great migrations of the early 1900s have been equally victimized by stereotypes engendered by the Mexican-American War. The consequence in recent years has been an increasing social and political consciousness to the point of demanding reformation of the socio-economic structure which has kept them subordinated these many years. And with this increasing social and political consciousness has come also the awareness of their literary heritage.

The decade of the '60s has seen the renaissance of the Mexican-American, and the decade of the '70s promises to be one in which this renaissance will exert an ever-growing awareness in Mexican-Americans not only in terms of creative efforts in drama, fiction, and poetry but in terms of seeking a more substantial literary identity in the ever-widening mainstream of American literature.

While this anthology deals with fairly modern and contemporary Mexican-American writers, it will show—I hope—that Mexican-Americans have indeed contributed to American letters in substantial measure. We cannot undo what has been done to the Mexican-American in American literature, but we can take steps in a new direction.

Part I

PERSPECTIVES

1 • BACKGROUNDS

There is no accurate count of the number of Mexicans residing in the northern Mexican states at the time the territory was ceded to the United States, nor is there any accurate count of the number who decided to stay and become citizens. According to the terms of the Treaty of Guadalupe-Hidalgo in 1848 and of the Gadsden Treaty of 1853, "Mexican citizens living in the area were given the choice of returning to Mexico under no penalty or tax, or of remaining and becoming American citizens automatically after one year, following the ratification of the treaty. Property rights were to be respected during the interim period and all rights of citizenship were conferred upon those who elected to stay." Most of the Mexican settlers decided to stay, taking advantage of the provisions of the treaty or else becoming citizens by default.

After the Mexican-American War, immigration from Mexico to the United States increased steadily until the end of the nineteenth century, first as a consequence of the French occupation of Mexico in the 1860s, then as a result of the police-state repression of the presidential dictator, Porfirio Díaz. But the great waves of immigration to the United States were not to come until after the turn of the century when Porfirismo became unbearable and the Mexican Revolution turned Mexico into an armed camp, impoverishing the nation and driving *los de abajo* (the oppressed) to seek a "better" life elsewhere. Of course, travel across the Mexican-American border either way was rather easy until the 1920s.

The Mexican-American border, devoid of really natural barriers, has been described as "an immense frontier

3

varying in length, with changing boundaries, from more than three thousand to less than two thousand miles." Indeed, in places the boundaries are nothing more than a line staked out by markers, a barbed-wire fence, or an almost dry river bed during certain seasons, supporting an undergrowth of chaparral and mesquite. And for the most part, Mexicans and Americans have crossed back and forth with relative ease. Mexicans settled easily in the Southwest, in surroundings not unlike those of their homeland. Unlike European immigrants, Mexicans were really emigrating to an area which had once been part of Mexico and which was still inhabited by the descendants of those Mexicans who came with the conquered land.

All in all, Mexican-Americans were regarded poorly by the vast majority of Anglo-Americans who came into contact with them, and many of the literary portraits of Mexican-Americans by Anglo-American writers were to unduly influence generations of Americans down to our own time. Disparaging images of Mexican-Americans by Easterners were reinforced by such American writers as Richard Henry Dana who in *Two Years Before the Mast,* published in 1840, described the soon-to-be Mexican-Americans as "an idle, thriftless people" who could "make nothing for themselves." And in 1852 Colonel Monroe reported to Washington that "The New Mexicans are thoroughly debased and totally incapable of self-government, and there is no latent quality about them that can ever make them respectable." He continued, "They have more Indian blood than Spanish, and in some respects are below the Pueblo Indians, for they are not as honest or as industrious."

Four years later W. W. H. Davis, United States Attorney for the Territory of New Mexico, wrote à propos his experiences with Mexican-Americans that "they possess the cunning and deceit of the Indian, the politeness and the spirit of revenge of the Spaniard, and the imaginative temperament and fiery impulses of the moor." He describes them as smart and quick but lacking the "stability and character and soundness of intellect that give such vast superiority to the Anglo-Saxon race over every other people." He ascribed to them the "cruelty, bigotry, and superstition" of the Spaniard, "a marked characteristic from earliest times." Moreover, he saw these traits as "constitutional and innate in the race." In a moment of kindness, though, Davis suggested that the fault lay no doubt on their "spiritual teachers," the Spaniards, that is, who never taught them "that beautiful doctrine which teaches us to love our neighbors as ourselves."

What most characterized the post-Civil War period in the Southwest was the quest for statehood by the territories of Colorado, Utah, Nevada, Arizona, and New Mexico. The admission of Texas into the Union in 1846, of course, precipitated the Mexican-American War. While the events of the Mexican-American War have been variously interpreted (see, for example, Ramón E. Ruiz, *The Mexican War: Was It Manifest Destiny?*), essentially those events include what President Polk called Mexican provocation on Texas soil and the Mexican response to what it regarded as simply an American scheme to annex the self-proclaimed republic of Texas which Mexico still regarded as part of its national territory. In May, 1846, President Polk sent a message to Congress claiming Mexicans had spilled American blood on American soil (Texas), since it had already annexed Texas in 1845. Mexico thus lost not only Texas but almost half of her national territory by the terms of the Treaty of Guadalupe-Hidalgo in 1848. But the fact of statehood allowed Texas a measure of "progress" which was not realized in the parts of the acquired territories until later in the nineteenth and twentieth centuries. California, like Texas, reaped the benefits of statehood early in 1850. And while Colorado became a state in 1876, Utah in 1896, Oklahoma in 1907, Arizona and New Mexico did not become states until 1912. The delay has been attributed to the fact that the preponderance of Mexican-Americans made statehood unpalatable to the rest of the nation. In fact, Senator Albert Beveridge's committee report for the minority as late as 1902 objected to statehood for the New Mexico Territory on the grounds that "the majority of people in New Mexico were Spanish, and a large percentage of the people could speak only their native tongue, necessitating such practices as the use of interpreters in court proceedings."

Throughout the Southwest Mexican-Americans were the butt of injustice after injustice, and their lands, though supposedly secured by the Treaty of Guadalupe-Hidalgo, were craftily secured by squatters, shyster lawyers, and con artists who shamelessly bilked them because of their disadvantage with the English language. In 1877, for example, an Anglo-American purchased for fifteen dollars from the sheriff of Hidalgo County in Texas 3,027 acres of land confiscated from a Mexican-American for back taxes.

Against this background emerged the rags-to-riches mystique which was to influence American life well into the twentieth century. Horatio Alger's characters, Tattered Tom, Ragged Dick, and Phil the Fiddler, became the American standard for success via hard work. In contradistinction to this tradition stood the Mexican-American who was thought of as indolent and afraid of hard work. A Mexican-American's "wealth" was judged as the product of connivance rather than of fortitude and application. When, for example, by 1865, the Mexican-American Lugo family of southern California lost its wealth, Benjamin Hayes quickly suggested that it was the finger of Providence which was responsible for the decay of the Mexican-Americans.

Even Mariano Vallejo, last of the military governors of Mexican California and a man who most eagerly welcomed the American takeover, asked bitterly in his old age, "What has the . . . government done for the Californians since the victory over Mexico? Have they kept the promises with which they deluded us? I do not ask for miracles; I am not and never have been exacting; I do not demand gold, a pleasing gift only to abject peoples. But I ask and I have a right to ask for an answer" (cited in W. Storrs Lee [ed.], *California: A Literary Chronicle*). The question was unanswered, and it was to be asked again by George I. Sánchez in 1940 in his work *Forgotten People*. Professor Sánchez raised the question again in

1967 with the reissue of *Forgotten People*. He wrote sadly, "In those distant younger days, though I did not ignore reality, I did harbor a modicum of optimism. Maybe, somehow, the forgotten people of my homeland would be remembered and redeemed. Maybe as the nation grew more affluent, and wiser perhaps, it would roll back the pages of history and pay the long overdue debt it incurred when it forced itself on my people. I had hopes, though very slim ones, that, at the very least, a repentant nation would help us lift ourselves by our bootstraps. Instead, it took away our boots."

In seeking to assert his literary heritage, the modern Mexican-American writer must confront foursquare the question of the Mexican-American War and its consequences on the psyche of the Mexican-American. Moreover, the modern Mexican-American writer has sought to dispel the mistaken Anglo-American notions about Mexican-Americans which have resulted in their socio-economic, political, and literary suppression. While George Sánchez had the courage to raise the question of Mexican-American rights, Sabine Ulibarri and Jacinto Quirarte express the positive considerations of the Mexican-American heritage. Feliciano Rivera addresses himself to the necessity of writing a "real" history of the United States, eighty-some years after Charles Lummis had expressed a similar need.

"Stepchildren of a Nation" (Héctor Melgoza)

George I. Sánchez

George I. Sánchez was professor of International Education at the University of Texas at Austin until his death early in 1972. Dr. Sánchez was in the forefront of securing civil rights for Chicanos, starting with his definitive study, *Forgotten People: A Study of New Mexicans*. Since 1940 *Forgotten People,* from which the following selection was excerpted, has become a cornerstone in the development of the Chicano movement.

STEPCHILDREN OF A NATION

> We come among you for your benefit, not for your injury.
> —Kearny, August 15, 1846

With these words, General Stephen Watts Kearny addressed the people of Las Vegas as he took possession in the name of the United States. Four days later he told the assembled populace at Santa Fe: "We come as friends, to better your condition . . . I am your governor—henceforth look to me for protection."

The common people of New Mexico did not, of course, comprehend the true significance of these words.

There were those among the New Mexicans, however, who appreciated the meaning of the events of the American Occupation. They were educated, knew of the outside world, had visited in Mexico, and had traded with the American settlements and outposts. They were aware that, under the American democracy, the condition of the New Mexican could be improved. They appreciated the promise of a new day. They were not unwilling that New Mexicans should become Americans.

The years immediately following the American Occupation proved disappointing. For five years the people of the region were denied territorial government. Civil and mil-

9

itary powers became hopelessly entangled. The judiciary established by the military was, in some instances, of doubtful competence and integrity. Army officials and their appointees exceeded their authority, violated their instructions from Washington, and were active in factional political movements.

After the treaty of peace in 1848, and until the organization of territorial government in 1851, the administration of public affairs in New Mexico was in turmoil. The region was neither territory nor state. Not only were Mexican laws not in force but the Congress of the United States had failed to provide for the regulation of the affairs of New Mexicans.

A populace, ignorant of modern ways, was thrown into a situation which would task the most enlightened societies. Centuries behind the times, without a democratic tradition, unaware of their rights and status, and incapable of voicing their views and feelings, they became cannon fodder for political guns.

The tragedy of this introduction was not solely a civic one. The opening of the area to American commerce opened the door to economic competition of a scale, and on a basis, far beyond the comprehension of the natives. Business relationships, legal technicalities, and sharp practices soon began to take their toll of the economic resources of the people. Urged to exercise their rights as free citizens, they, in their ignorance, entered into agreements which lost them their birthright.

Ruthless politicians and merchants acquired their stock, their water rights, their land. The land grants became involved in legal battles. Was a grant genuine, was it tax-free, was it correctly administered, was it registered? Who were the grantees, who the descendants, where the boundaries, and by whose authority? Defenseless before the onslaught of an intangible yet superior force, the economic foundations of New Mexican life were undermined and began to crumble. As their economy deteriorated so did the people, for their way of life was based on, and identified with, the agrarian economy which they had built through many generations.

Far-seeing leaders sought to bring about reforms that would stem the tide of political and economic regression. The memorable address of Governor Donaciano Vigil to the first Legislative Assembly (1847) indicates that native leaders had envisioned a plan for the incorporation of the New Mexican into the American fold. On that occasion he advocated reforms that would safeguard public revenues, that would protect the Indian, and that would give the small farmer adequate water rights. Above everything, he was interested in education for his people. This abiding faith in education he shared with other leaders such as Father Antonio Martínez.

Before 1890, there were virtually no public schools in the territory, and education had been left largely to private and church endeavor. In 1853, the Sisters of Loretto had opened at Santa Fe the Academy of Our Lady of Light, which, by 1890, had had a maximum enrollment of fifty boarders. During that period, this order opened several other boarding schools for girls elsewhere in the territory and, in connection with them, accepted a few day-students. The Christian Brothers had established the College of San Miguel in Santa Fe in 1859. In connection with this boarding school the brothers carried on a free day-school where, through the years, several hundred children received instruction. Later, they opened the La Salle Institute at Las Vegas and a school in Bernalillo. In 1892, these schools enrolled about 350 children. These schools, together with a few other small, private and denominational centers, constituted the chief educational institutions for the first forty years after the Treaty of Guadalupe-Hidalgo. To them came students from over the territory, from Arizona, Texas, Colorado, and Mexico.

After 1890, considerable progress was made in establishing public schools. Nevertheless, this progress was purely relative. As late as 1903, more than half of the school population was not in attendance in any school.

Though Congress made grants of land to the territory for educational purposes, the national government never made due recognition of its responsibilities to the native people of the region it acquired from Mexico. It failed to take note of the fact that those people were, in effect, subject peoples of a culture and a way of life radically different from that into which they were suddenly and unwittingly thrust by a treaty. The government also failed to appreciate the fact that the territory lacked the economic resources, the leadership, and the administrative devices necessary to launch an effective program of cultural rehabilitation.

Child of the barrio (Héctor Melgoza)

What has been said of education can be said with equal or greater force about other public services intended to raise the cultural level of a society. Health programs, the administration of justice, economic competition and development, the exercise of suffrage, land use and management—the vital aspects of the social and economic incorporation of a people were left up to the doubtful ministrations of improvised leadership. The New Mexican was placed at the mercy of those political and economic forces, of those vested interests, that could control the machinery of local government. In an area of cultural unsophistication and of economic inadequacy, he was expected to lift himself up by his own bootstraps.

Whereas the adoption of the New Mexican has been a casual matter for the United States, the New Mexican quickly and wholeheartedly accepted his foster parent. The American Occupation took place without the firing of a shot and without any bloodshed or disturbance whatsoever. The abortive revolt at Taos in 1847 can be attributed to a few malcontents who did not have the sympathies of the native leaders of the masses. The response made by New Mexico during the Civil War showed the loyalty of the people to the central government. The temper of that loyalty is best illustrated by the words of Colonel Manuel Antonio Chávez, a truly great Indian-fighter, frontiersman, and soldier of the West. On being offered a commission in the Confederate Army, he said: "When I took the oath of allegiance to the United States, I swore to protect the American flag, and if my services are needed I shall give them to the country of my adoption and her flag."

The Spanish-American War, and the World War likewise, gave New Mexicans an opportunity to evidence their loyalty. In the World War, New Mexico had more volunteers per capita than any other state. Sixty percent of these volunteers were of Spanish descent. As a matter of fact, New Mexico had so many volunteers that there were not enough able-bodied citizens left to fill the draft quota!

Thus have an humble people reacted to their adoption. Loyal and uncomplaining, they have sought to carry on in the face of forces beyond their ken. In view of the cir-

cumstances already referred to, it is not to wonder that
they have been unable to span completely the cultural and
economic gap between their traditional way of life and
modern America. The progress that has been made serves
but to suggest the levels that might have been attained had
a neglectful parent been more considerate of her children
—stepchildren that the nation adopted through treaty.

Sabine R. Ulibarri

Sabine R. Ulibarri is professor of Modern Languages at the University
of New Mexico in Albuquerque. His most recent book is *La Fragua
Sin Fuego* published by San Marcos Press. Among his many works
is the poignant collection of stories about *Tierra Amarilla* which has
recently been reissued by the University of New Mexico Press.

CULTURAL HERITAGE OF THE SOUTHWEST

In the beginning was the Word. And the Word was made
flesh. It was so in the beginning, and it is so today. The
language, the Word, carries within it the history, the culture, the traditions, the very life of a people, the flesh.
Language is people. We cannot even conceive of a people
without a language, or a language without a people. The
two are one and the same. To know one is to know the
other.

We are gathered here to consider this dual unity, this
single quality: a people and their language, in danger of
coming apart. This threatened split infinitive has become
a national problem. A wedge has been driven between the
Hispano and his language. As a result the Hispano is
floundering in confusion, and his language is dying on the
vine. A dynamic and aggressive Anglo culture has come
between him and his past and is uprooting him from the

soil, cutting him off from his ancestors, separating him from his own culture. Very little is being done to facilitate his transition from the culture of his ancestors, whose voice is silent, to the culture of the majority, whose voice makes his laws and determines his destiny. As his language fades, the Hispano's identity with a history, with a tradition, with a culture, becomes more nebulous with each passing day. His identity as an Anglo is not yet in sight. There is no assurance that such an identity is possible, or even desirable. A man is what he is, and if he isn't that, he isn't anything. In terms of the national interest, our greatest natural resources are our human differences, and it behooves us to cultivate those differences. It is one thing to homogenize milk; it is quite another thing to homogenize the citizenry. It would appear, therefore, that a loyal, productive, and effective Hispano citizen, proud of what he is and of what he has to give, has more to offer his country than a de-hispanized, disoriented Anglo with a dark skin, a mispronounced name, and a guilty conscience to boot.

From the standpoint of the preservation of our natural resources, every attempt must be made to save the Spanish language. It is the instrument that will make the English language available to the Spanish-speaking child through well-trained bilingual teachers. The voice of America must be multilingual if it is to be understood around the world. The best bilinguals in Spanish and English are coming out of the Spanish-speaking Southwest. This human resource, which our government and industry are utilizing most effectively, must not be allowed to dry up. For better or for worse our destiny is inextricably interwoven with the destiny of our Spanish-speaking friends to the south.

If we wish to hold on to the cultural heritage of the Southwest, we must preserve the Spanish language. If the language goes, the culture goes with it. This is precisely the spiritual crisis of the minorities of the United States. They are losing their native languages, and with the language they are losing a certain consciousness of their own existence. They are losing something of their vital polarity, something of their identity. They find themselves somewhat uprooted, somewhat disoriented. A manner of being a way of life, forged slowly since the beginning of history is lost with the loss of the language. Until a new consciousness, a new manner of being, is forged through and by the newly acquired language, these minorities will remain somewhat disoriented.

It is all a matter of language. It is a matter of economics. It is a matter of rural versus urban societies. Hispano children speak Spanish. Most of them are poor. Many of them live in the country. Many have recently moved to the city. Consequently, they are predestined to failure, frustration, and academic fatigue in our national public schools.

The Hispano child begins with a handicap the very first day he shows up in the first grade. English is the language of the classroom. He speaks no English, or he speaks inadequate English. The whole program is designed to make him an Anglo. He doesn't want to become an Anglo, or he doesn't know how. He comes from a father-dominated home and finds himself in a female-dominated classroom. The Anglo concepts and values that govern and prevail are unintelligible to him. In all likelihood he comes from a low social and economic class, and there he is in an Anglo middle class environment. Much too frequently he is fresh out of the country, and the city in general, and the school in particular, might just as well be on another planet. He probably feels very uncomfortable and self-conscious in the unfamiliar clothes he's wearing. He looks about him. The teacher, far from representing a mother image, must seem to him a remote and awe-inspiring creature. The children around him, so friendly with one another and so much at ease, look at him with suspicion. There is nothing in the atmosphere from which he can draw any comfort. Everything he sees is foreign. The climate of sound is confusing and frightening. The Hispano kid, José Pérez, finds himself in a hostile environment indeed. He will never, ever, forget this day, and this day will influence everything he does from then on. So the very first day in school, before he comes up to bat, he has two strikes against him. Before the coin is tossed, he has a penalty of a hundred yards against him. He has to be something very special, a star, a hero, in order to win.

Amazingly enough, he does much better in the primary grades than one would expect. It is later when he gets into deep trouble. In the primary grades the language of the classroom is primarily what the linguists call "sign language," that is, the kind of language a dog would understand: "stand up," "sit down," "go to the blackboard," "open your books," "let's sing." The Hispano kid falls behind in the first grade, but not too much; his intuition and native intelligence keep him afloat.

Each successive year he falls farther behind, and as time goes on, as the language becomes more abstract and more transparent, the gap of deficiency becomes wider and wider—until he becomes a drop-out. We hear a great deal about the high school drop-out. We are going to hear more and more about the university drop-out. Imagine if you will the young Hispano with his high school diploma in his hot little hand who appears at the university. He's highly motivated, eager, and full of illusions. He has been more successful than most. His family is very proud of him. He is going to be a somebody. Then comes the shock. He finds out. He doesn't know how to read! His teachers never taught him how to read. How could they? They didn't know Spanish. They didn't understand his culture. No teacher can teach a second language effectively without knowing the native language of her students and understanding their culture. So the kid is suspended. No one can blame him if he feels cheated, betrayed, and frustrated. He earned that high school diploma in good faith, and he put in more than the normal effort to earn it. And a valuable asset to our society is lost in anger and despair.

Education is the answer. School boards, school administrators, and teachers must stop wringing their hands, or looking the other way, hoping the problems will vanish. They must face the issue and seek educational and social solutions. Admittedly, the problem is bigger than they are. Let them confess it. Then let them find the answers and the advice they need, outside the college of education if that is where they are to be found. Hispano parents must

"The Hispano should be educated in his own culture. . . .

learn to place their confidence and cooperation in the
schools. Employers must be educated too. They must find
out that discrimination is detrimental to them and to the
nation they profess to serve.

Above all, the Hispano should be educated in his own
culture, his own history, his own contribution to the life-
stream of his country. An American citizen of Jewish ex-
and brighter *mañana*. If he's got the stuff he'll make it
himself, to his people, and to the United States than one
who is not. An Hispano who doesn't speak Spanish must
choke on his chile. But before anyone can be proud of
being an Hispano or a Jew, or anything else, one must be
proud of being a human being. This is not easy in the
poverty puddles in which many an Hispano exists in a
subhuman level, according to American standards, his
grace, dignity, and pride eroded by more than a hundred
years of privation, denial, and dishonor. This nation can

(Salvador Valdez, courtesy of *Nosotros* Magazine)

certainly give this man the tools and the materials with which he can build himself a ladder, and the dream that will make it worthwhile, with which to climb to a better and brighter *mañana*. If he's got the stuff he'll make it, and he'll be a better man for it, and the United States will be the richer because of it. In the name of the Virgin Guadalupana or a Cristo de Velázquez don't offer him an elevator! The Statue of Liberty, the Constitution of the United States, and the great American dream promise opportunity to compete, the chance to challenge, the hope to cope with the imponderables of our times and circumstances.

And we must educate the child! We must begin with that first-grader. Let us catch him before the traumatic first day in the first grade. Let us give him a preschool orientation where we work him in slowly with toys, games, puzzles, and songs into the new fabric that is going to be the pattern of his life. Let this happen with other children like him and a teacher that looks like his mother, his aunt, or his grandmother, and who speaks his language. Let us decorate his classroom with things he can identify and provide him with coloring books with people and events he can recognize.

In the first grade, and throughout the primary grades, let us give him instruction in both Spanish and English. Being, in most cases, illiterate, the printed word is as far off as the stars on the dark side of the moon to him. The printed word in English is practically null and void, since it often does not look at all like the spoken word. The Spanish printed word, however, is written exactly as it sounds, and thus is not nearly as remote. So, from a pedagogical standpoint, it makes sense to introduce the little savage to the concept of print and writing through a system of symbols he can understand. This is relatively easy because the spoken language with which the child is familiar corresponds point for point with the symbols that appear on the printed page. Once he accepts the idea of silent and visual communication, he can be eased into a similar experience in English. The teacher, it goes without saying, must know both languages perfectly. It would help tremendously if the child could have the same teacher for the first three years. English, of course, should be taught as a second language by a teacher who knows the score. This kind of approach would give the Hispano child a status he sorely needs. Furthermore, it would give him the sweet taste of success. Success in one area can cast a glow that will illuminate other areas.

As this Hispano child progresses through school, cultural content should infiltrate his program. The history of the conquest and colonization of the new world. The conquest and colonization of his state. The heroes of Spain and Spanish America. All of these will give him money to spend in the world's fair, will make him a person to be considered in the social arena that is so important to big and little people. In the process, Hispanic culture and all it has to enrich our Anglo-American culture will endure, aesthetically, practically, and vitally.

Jacinto Quirarte

Jacinto Quirarte is presently Dean of the School of Fine Arts at the University of Texas at San Antonio. He is primarily an art historian, and his interest in the art of Mexican-America has led to this article and to a book of the same title published by the University of Texas Press.

THE ART OF MEXICAN-AMERICA

The Mexican-American artist is not difficult to identify in the twentieth century. His parents, grandparents, or great-grandparents may have come originally from Mexico. He may have been born in Mexico himself but spent a good part of his life in the United States. He may be a first- or a sixth-generation American. The important thing is that somewhere there is a tie with Mexico, or New Spain before that. Thus he is part American, part Mexican, and part Spanish. Which part plays the dominant role in his life depends upon many variables, all of which are tempered by his own talents and intelligence.

The contributions that American artists of Mexican ancestry have made in the past are far more difficult to establish. In order to do this we have to determine exactly when and how this identity was assumed. When do we begin to speak of Mexican-Americans and not Mexicans or Spaniards?

The dates of exploration, conquest, and evangelization by the Spaniards of the lands and peoples now comprising Mexico and parts of the United States took place between 1521 and 1821. The nineteenth century saw far-reaching and rapid political change take place: first, the independence of Mexico, declared in 1810 and attained in 1821;

then its fragmentation with part of its northern frontier (Texas) breaking away in 1835; and finally the loss within ten years of the area now comprising the American states of New Mexico, part of Colorado, Arizona, and California.

Is it proper, then, to speak of the peoples living in these areas at the time of the American conquest as Mexican-Americans? Technically, this would be correct, even though the area had been under Spanish control for a much longer period of time. Obviously, these designations based solely on national distinctions are only part of the picture. Those who settled and built the first missions in the American Southwest were New Spaniards; these were the same people who later became Mexicans and then Americans.

The first mission in the Southwest was established some thirty miles north of Santa Fe on July 11, 1598. Within the next thirty years forty-three other missions were built. One of the most impressive of these is San Estevan Mission in Acoma, New Mexico. Missions in Texas and Arizona were inaugurated in 1690. Major examples are San José (1720–1731), whose architect and sculptor was Pedro Huízar, and Purísima Concepción (1731), both in San Antonio, and San Xavier de Bac (1784–1797) in Tucson. The twenty missions of California were founded between 1769 and 1823.

The artisans who worked during this initial period are called *santeros,* or makers of *santos,* Spanish for saints. This is a reference to a carved or painted representation of holy persons, not exclusively restricted to saints. The Holy Family and the Crucifixion as well as saints were represented either in figures in the round, called *bultos,* or painted on altarpieces or other panels, called *retablos.* Bultos made of cottonwood were assembled with dowels, never with nails, and then painted in red, yellow, blue, and green. The small wooden panels or retablos, usually made of pine, were especially prepared with a gesso ground and painted with tempera colors.

Most of the artisans are anonymous, although a few are identifiable by name during the early decades of the nineteenth century: José Aragón of Chamisal (heart of the Sangre de Cristo Range), working in the 1820s and '30s, and José Rafael Aragón (no relation) of Córdova, active between 1829 and 1855. . . .

With time, the artisans simplified the forms in their works until these became the prototypes for a well-defined folk tradition in New Mexico. . . . Some of the artists who have worked in this tradition are Patrocino Barela (1908–1964), George López (b. 1900), and Joe Mondragón (b. 1931).

The first phase of the Mexican-American tradition spans the period of time during which New Spain and then Republican Mexico controlled the area. American conquest definitely put an end to it, although the breakdown process had already started some decades earlier under Mexican rule. . . .

The second phase of Mexican-American art is dominated by artists actually born in Mexico. This includes all of the major Mexican muralists, José Clemente Orozco (1883–1949), Diego Rivera (1886–1957), David Alfaro Siqueiros (b. 1898), and Rufino Tamayo (b. 1899). Al-

Departure of Quetzalcoatl, 1932–1934 by José Clemente Orozco
(Courtesy of the Trustees of Dartmouth College)

La Jardinera del Kiosco, 1969 by Chelo González Amezcua

though these men never became American citizens they lived and worked in this country for many years. . . .

The '20s and '30s then were dominated by the muralists whose influence on American artists of this period (beyond their obvious impact on the short-lived PWAP-sponsored muralists) has not been properly assessed, particularly in regard to the work of Jackson Pollock and other Abstract Expressionists of the '40s.

The next generation of Mexican-American artists bridges both cultures. Some are self-taught, like Octavio Medellín (b. 1907), Chelo González Amezcua (b. 1903), and Porfirio Salinas (b. 1912). Others, like Antonio García (b. 1901) and Margaret Herrera-Chávez (b. 1912), have received most of their formal art training in the United States. Still, close ties with Mexico have been retained. . . .

Octavio Medellín's works in wood or stone, usually based on representations of a figure or animal, are strong and monumental regardless of their size. His subjects are depicted in broad, firm strokes. He has a high regard for the native and primitive crafts of Mexico, particularly those of Veracruz and Yucatan. The functional art of the Indians and the integral part it plays in their daily lives have influenced his work. Medellín has taught in several Texas colleges and universities and, since 1966, has run his own school of sculpture in Dallas.

Porfirio Salinas has chosen a far more particularized path in his devotion to recording the landscapes of the Southwest with special reference to the environs of San Antonio. It is this immediate recognition and emotional attachment to the land that Texans feel that have brought him such acclaim in his home state. One of his earliest admirers was Lyndon Johnson, who began to buy his works in the '40s and whose elevation to the Presidency brought national attention to Salinas' work. His paintings have been reproduced in articles, books, and other publications, especially his renditions of the fields of bluebonnets which grow in profusion in Central Texas. . . .

Edward Chávez (b. 1917) and Michael Ponce de León (b. 1922) are two truly outstanding members of the next

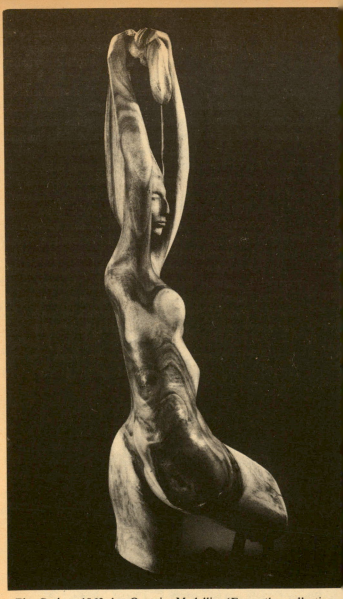

The Bather, 1963 by Octavio Medellin (From the collection
of Mr. & Mrs. Harold Simmons, Dallas, Texas)

generation of artists whose formative years span the '30s and '40s. They have achieved national prominence, with their works being exhibited in every major museum of this country. Primarily an easel painter, Chávez has painted murals in several states and Brazil. His work is based on the new pictorial languages developed by European artists before World War I, abstraction based on a cubist spatial grid. . . . Chávez has taught in many colleges and universities since the '50s. At present he is teaching at Dutchess Community College in New York State.

Michael Ponce de León, printmaker and teacher at the Pratt Graphic Center in New York, is well known for his relief prints made with a press of his own design. He creates bas-reliefs with special papers and a press that applies 10,000 pounds of pressure per square inch. He explains his approach by saying, "I bring into my work all the insights gained from sculpture, paintings, cinematography, and music, and by combining their resources and wedding these traditionally separate media through a single image, a new form emerges. My research, therefore, is not based on new ways of graphics per se, but in discovering a new meaning of art through graphics." Ponce de León's prints and his teaching have influenced artists from all parts of the country. . . .

The third generation, which came to maturity in the '50s, represents the diverse directions that American art was beginning to take at the time. The works of Manuel Neri (b. 1930) and Ralph Ortiz (b. 1934), both sculptors, reflect the prevailing modes of the '50s and '60s respectively. Neri, a San Francisco artist, has continued to work in a figurative tradition, using plaster and paint in his relief and full-round pieces. This effective tension between medium and thematic structure is related to the Abstract Expressionist approach of the '50s. Ortiz, the leading destructive artist in this country, best exemplifies the artist of the '60s who has abandoned the concept of the artist as a constructor of objects. He, along with others, has sought to redefine the role of the artist and his work. He is best known for his "Piano Destruction" which he has performed on national television, in London, New York, Vancouver, and elsewhere. He explains, "To realize our destructions within the framework of art is to finally rescue ourselves and civilization from the havoc reaped by our depersonalized psychologies. Destruction theater is the symbolic realization of those subtle and extreme destructions which play such a dominant role in our everyday lives, from our headaches and ulcers to our murders and suicides." His sculpture, exhibitions, concerts, and theater performances have been seen, heard, and experienced in major cities of both coasts and Europe.

Other Mexican-American artists of this generation working in the Southwest and other parts of the country include Ishmael Soto (b. 1932), a ceramist and sculptor who teaches at the University of Texas at Austin. His studio is well known throughout the area and is a meeting ground for patrons and young artists who are able to study and work there. Mel Casas (b. 1930), a painter who teaches at San Antonio College, paints large canvasses with garishly loud representations of amply endowed females in various settings, usually related to television and the movie screen. He calls these "Humanscapes." These works, with their strong thematic and pictorial tensions, draw us in, ask us to participate and identify with the passive viewer placed in front of the projected images.

In California, there is Louis Gutiérrez (b. 1933), who is noted for his low-keyed collage paintings based on geometric configurations in whites, grays, and off-whites, and recently in a richer palette. Esteban Villa (b. 1930), a teacher at Sacramento State College, is a leading member of a group of California artists that is actively seeking recognition of Chicano artists.

Of the younger artists, Luis Jiménez, born in Texas in 1940 and now working in New York, is perhaps the outstanding example. Like Mel Casas, he uses the typical American phenomenon of the pop sex goddesses and the motorcycle, but adds an even more devastating dimension to his works. . . . his large, shiny, polychromed sculptures are fashioned of fiberglass and epoxy. . . .

Serious students of contemporary art would find it difficult to identify an artist by nationality if confronted with the works and no other information. In this respect, American artists of Mexican descent, outside the small towns of northern New Mexico where artisans have continued to work in the old ways, are indistinguishable from other American artists. They have been affected by the same events which have revolutionized twentieth-century art. Still, antecedents have to be kept in mind. The Mexican-American artist straddles several traditions which at times seem irreconcilable. On the one hand he is indirectly related to the Spanish Colonial and Mexican Republican periods of American history and directly involved with American culture of the twentieth century. On the other hand, the ties with Mexico remain strong and in certain parts of the Southwest there appears to be a concerted effort to emphasize the latter more strenuously than ever before.

Feliciano Rivera

Feliciano Rivera is professor of History and Mexican-American Studies at San Jose State College in California. Dr. Rivera has authored numerous works on the history of Mexican-Americans. He is co-author of *The Chicanos: A History of Mexican-Americans.*

TOWARD A HISTORY
OF THE MEXICAN-AMERICAN

History does, indeed, tell us *who* we are. In studying the history of the Mexican-American, one must ask why the Mexican-American has been neglected in our history textbooks. First, the perpetuators of our history have, of course, been the historians; most historians, when they

write history, establish a conclusion and then aim their
research toward this. Secondly, society has depended on
our historians, who have been largely of Anglo-Saxon ex-
traction; in spite of their efforts to overcome their backgrounds, they have been the very victims of it: they remain
confined and restricted by their backgrounds.

Naturally, the history of the Mexican-American people
does *not* have the same roots as the Anglo-American's but
rather distinctly different ones. This is why the Mexican-
American can*not* relate to the eastern seaboard experience
of the "founding fathers," the bases of which are *England
and northern Europe.* Mexican-Americans, because of
their Indian heritage, are *indigenous* to their area. Up to
1821 their history is the *colonial history of the Spanish
Empire;* from 1821 to 1848 it becomes the history of the
Mexican nation, Mexico having achieved independence

Neglected Americans (Héctor Melgoza)

from Spain in 1821. From 1848 to the present time the history of the Mexican people is unique: their cultural and social history having been a bi-cultural experience differentiates the Mexican-Americans from the Mexicans raised *south* of the border.

Furthermore, in terms of political history, the Mexican-Americans have had little to say; and, except as spectators, they have not been permitted to become involved in the building of the political history of the United States of America. What has occurred has been affected by the fact that the border set up under the Treaty of Guadalupe-Hidalgo (and later changed somewhat by the Gadsden Purchase) has been but a *political* border and not a *cultural* border.

The movement of the people north from Mexico has continued to be more a *migration* than an *immigration*. The border has been and continues to be a very nebulous and mythical one, especially as it relates to the social and cultural makeup, for the continued migration north from Mexico has invalidated the border as a cultural one; it continues to be a political border. Above all, the major differences of the Americans of Mexican descent are that (a) they are indigenous to the area because of their Indian heritage, which no other groups can claim; and (b) no other group within the political or continental limits of the United States has received the continued reinforcement of those elements that make for a distinct people and culture (e.g., food, language, traditions, music, etc.).

The complete history of the Mexican-American people of the United States of America has yet to be written, especially as it pertains to the Southwest and the West. *The only sound and valid approach now is a tri-cultural approach:* that is, through the *Indian* experience, the *Mexican-Hispanic* experience, and the *Anglo* experience; the fusion of these three experiences produces a unique human phenomenon.

2 • FOLKLORE

By 1900 Anglo-Americans in the Southwest had so taken over the Mexican Southwest that what had once been Mexican and Spanish had been neatly appropriated and transformed into an American "tradition." Mexican water and mining laws were retained in principle by Anglo-American settlers and governments. Spanish words were transformed into English equivalents. *La riata* became *lariat; juzgado* became *hoosegow; calabozo* became *calaboose; chiapas* became *chaps,* and so on. The American *cowboy* became simply an altered reflection of the Mexican *vaquero*—saddle, ten-gallon hat, and all. The American language had absorbed a considerable Mexican vocabulary, but the Mexican-Americans themselves were kept at arm's length as "outsiders," to be forgotten for another fifty years.

During these years Mexican-American literature was undergoing the rigors of change from one social order to another. Mexican-American writers continued writing in Spanish, their sentiments and outlook still rooted in the literary tradition from which they sprang. The transition from writing in Spanish to writing in English was a process encompassing the latter half of the nineteenth century. Throughout this time, Mexican-American writers were still focusing on their past. Published expositions of the grim realities Mexican-Americans faced daily were still decades away.

Mexican-American scholars and writers like Aurelio M. Espinosa were busily engaged in preserving the literary roots of their heritage. In 1910 Professor Espinosa pointed out the paucity of Mexican-American folklore studies in an article entitled "New Mexican Spanish Folk-Lore" (in *The Journal of American Folklore*). "Folk-lore studies in Spanish North America," he wrote, "have been entirely neglected. With the single exception of a short article by John G. Bourke, published in . . . 1896, I do not know of any American publication on Spanish-American folk-lore. The field is very rich, and will repay the labors of anyone. The abundant material which has already been found in New Mexico and Colorado would seem to furnish ample proof that vast treasures of folk-lore are to be found in Texas, California, and Arizona, not to speak of Mexican folk-lore studies, which, to my knowledge, no one ever touched upon."

With the Mexican-American inhabitants of the land and the new immigrants came a rich cultural heritage. The fact of the matter was that the Hispano-Americans were a highly literate people, as the inventories of personal and church libraries attest. It should be remembered that no sooner had the Spanish established their hold on Mexico than they started a printing press in Mexico City in 1529, more than a century earlier than any established in the British colonies of North America.

In the Southwest the people who had come with the land continued to tell and retell the tales which their forebears had brought from the Old World and from Mexico. These folktales had been passed on from generation to generation until they had come to represent a decidedly oral tradition.

By the time of the Mexican-American War the Mexican Southwest had been thoroughly nurtured on drama, poetry, and folktales of a literary tradition reaching back several hundred years. Mexicans who became Americans continued the Hispanic literary tradition not only by preserving the old literary materials but by creating new ones with a superimposed American political ambience.

There is still an abundance of folklore material to be mined out of the Mexican-American Southwest, material which focuses on both the Hispanic and Indian roots of Mexican-American culture. To date, much of the Mexican-American folklore seems to emphasize nostalgically a way of life in the Hispanic Southwest which was more Spanish than Mexican, more Hispanic than Indian. Looking backward some Mexican-American writers were influenced by the literary imperatives of the highly touted Spanish templar tradition, a way of life which upon first view might be seen as romantic and charming but which, upon closer examination, reveals the rigors of the rugged kinds of existence the forebears of Mexican-Americans endured in the Southwest. While life in the Spanish and Mexican Southwest was not without its compensations, it was nevertheless a harsh and demanding one. Adelina Otero could write that "my people are a simple people. There are no complexities which harass us. We live—we love—we die. We laugh in joy and weep in sadness."

The selections in this section represent two distinct perspectives on Mexican-American folklore. The first work, by Nina Otero, represents the spatial view, looking back to a time that was rooted in the memory of the people, a memory of exploration, settlement, and colonization. This point of view stems directly from identification with the original families of the conquest and subsequent *entradas* into the Southwest. The works by Josefina Escajeda and Jovita González reflect the experiential view on Mexican-American folklore. The works deal with the day-to-day considerations of life in the lands so far to the north and so removed from the central administrations of either Mexico City or Washington, D.C. And while the tales and sketches have touches of the spatial view of the Hispanic Southwest, they nevertheless attempt a portrayal of life in its leaps and bounds as it was lived then. *The Legend of Gregorio Cortez* by Américo Paredes represents the heroic view of Mexican-American folklore. Indeed, in a time of troubles and oppression a people need a popular hero to sustain them in their own griefs. Robin Hood was such a figure for the oppressed in Nottingham, England, during a time of great distress. Mexican-Americans could look to characters like Juan Cortina and Gregorio Cortez and realize a measure of hope that somewhere Mexican-Americans were standing up for what they believed and for what was right. But the pastoral concept of the Spanish, Mexican, and American Southwest was giving way to the everyday realities Mexican-Americans suffered and endured.

Nina Otero

Nina Otero was a New Mexican writer whose family was among the earliest of the Hispanic pioneers in the Southwest. She wrote sensitively about the life of her people.

COUNT LA CERDA'S TREASURE

The Manzano mountains divide the Estancia plains from the Bernalillo valley. In the Estancia, there were long ago small lakes of fresh water. The Indians tell of their being filled with fish, but they say the lakes were accursed, for the fresh water became bitter and unfit to drink, the fish disappeared, and finally the water seeped through the sand, leaving dry lakes of salt. Various sorts of people followed each other in this country: the early Indians hunted the antelope over these plains; the Pueblo Indians built villages which they later abandoned. In the seventeenth century, missions were established here by the Franciscans and they flourished for a long period of years. The Spanish explorers and settlers in search of greater wealth and more territory came and built their villages on the ruins of the pueblos; even Brazilian gypsies were lured there by leaders more eager for wealth than safety. The settlers made a brave effort for years to establish their homes, but constant raids by the Apache and Comanche Indians caused so much loss of life and property that they finally had to abandon the valley. The villages, legend says, "died of fear."

It is in this valley that the famous Gran Quivira is located. This is the legendary name for what was once the Indian pueblo of Tabirá. Tradition said that there was a large quantity of gold and silver buried there by a former explorer. This story probably grew because Gran Quivira was confused with Quivira of Coronado's time, a mythical city of Kansas, to which Coronado, the Conqueror, was lured in search of gold. He and his army were led through the Staked Plains in 1541 by an Indian called El Turco, on and on into what is now the state of Kansas, there to find that they had been deceived by this guide, for the "great city" turned out to be only Indian settlements of straw huts in which the Wichita Indians lived.

In about the year 1900 a band of Brazilian gypsies came to the Gran Quivira, with their leader who called himself Count La Cerda. He had heard of the enormous hidden wealth, supposedly buried in the Gran Quivira country. In wagons and buckboards this caravan of gypsies wound their way over the passes and through the canyons of the Manzano mountains; on New Year's day they arrived at the village of Chilili, where, in the old cemetery, they started their excavations. Here they found a stone box which contained Spanish coins. This was not the great treasure that La Cerda had crossed countries to claim. He left his companions and the small box containing the Spanish coins and continued his journey to Tajique, and thence to Gran Quivira. The gypsy band were content to set up their camp in Chilili. They followed their leader because of what they thought were the possibilities in a new country. In Chilili, they could follow their professions of fortune-telling and stealing. Their patron saint was San Dímas, the good thief, crucified with Our Lord. They, too, had someone to plead for them with the Divine Judge!

While in Tajique, Count La Cerda met a Spanish girl with whom he fell in love. She was, however, engaged to a young Mexican boy. The two men had an encounter which left the Mexican boy, presumably, dead. La Cerda jumped at once into his buckboard and crossed the mountains, arriving in the county of Valencia where he surrendered to the sheriff. After a preliminary hearing, La Cerda was put in jail to await the action of the grand jury, as he was unable to furnish a twenty-five-thousand-dollar bond.

La Cerda cabled his brother, who he claimed was a wealthy man, living in Brazil, and within a certain time the report came that his brother had left his country on his way to New Mexico. La Cerda, when questioned by the examining authorities, said:

"I had an aunt who was a *marquesa* of Spain. When she learned that I was coming to America, she told me that from some ancient papers she had learned there was a great treasure, thirty millions, buried in the Gran Quivira by her Spanish forefathers. She gave me a map, showing where the treasure lay, and this map indicated the location of the treasure. The directions were marked by arrows and crosses. She explained that at a certain point, so many feet west from the old church, I would find an old cottonwood tree and, so many feet north and the same distance east from this cottonwood tree I must dig, and when I found the proper point by measure, I should go down fifteen feet where I would find a slab with an iron ring in the center. This I must remove and descend the steps leading to a door, but the door must not be entered until the following day.

"On opening the door I would find a passageway of about twenty-five feet, at the end of which I would arrive at a second door which, again, must not be entered until the following day. This I must continue until I reached the ninth door, waiting each time one day before crossing the threshold of the respective doors. That on arriving at the ninth door, I must wait two days before crossing that threshold and then I must be dressed in white satin.

"When I opened that ninth door I would find myself in a moderately sized room, and in this room would be some forty or fifty boxes made of stone slabs, in which I would find thirty millions in gold and foreign coins. She then told me that I should divide this gold among those of my tribe who went with me and assisted me;

that my compensation would be found behind the door; that there I would find a diamond weighing one hundred pounds which I should immediately take to Spain."

The Count's brother arrived and was entertained at an old Spanish hacienda. News came that the Mexican boy with whom the Count had fought was recovering. As the Count's brother and his host discussed the adventures of Count La Cerda, the Spaniard heard something heavy fall to the ground. It was a moonlit night but the *portal* was in shadow and it was difficult to determine what had dropped. It sounded like a weapon. The stranger, seeing his host startled, explained that he would show him the heavy object he had dropped by accident as soon as they entered the lighted room. The Spaniard, unable to bear the suspense, led his guest to the reception room, where the stranger placed on the table a leather belt filled with gold coins—Spanish, Portuguese, and French—amounting to fifty thousand dollars. This the Brazilian intended to use for the release of his brother. The Brazilian told his astonished host that Count La Cerda suffered from mental trouble; that he had no aunt in Spain; that he was ignorant of buried treasure. He said that La Cerda was rather a rascal and a great trial to their father, head of the gypsies of Brazil; that they were a large family, and no one had ever disgraced their name except this wayward brother. He would return to Brazil, taking with him La Cerda and the gypsies he had tricked into believing there was buried treasure in New Mexico. His father would then deal with the miscreant as he saw fit.

The following day an attorney was employed, the bond reduced, foreign coins put up to meet the bond, and the Brazilian gypsies left the country. They left the cities that "died of fear" for others to excavate and resurrect, for others who would believe in the myth of the Gran Quivira. Others came, Spaniards, Frenchmen, English, and Yankees, hungry for the buried treasure of the *Dons* of old.

The legend ranks with the illusions of the hidden treasure of the Moors of Granada, with the buried gold of the Incas of Peru. There are those today who believe that hidden treasures have been found, but the superstition is that to find these treasures one must be the seventh son of a seventh son born on a Friday, the day obscured by the sun.

Josefina Escajeda

Josefina Escajeda is a Texas writer whose interest in Mexican-American folklore has produced numerous accounts of the type presented in *Tales from San Elizario*.

TALES FROM SAN ELIZARIO

Twenty miles down the river from El Paso is San Elizario, a small Spanish-speaking community with few pretensions to importance other than that of the past. For nearly two centuries it maintained its dignity as one of the chief towns of the region; its legal and mercantile business was extensive; its old families maintained the Spanish tradition of courtesy and hospitality. A considerable folklore grew up before El Paso and Ciudad Juárez drained the town of inhabitants and prestige. For generations one particular family was regarded as possessed of supernatural powers, and many hair-raising stories concerning the doings of its members grew up.

Remnant of San Elizario's past (Salvador Valdez,
courtesy of *Nosotros* Magazine)

THE WITCH OF CENECÚ

Eutiquio Holquín was a healthy young animal. No one
in San Elizario could excel him in dancing the *fandango,*
and he was always among the winners when on Sunday
afternoon the young men gathered together to play *la
chueca* and *la quemada.* But quite suddenly he was strick-
en with a strange malady. He lost the use of his limbs
and had to lie in bed as helpless as a babe.

His mother tried every remedy she knew of, but Eutiquio did not improve. Soon he began to tell queer stories
of a woman who came at night when everyone was asleep
and forced him to take strange herbs and potions. Now it
was clear why the remedies of his mother were of no
avail. Eutiquio was bewitched.

One night his family were startled from their sleep by
the cry, "Look! Look! Here I have her! Come quick! She
takes me dragging!"

They hurried to his room. There a strange sight met

their eyes. Eutiquio was being dragged toward the door—*but the person who dragged him was invisible*. Suddenly, near the door, he fell. His mother and his sisters rushed to him. With great effort they managed to get him back in bed. Eutiquio could not move.

"Didn't you see her?" he asked. "It was the *bruja*. When she leaned toward me to make me eat, I managed to catch her by the hands. Then I called you. She tried to get away, and, not being able to release herself, she dragged me toward the door. My strength left me, and she escaped. But I recognized her. She is a *bruja* from Cenecú."

After this episode Eutiquio began to improve. Gradually he recovered his strength and was soon able to walk around a little. When he was well enough to get on a horse again, he determined to go to Cenecú to punish the witch who had caused him so much suffering.

He arrived in Cenecú one afternoon and went straight to the house of the *bruja*. The girl who came to the door told him her mother was at the church helping to clean it for the *fiesta*. In spite of her protests, Eutiquio dismounted and walked into the house. After satisfying himself that the *bruja* was not there, he demanded that the girl show him where her mother kept her *monos*. She hesitated, but when Eutiquio threatened her with his quirt, she showed him an immense gourd under the bed.

Eutiquio took this gourd to the kitchen and began to examine its contents. There were rag dolls of every size. Some had a thorn in the head, others in an eye, others through the stomach, others through an arm or a leg. Each *mono*, or figurine, represented some victim of the *bruja's* evil powers.

Eutiquio stirred up the fire and threw all these *monos* into it. No sooner had he done this than the *bruja* was seen running toward her home, crying at the top of her voice. She rushed into the kitchen. Her dolls were ashes.

Overcome by the calamity that had befallen her precious *monos*, she fell to the floor in a faint. Never again could she be a *bruja*. With the destruction of her *monos* her powers had also been destroyed.

DOÑA CAROLINA LEARNS A LESSON

Nicolás and his *compadre* were jogging along in a rickety wagon on their way to the *bosque* to cut wood. They had left El Paso del Norte, now Ciudad Juárez, before daybreak, and were now near Cenecú. Nicolás looked up. He could not believe his eyes.

"Look, *compadre!* There comes a woman. She looks like Doña Carolina, the wife of our good friend Don Ricardo."

"It cannot be, *compadre.* What would a rich *señora* be doing out here in the *monte?*"

They hurried to meet her. It was Doña Carolina—a very much subdued and penitent Doña Carolina. This is the story she told them:

"My husband has gone to Chihuahua on business. He has been away longer than usual, and I began to wonder what could be keeping him so long. Yesterday morning I went to the house of Agapito, the *brujo,* and asked him to help me. He agreed to take me to a place where I could see what my husband was doing if I would promise to do just as he told me.

"Last night, at the appointed hour, Agapito presented himself at my house. *'Señora,'* he said, 'you must solemnly promise not to invoke God or the saints, no matter what happens.'

"Dios me perdone. I promised to do as I was told. Agapito blindfolded me and took me by the hand. I felt myself going up and up. We seemed to be flying through the air. At last I felt my feet on firm ground. Agapito uncovered my eyes. We were just outside a large cave. It was well lighted, but there seemed to be no one in it.

"Agapito spoke to me: 'If you are wearing a scapular, a medal, or a crucifix, take it off and hang it on that mesquite that you see near you. After you have done this, you may enter the cave and take the seat that you see there. Remember—do not invoke God or the saints no matter what happens.'

"I did as I was told and took my seat. I was alone in the

cave. Everything was so quiet that I could hear myself breathing. Suddenly I heard a great commotion, and a huge billy goat rushed toward me. His eyes were balls of fire, and the tips of his horns gave off sparks. I felt faint when he passed me, but, mustering all my courage, did not cry out.

"I had hardly recovered from this frightful scare when the largest snake I have ever seen came from the same direction from which the goat had come. It crawled closer and closer. Still I managed to control myself. Then, *señores,* this terrible creature came right up to me and began to wind itself around me. This was more than any mortal could stand. I cried out, *'Jesús, María y José, me favorezcan!'*

"At once the cave went dark. There was a terrible explosion. When I recovered consciousness, I was lying out here in the *monte.* I was beginning to despair of being rescued when I saw you coming. God must have sent you this way. May He have mercy on my sinful soul."

Nicolás and his *compadre* took Doña Carolina back to her home. Everyone noticed the great change in her. She was no longer the haughty, arrogant woman of former days. But only Nicolás and his *compadre* knew what had brought about this change, and they had promised never to tell.

LA CASA DE LA LABOR

Until some fifty years ago, the people of San Elizario made the sign of the cross whenever they passed a certain heap of ruins. There La Casa de la Labor, the largest and finest *rancho* in the vicinity, once stood. But the hand of God had fallen heavily upon it and destroyed it together with its mistress.

Doña Fidencia Ortega was the woman's name. Since the death of her husband she had managed her great *rancho.* Her servants feared and hated her, for many of them had felt the sting of her *cuarta.*

The previous year had been a dry one. The vineyards

ɪad borne but little fruit. It would soon be the feast of
San Isidro, the patron of farmers; and there was no wine
for the mass. There was just one thing to do, for Doña
Fidencia was the only one who had wine.

Father Pedro set out toward La Casa de la Labor.
Surely Doña Fidencia would not refuse a little wine for
the feast of San Isidro. Surely she must see how much
the people needed the protection of this *santo*. Another
dry year would cause untold suffering. Tired but full of
hope, the good old priest arrived at La Casa de la Labor.

Doña Fidencia was relentless. Yes, she had wine. But
it was barely enough for her own needs. Not one drop
would she give. What did she owe to Father Pedro or his
Church? Let him go about his business and leave her
alone.

Slowly, disconsolately, Father Pedro returned to the
curato. His eyes filled with tears and he shook his head.
"Dios que la perdone." How could anyone refuse to give
a little wine for the Holy Sacrifice of the Mass?

The next day La Casa de la Labor had disappeared.
Not a sheep, not a horse was left. Only smoldering ruins
remained to give testimony of the wrath of God.

What had become of Doña Fidencia? There were those
who afterward said that they had seen her riding to the
laguna on a bull that snorted fire, and that they had heard
her laugh a diabolical laugh and cry, as she plunged into
the water, never to be seen again, *"Hasta el infierno!"*

AGAPITO BRINGS A TREAT

It was growing dark when *la conducta* from San Elizario
stopped for the night. For days the men and their pack
mules had been traveling from early morning until twilight.
Many more days of hardship lay ahead of them before
they should reach Chihuahua with their *carga* of salt and
wine. The men were tired—tired of the road—tired of the
food which they themselves were obliged to prepare while
on *conducta*. Grumbling, they made ready to cook their
scant fare.

Agapito Cercas spoke up: "Don't bother to cook any thing. This very day a hog was slaughtered at my home Just wait a little moment. I am going to bring you *carne adobada, chile con asadura,* and *tortillas calientes!*" The men only laughed and went on with their work. Agapito withdrew from the group. Clemente Durán followed him One by one, Agapito began to remove his garments and drop them to the right and to the left. When he had taken off all his clothes, he stood for a moment perfectly still Then he vanished. Again and again Clemente called him There was no answer.

Clemente gathered up Agapito's discarded clothing and returned to his companions to relate the strange things he had seen. The men about the campfire were discussing these singular actions when Agapito's voice startled them into silence.

"Clemente, throw me my clothes. How do you expect me to come back without them?"

Clemente took the clothes and threw them in the direction from which the voice had come. In just a few minutes Agapito appeared. Before their astonished eyes he laid a *cazuela* (bowl) of *chile con asadura,* another of *carne adobada,* and a cloth full of piping hot *tortillas de maíz.*

At sight of such delicious food, a few of the men forgot all fear and ate it *con mucho gusto.* But the others refused it as tactfully as possible. For was it not clearly the work of a *brujo?*

A HANGED MAN SENDS RAIN

Many of the old people of San Elizario remember the summer of 1868 for two reasons: it was unusually dry, and the first man to be executed in El Paso County was hanged there in August.

Bartolo Mendoza [had been] convicted of the murder of his stepdaughter. He did not deny his guilt, but, as the time for his execution drew near, his remorse was great. He passed his days in prayer. As he paced back and forth in his cell, he would raise his voice in the prayers of the rosary and the litanies. For eight days before he was hanged, he attended mass and received communion daily. Bartolo was ready for death.

The night before the execution, the condemned man was saying his beads when one of the guards entered. "Bartolo," he said, "you will soon be face to face with God. Won't you please tell Him to send us a little rain? A few more days of this terrible drought and all our crops will be ruined."

A look impossible to describe came over Bartolo's face. "Stop worrying," was all he said.

The next day dawned bright and clear. Not a cloud could be seen. The sun seemed to grow hotter with each moment that passed. At three o'clock it beat down mercilessly on the procession that was slowly making its way to the gallows.

Father Borrajo walked with the prisoner. As the priest intoned the prayers of the litany, the people joined in the responses. Slowly, praying as they went, the procession moved on.

At last they reached the gallows. With steady steps Bartolo mounted the platform, accompanied by Father Borrajo. He knelt to receive the priest's blessing. Then he got up, looked around him, and took his place. The noose was adjusted. In a second the trap had been sprung.

Hardly had he been pronounced dead when the sky began to cloud. By the time the procession with his body reached the church, a few drops of rain were falling. Before long it was raining hard, and the rain continued all through the night and all the next day.

Can anyone doubt that the soul of Bartolo Mendoza went straight to heaven?

Jovita González

Jovita González was born at Roma on the Texas-Mexican border and spent much of her time there. Later she was a teacher of Spanish at St. Mary's Hall in San Antonio. She contributed extensively to the *Journal of the Texas Folklore Society* when J. Frank Dobie was its editor.

DON TOMÁS

On the ground was a youth, seminaked, his back and chest crossed with thick welts from which blood streamed. Above him towered a lean, gray-headed giant, rawhide rope in hand, beating the prostrate form mercilessly. With a cry of anguish and pain, the youth staggered from the ground, only to fall back in a faint. Seeing this, the older man gathered the blood-covered form of the youth gently in his arms, took him indoors, and laid him on a cot. In a corner of the room three weeping women huddled together. The oldest of the group fell on her knees in front of the cot, kissed the pale face of the youth, and cried in an anguished voice,

"Tomás, you have killed our son!"

"No," the man replied proudly, "I have merely taught him not to steal cattle again. Bring water and salve and I'll dress his wounds."

Such was patriarchal justice among the Mexican *rancheros* of the border land. The stern father was Don Tomás, a well-known character of the border country. Materially, Don Tomás was not a rich man. In the center of his few thousand acres of brush-covered land and near a stream was his home, a big, thatch-covered *jacal*. Close by, separated by a *portal*, another *jacal* served as kitchen

"Don Tomás" (José Medina)

and dining room. And beyond, near the stream, were the *corrales* for his cows and goats.

He believed in parental dominion. He was head of the family. His word was authority; no other law was needed and there was no necessity for civil interference. He was the sole judge of his children's actions, whether they were married or single.

His ranch was near my grandfather's, and although he did not belong to what was considered the landed gentry, he and my grandfather were the best of friends and *compadres*. My earliest recollection of Don Tomás is of seeing him ride up on a spirited *bayo potro,* descend from it with a leap, and tie it to a salt cedar tree by the gate. Although he was a *texano,* he dressed like a Mexican *ranchero,* always in brown, with a black silk sash around his waist, a bright-colored sarape over one shoulder, and a Mexican *sombrero* on his head. He was tall and slender, and in spite of his sixty-odd years was the champion wrestler of the community. I remember him well as he would walk arrogantly about, his silver spurs clinking on the brick floor of the patio. His lean face with its gray, pointed beard was striking because of the clear-cut features and deep-set gray eyes. What as a child I used to think were blue freckles were grains of gunpowder from a shotgun that had once exploded in his hands.

He knew more about setting bones, treating snake bites, and curing sunstroke than any other man in the region. He applied the same cures to man and beast, and his boast was that he had never lost a patient. A strip of deerskin tied around the victim's neck, for instance, would cure anyone of a snake bite. But although Don Tomás might cure any disease or wound, there was one thing which was beyond him—witchcraft. And this was the cause of the ruin and disintegration of his family and his patriarchal rule.

All of his married sons lived on his ranch. And if little birds in their own nest cannot agree, neither can sisters-in-law. The quarrel started when one daughter-in-law accused the child of another of having stolen a ring. After much bickering and quarreling, the offended party swore that some day all concerned would be sorry for the insult she and her child had suffered.

Some time later, when the families were gathered together at Don Tomás' house in the evening, a shrill whistle broke the stillness of the twilight. It was a screech owl, the bird of ill-omen, the messenger of the witches.

Things happened after that. Don Tomás' wife was the first to be stricken. She was bewitched and went insane. The next day a daughter went raving mad, and was taken to the county jail for safe-keeping. One of the sons imagined himself a cat, crawled on all fours, lapped milk from a saucer, and perched himself on a beam of the house. Another one became a general, rallied the ranch children together, and drilled them all day in military fashion. Worst of all, a second daughter was possessed of the Evil Spirit, who attempted to strangle her in the darkness of night. Next day her neck and face were bruised and showed the marks that the Evil One had left. The food prepared for the stricken turned to worms, and the fruit from a can of peaches that was opened one day became stones. Exotic flowers, never seen before at the ranch, were placed in vases about the house.

One day, a Friday to be exact, the bewitched became worse and a shower of ashes fell upon the place, killing all growing things. Even the dogs went blind and staggered about the place in a most pitiable manner. That night the daughter in jail died, the other was strangled, and Pancho, perched on the beam, mewed in the most terrifying manner, while screech owls held a concert over the roof. A priest who was called blessed the ranch and spoke to Don Tomás in strong terms about the nonexistence of witchcraft.

"You may know a great deal about religion, *padre*, but you know nothing about the witches."

And evidently the good *padre* did not, for when a *curandero* was called, this was his decree: all had been bewitched by a member of the family, and the welfare of all concerned depended upon the death of the sorceress. The daughter-in-law's threat was remembered, and everyone believed she was the guilty person.

One of Don Tomás' sons, crazed by his fear of the evil spirits and athirst to avenge the sufferings of his family, took it upon himself to release them from the evil influence that possessed them. Early the following morning he went to his sister-in-law's house and, while she was still in bed, stabbed her seven times with a machete.

After the incident the three remaining patients regained their health, but the liberator of the family was given a life sentence.

I went to the border a few months after the event and made it a point to visit Don Tomás. He was a broken man. His son's disgrace and the misfortunes of his family had crushed his proud spirit.

"That's American law," he said, shaking his fist at his imaginary enemy. "It does away with paternal discipline. It tears your heart and disgraces an honorable name. I could have dealt with my youngest as I did with my eldest years ago."

My stay at the ranch was brief. I could not stand the atmosphere of dread that permeated the place. Don Tomás told me such harrowing tales of the supernatural, of the occult power of the witches, that when at night the owls called to each other I imagined myself in the clutches of some evil spirit. And so I left.

Américo Paredes

Américo Paredes is professor of English and Anthropology at the University of Texas at Austin. Until recently he was director of the Mexican-American Studies Center at U.T. Austin. His works on folklore and anthropology appear in leading professional journals. His study of Gregorio Cortez has contributed significantly to our understanding of the *corrido* as a literary art form of the border.

The following legend was written by Américo Paredes, a Mexican-American, after tape-recording many versions of it told by people still living along the Mexico-Texas border. "El Corrido de Gregorio Cortez," the border ballad or *corrido,* was the subject of Paredes' doctoral dissertation and his book *With His Pistol in His Hand* (1958). In his research Paredes found that a real Gregorio Cortez did exist and that the legend was based largely on truth. The real Cortez was born in 1875 on the Mexican side of the border on a ranch between Matamoros and Reynosa. When he was twelve the family crossed the border and moved to the Austin area of Texas. His brother's name was Romaldo rather than Román, and the incidents of the legend took place in Karnes County, pronounced in Spanish similarly to "El Carmen" of the legend.

THE LEGEND OF GREGORIO CORTEZ

They still sing of him—in the *cantinas* and the country stores, in the ranches when men gather at night to talk in the cool dark, sitting in a circle, smoking and listening to the old songs and the tales of other days. Then the *guitarreros* sing of the border raids and the skirmishes, of the men who lived by the phrase, "I will break before I bend."

"I will break before I bend." (Alejandro Morales)

They sing with deadly-serious faces, throwing out the words of the song like a challenge, tearing savagely with their stiff, callused fingers at the strings of the guitars.

And that is how, in the dark quiet of the ranches, in the lighted noise of the saloons, they sing of Gregorio Cortez.

After the song is sung there is a lull. Then the old men, who have lived long and seen almost everything, tell their stories. And when they tell about Gregorio Cortez, the telling goes like this:

HOW GREGORIO CORTEZ CAME TO BE
IN THE COUNTY OF EL CARMEN

That was good singing, and a good song; give the man a drink. Not like these *pachucos* nowadays, mumbling damn-foolishness into a microphone; it is not done that way. Men should sing with their heads thrown back, with their mouths wide open and their eyes shut. Fill your lungs, so they can hear you at the pasture's farther end. And when you sing, sing songs like *El Corrido de Gregorio Cortez*. There's a song that makes the hackles rise. You can almost see him there—Gregorio Cortez, with his pistol in his hand.

He was a man, a border man. What did he look like? Well, that is hard to tell. Some say he was short and some say he was tall; some say he was Indian brown and some say he was blond like a newborn cockroach. But I'd say he was not too dark and not too fair, not too thin and not too fat, not too short and not too tall; and he looked just a little bit like me. But does it matter so much what he looked like? He was a man, very much of a man; and he was a border man. Some say he was born in Matamoros; some say Reynosa; some say Hidalgo county on the other side. And I guess others will say other things. But Matamoros, or Reynosa, or Hidalgo, it's all the same border; and short or tall, dark or fair, it's the man that counts. And that's what he was, a man.

Not a gunman, no, not a bravo. He never came out

of a *cantina* wanting to drink up the sea at one gulp. Not that kind of man, if you can call that kind a man. No, that wasn't Gregorio Cortez at all. He was a peaceful man, a hardworking man like you and me.

He could shoot. Forty-four and thirty-thirty, they were the same to him. He could put five bullets into a piece of board and not make but one hole, and quicker than you could draw a good deep breath. Yes, he could shoot. But he could also work.

He was a *vaquero,* and a better one there has not ever been from Laredo to the mouth. He could talk to horses, and they would understand. They would follow him around, like dogs, and no man knew a good horse better than Gregorio Cortez. As for cattle, he could set up school for your best caporal. And if an animal was lost, and nobody could pick up a trail, they would send for Gregorio Cortez. He could always find a trail. There was no better tracker in all the border country, nor a man who could hide his tracks better if he wanted to. That was Gregorio Cortez, the best *vaquero* and range man that there ever was.

But that is not all. You farmers, do you think that Gregorio Cortez did not know your business too? You could have told him nothing about cotton or beans or corn. He knew it all. He could look into the sky of a morning and smell it, sniff it the way a dog sniffs, and tell you what kind of weather there was going to be. And he would take a piece of dirt in his hands and rub it back and forth between his fingers—to see if the land had reached its point—and you would say he was looking into it. And perhaps he was, for Gregorio Cortez was the seventh son of a seventh son.

You piddling modern farmers, vain of yourselves when you make a bale! You should have seen the crops raised by Gregorio Cortez. And when harvesting came, he was in there with the rest. Was it shucking corn? All you could see was the shucks fly and the pile grow, until you didn't know there was a man behind the pile. But he was even better at cotton-picking time. He would bend down and never raise his head till he came out the other end, and he would be halfway through another row before the next man was through with his. And don't think the row he went through wasn't clean. No flags, no streamers, nothing left behind, nothing but clean, empty burrs where he had passed. It was the same when clearing land. There were men who went ahead of him, cutting fast along their strip in the early morning, but by noontime the man ahead was always Gregorio Cortez, working at his own pace, talking little and not singing very much, and never acting up.

For Gregorio Cortez was not of your noisy, hell-raising type. That was not his way. He always spoke low, and he was always polite, whoever he was speaking to. And when he spoke to men older than himself he took off his hat and held it over his heart. A man who never raised his voice to parent or elder brother, and never disobeyed. That was Gregorio Cortez, and that was the way men were in this country along the river. That was the way they were before these modern times came, and God went away.

He should have stayed on the border; he should not have gone up above, into the north. But it was going to be that way, and that was the way it was. Each man has a certain lot in life, and no other thing but that will be his share. People were always coming down from places in the north, from Dallas and San Antonio and Corpus and Foro West. And they would say, "Gregorio Cortez, why don't you go north? There is much money to be made. Stop eating beans and tortillas and that rubbery jerked beef. One of these days you're going to put out one of your eyes, pull and pull with your teeth on that stuff and it suddenly lets go. It's a wonder all you border people are not one-eyed. Come up above with us, where you can eat white bread and ham."

But Gregorio Cortez would only smile, because he was a peaceful man and did not take offense. He did not like white bread and ham; it makes people flatulent and dull. And he liked it where he was. So he always said, "I like this country. I will stay here."

But Gregorio Cortez had a brother, a younger brother

named Román. Now Román was just like the young men
of today, loud-mouthed and discontented. He was never
happy where he was, and to make it worse he loved a
joke more than any other thing. He would think nothing
of playing a joke on a person twice his age. He had no
respect for anyone, and that is why he ended like he did.
But that is yet to tell.

Román talked to Gregorio and begged him that they
should move away from the river and go up above, where
there was much money to be made. And he talked and
begged so that finally Gregorio Cortez said he would go
with his brother Román, and they saddled their horses
and rode north.

Well, they did not grow rich, though things went well
with them because they were good workers. Sometimes
they picked cotton; sometimes they were *vaqueros,* and
sometimes they cleared land for the Germans. Finally they
came to a place called El Carmen, and there they settled
down and farmed. And that was how Gregorio Cortez
came to be in the county of El Carmen, where the tragedy
took place.

ROMÁN'S HORSE TRADE AND WHAT CAME OF IT

Román owned two horses, two beautiful sorrels that were
just alike, the same color, the same markings, and the
same size. You could not have told them apart, except
that one of them was lame. There was an American who
owned a little sorrel mare. This man was dying to get
Román's sorrel—the good one—and every time they met
he would offer to swap the mare for the horse. But Román
did not think much of the mare. He did not like it when
the American kept trying to make him trade.

"I wonder what this Gringo thinks," Román said to
himself. "He takes me for a fool. But I'm going to make
him such a trade that he will remember me forever."

And Román laughed a big-mouthed laugh. He thought
it would be a fine joke, besides being a good trade. There
were mornings when the American went to town in his

buggy along a narrow road. So Román saddled the lame sorrel, led him a little way along the road, and stopped under a big mesquite that bordered on the fence. He fixed it so the spavined side was against the mesquite. Román waited a little while, and soon he heard the buggy coming along the road. Then he got in the saddle and began picking mesquites off the tree and eating them. When the American came around the bend, there was Román on his sorrel horse. The American stopped his buggy beside Román and looked at the horse with much admiration. It was a fine animal, exactly like the other one, but the American could not see the spavined leg.

"Changed your mind?" the American said.

Román stopped chewing on a mesquite and said, "Changed my mind about what?"

"About trading that horse for my mare."

"You're dead set on trading your mare for this horse of mine?" Román said.

"You know I am," the American said. "Are you ready to come round?"

"I'm in a trading mood," said Román. "With just a little arguing you might convince me to trade this horse for that worthless mare of yours. But I don't know; you might go back on the deal later on."

"I never go back on my word," the American said. "What do you think I am, a Mexican?"

"We'll see, we'll see," said Román. "How much are you willing to give in hand?"

"Enough to give you the first square meal you've had in your life," the American said.

Román just laughed, and it was all he could do to keep from guffawing. He knew who was getting the best of things.

So they made the deal, with Román still sitting on his spavined horse under the tree, chewing on mesquites.

"Where's the mare?" Román said.

"She's in my yard," said the American, "hung to a tree. You go get her and leave the horse there for me because I'm in a hurry to get to town."

That was how Román had figured it, so he said, "All right, I'll do it, but when I finish with these mesquites."

"Be sure you do, then," the American said.

"Sure, sure," said Román. "No hurry about it, is there?"

"All right," the American said, "take your time." And he drove off leaving Román still sitting on his horse under the mesquite, and as he drove off the American said, "Now isn't that just like a Mexican. He takes his time."

Román waited until the American was gone, and then he stopped eating mesquites. He got off and led the horse down the road to the American's yard and left him there in place of the little sorrel mare. On the way home Román almost fell off his saddle a couple of times, just laughing and laughing to think of the sort of face the American would pull when he came home that night.

The next morning, when Gregorio Cortez got up he said to his brother Román, "Something is going to happen today."

"Why do you say that?" asked Román.

"I don't know," said Gregorio Cortez. "I just know that something is going to happen today. I feel it. Last night my wife began to sigh for no reason at all. She kept sighing and sighing half the night, and she didn't know why. Her heart was telling her something, and I know some unlucky thing will happen to us today."

But Román just laughed, and Gregorio went inside the house to shave. Román followed him into the house and stood at the door while Gregorio shaved. It was a door made in two sections; the upper part was open and Román was leaning on the lower part, like a man leaning out of a window or over a fence. Román began to tell Gregorio about the horse trade he had made the day before, and he laughed pretty loud about it, because he thought it was a good joke. Gregorio Cortez just shaved, and he didn't say anything.

When what should pull in at the gate but a buggy, and the American got down, and the major sheriff of the county of El Carmen got down too. They came into the yard and up to where Román was leaning over the door, looking out.

The American had a very serious face. "I came for the ¹are you stole yesterday morning," he said.

Román laughed a big-mouthed laugh. "What did I tell ꭐu, Gregorio?" he said. "This Gringo Sanavabiche has ꭓacked down on me."

Now there are three saints that the Americans are ꭤpecially fond of—Santa Anna, San Jacinto, and Sanavaꭜche—and of the three it is Sanavabiche that they pray ꭐ most. Just listen to an American anytime. You may ꭐt understand anything else he says, but you are sure to ꭐar him say, "Sanavabiche! Sanavabiche! Sanavabiche!" ꭐvery hour of the day. But they'll get very angry if you say ꭐ too, perhaps because it is a saint that belongs to them ꭐone.

And so it was with the major sheriff of the county of ꭐl Carmen. Just as the words "Gringo Sanavabiche" came ꭐut of Román's mouth, the sheriff whipped out his pistol ꭐnd shot Román. He shot Román as he stood there with ꭐis head thrown back, laughing at his joke. The sheriff ꭐhot him in the face, right in the open mouth, and Román ꭐll away from the door, at the major sheriff's feet.

And then Gregorio Cortez stood at the door, where his ꭜrother had stood, with his pistol in his hand. Now he ꭐnd the major sheriff met, each one pistol in hand, as ꭐen should meet when they fight for what is right. For it ꭐ a pretty thing to see, when two men stand up for their ꭐight, with their pistols in their hands, front to front and ꭐithout fear. And so it was, for the major sheriff also was ꭐ man.

Yes, the major sheriff was a man; he was a gamecock ꭐhat had won in many pits, but in Gregorio Cortez he met ꭐ cockerel that pecked his comb. The major sheriff shot ꭐrst, and he missed; and Gregorio Cortez shot next, and ꭐe didn't miss. Three times did they shoot, three times did ꭐhe major sheriff miss, and three times did Gregorio ꭐortez shoot the sheriff of El Carmen. The major sheriff ꭐll dead at the feet of Gregorio Cortez, and it was in this ꭐay that Gregorio Cortez killed the first sheriff of many ꭐhat he was to kill.

When the major sheriff fell, Gregorio Cortez looked up,

and the other American said, "Don't kill me; I a
unarmed."

"I will not kill you," said Gregorio Cortez. "But you
better go away."

So the American went away. He ran into the brush a
kept on running until he came to town and told all t
other sheriffs that the major sheriff was dead.

Meanwhile, Gregorio Cortez knew that he too must
away. He was not afraid of the law; he knew the la
and he knew that he had the right. But if he stayed, t
rangers would come, and the rangers have no regard f
law. You know what kind of men they are. When t
governor of the state wants a new ranger, he asks h
sheriffs, "Bring all the criminals to me." And from t
murderers he chooses the ranger, because no one can
a ranger who has not killed a man. So Gregorio Corte
knew that the best thing for him was to go away, an
his first thought was of the border, where he had bee
born. But first he must take care of his brother, so he p
Román in the buggy and drove into town, where h
mother lived.

Now there was a lot of excitement in town. All t
Americans were saddling up and loading rifles and pisto
because they were going out to kill Cortez. When all of
sudden, what should come rolling into town but the bugg
driven by Gregorio Cortez. They met him on the edg
of town, armed to the teeth, on horseback and afoo
and he on the buggy, holding the reins lightly in his hand
Román was in the back, shot in the mouth. He coul
neither speak nor move, but just lay there like one wh
is dead.

They asked him, "Who are you?"

And he said to them, "I am Gregorio Cortez."

They all looked at him and were afraid of him, becaus
they were only twenty or twenty-five, and they knew tha
they were not enough. So they stepped aside and let hi
pass and stood talking among themselves what would b
the best thing to do. But Gregorio Cortez just drov
ahead, slowly, without seeming to care about the me
he left behind. He came to his mother's house, and ther

e took down his brother and carried him in the house. He stayed there until dawn, and during the night groups of armed men would go by the house and say, "He's in here. He's in there." But none of them ever went in.

At dawn Gregorio Cortez came out of his mother's house. There were armed men outside, but they made no move against him. They just watched as he went down the street, his hands resting on his belt. He went along as if he was taking a walk, and they stood there watching until he reached the brush and he jumped into it and disappeared. And then they started shooting at him with rifles, now that he was out of pistol range.

"I must get me a rifle," said Gregorio Cortez, "a rifle and a horse."

They gathered in a big bunch and started after him in the brush. But they could not catch Gregorio Cortez. No man was ever as good as him in hiding his own tracks, and he soon had them going around in circles, while he doubled back and headed for home to get himself a rifle and a horse.

HOW GREGORIO CORTEZ RODE THE LITTLE SORREL MARE ALL OF FIVE HUNDRED MILES

He went in and got his thirty-thirty, and then he looked around for the best horse he had. It is a long way from El Carmen to the border, all of five hundred miles. The first thing he saw in the corral was the little sorrel mare. Gregorio Cortez took a good look at her, and he knew she was no ordinary mare.

"You're worth a dozen horses," said Gregorio Cortez, and he saddled the little mare.

But by then the whole wasps' nest was beginning to buzz. The President of the United States offered a thousand dollars for him, and many men went out to get Gregorio Cortez. The major sheriffs of the counties and all their sheriffs were out. There were rangers from the counties, armed to the teeth, and the King Ranch rangers from the capital, the meanest of them all, all armed and looking for Cortez. Every road was blocked and every bridge guarded. There were trackers out with those dogs they call hounds, that can follow a track better than the best tracker. They had railroad cars loaded with guns and ammunition and with men, moving up and down trying to head him off. The women and children stayed in the houses, behind locked doors, such was the fear they all had of Gregorio Cortez. Every town from the capital to the border was watching out for him. The brush and the fields were full of men, trying to pick up his trail. And Gregorio Cortez rode out for the border, through brush and fields and barbed-wire fences, on his little sorrel mare.

He rode and rode until he came to a great broad plain, and he started to ride across. But just as he did, one of the sheriffs saw him. The sheriff saw him, but he hid behind a bush, because he was afraid to take him on alone. So he called the other sheriffs together and all the rangers he could find, and they went off after Gregorio Cortez just as he came out upon the plain.

Gregorio Cortez looked back and saw them coming. There were three hundred of them.

"We'll run them a little race," said Gregorio Cortez.

Away went the mare, as if she had been shot from a gun, and behind her came the sheriffs and the rangers, all shooting and riding hard. And so they rode across the plain, until one by one their horses foundered and fell to the ground and died. But still the little mare ran on, as fresh as a lettuce leaf, and pretty soon she was running all alone.

"They'll never catch me like that," said Gregorio Cortez, "not even with those dogs called hounds."

Another big bunch of sheriffs rode up, and they chased him to the edge of the plain, and into the brush went Cortez, with the trackers after him, but they did not chase him long. One moment there was a trail to follow, and next moment there was none. And the dogs called hounds sat down and howled, and the men scratched their heads and went about in circles looking for the trail. And Gregorio Cortez went on, leaving no trail, so that people thought he was riding through the air.

There were armed men everywhere, and he could not stop to eat or drink, because wherever he tried to stop, armed men were there before him. So he had to ride on and on. Now they saw him, now they lost him, and so the chase went on. Many more horses foundered, but the mare still ran, and Gregorio Cortez rode on and on, pursued by hundreds and fighting hundreds every place he went.

"So many mounted rangers," said Gregorio Cortez, "to catch just one Mexican."

It was from the big bunches that he ran. Now and again he would run into little ones of ten or a dozen men, and they were so scared of him that they would let him pass. Then, when he was out of range, they would shoot at him, and he would shoot back at them once or twice, so they could go back and say, "We met up with Gregorio Cortez, and we traded shots with him." But from the big ones he had to run. And it was the little sorrel mare that took him safe away, over the open spaces and into the brush, and once in the brush, they might as well have been following a star.

So it went for a day, and when night fell Cortez arrived at a place named Los Fresnos and called at a Mexican house. When the man of the house came out, Cortez told him, "I am Gregorio Cortez."

That was all he had to say. He was given to eat and drink, and the man of the house offered Gregorio Cortez his own horse and his rifle and his saddle. But Cortez would not take them. He thanked the man, but he would not give up his little sorrel mare. Cortez was sitting there, drinking a cup of coffee, when the major sheriff of Los Fresnos came up with his three hundred men. All the other people ran out of the house and hid, and no one was left in the house, only Gregorio Cortez, with his pistol in his hand.

Then the major sheriff called out, in a weepy voice, as the *corrido* says. He sounded as if he wanted to cry, but it was all done to deceive Gregorio Cortez.

"Cortez," the major sheriff said, "hand over your weapons. I did not come to kill you. I am your friend."

"If you come as my friend," said Gregorio Cortez, "why did you bring three hundred men? Why have you made me a corral?"

The major sheriff knew that he had been caught in a lie, and the fighting began. [Cortez] killed the major sheriff and the second sheriff under him, and he killed many sheriffs more. Some of the sheriffs got weak in the knees, and many ran away.

"Don't go away," said Gregorio Cortez. "I am the man you are looking for. I am Gregorio Cortez."

They were more than three hundred, but he jumped their corral, and he rode away again, and those three hundred did not chase him anymore.

He rode on and on, until he came to a river called the San Antonio. It is not much of a river, but the banks are steep and high, and he could not find a ford. So he rode to a ranch house nearby, where they were holding a *baile* because the youngest child of the house had been baptized that day, and he asked the man of the house about a ford.

"There are only two fords," the man said. "One is seven miles upstream and the other is seven miles down."

"I will take another look at the river," said Gregorio Cortez. He left the *baile* and rode slowly to the river. It was steep, and far below he could see the water flowing: he could barely see it because it was so dark. He stood there thinking, trying to figure out a way, when he heard the music at the *baile* stop.

He knew the rangers were at the *baile* now. So he leaned over in his saddle and whispered in the mare's ear. He talked to her, and she understood. She came to the edge of the bank, with soft little steps, because she was afraid. But Gregorio Cortez kept talking to her and talking to her, and finally she jumped. She jumped far out and into the dark water below, she and Gregorio Cortez.

The other bank was not so high, but it was just as steep. Gregorio Cortez took out his *reata,* and he lassoed a stump high on the bank. He climbed up the rope and got a stick, and with the stick he worked on the bank as fast as he could, for he could hear the racket of the dogs. The ground was soft, and he knocked off part of

he top, until he made something like a slope. Then he
pulled and talked until the mare struggled up the bank to
where he was. After that they rested up a bit and waited
for the rangers. Up they came with their dogs, to the spot
where the mare had jumped. When they came up to the
river's edge, Cortez fired a shot in the air and yelled at
them, "I am Gregorio Cortez!"

Then he rode away, leaving them standing there on the
other side, because none of them was brave enough to do
what Cortez had done.

He rode on and on, and sometimes they chased him and
sometimes he stood and fought. And every time he fought
he would kill them a ranger or two. They chased him
across the Arroyo del Cíbolo and into the oak grove,
and there they made him a corral. Then they sent the dogs
away and sat down to wait, for they wanted to catch him
asleep. Gregorio Cortez thought for a little while what
he should do. Then he made his mare lie down on the
ground, so she would not be hurt. After that Gregorio
Cortez began talking to himself and answering himself in
different voices, as if he had many men. This made the
rangers say to one another, "There is a whole army of men
with Gregorio Cortez." So they broke up their corral and
went away, because they did not think there were enough
of them to fight Gregorio Cortez and all the men he had.
And Gregorio Cortez rode away, laughing to himself.

He kept riding on and on, by day and by night, and if
he slept the mare stood guard and she would wake him up
when she heard a noise. He had no food or cigarettes, and
his ammunition was running low. He was going along
a narrow trail with a high barbed-wire fence on one side
and a nopal thicket on the other, and right before he hit
a turn he heard horses ahead. The first man that came
around the turn ran into Gregorio Cortez, with his pistol
in his hand. There was a whole line of others behind the
first, all armed with rifles, but they had to put the rifles
away. Then Gregorio Cortez knocked over a tall nopal
plant with his stirrup and made just enough room for his
mare to back into while the rangers filed by. He stopped

the last one and took away his tobacco, matches, and ammunition. And then he rode away.

He rode on to La Grulla, and he was very thirsty, because he had not had water in a long time, and the mare was thirsty too. Near La Grulla there was a dam where the *vaqueros* watered their stock. But when Gregorio Cortez got there, he saw twenty armed men resting under the trees that grew close to the water. Gregorio Cortez stopped and thought what he could do. Then he went back into the brush and began rounding up cattle, for this was cattle country and steers were everywhere. Pretty soon he had two hundred head, and he drove them to water and while the cattle drank he and the mare drank too. After he had finished, some of the rangers that were resting under the trees came over and helped him get the herd together again, and Gregorio Cortez rode off with the herd, laughing to himself.

He rode on and on, and by now he knew that the Rio Grande was near. He rode till he came to Cotulla, and there he was chased again. The little mare was tired, and now she began to limp. She had cut her leg and it was swelling up. Gregorio Cortez rode her into a thicket, and the rangers made him a corral. But once in the brush, Gregorio Cortez led the mare to a coma tree and tied her there. He unsaddled her and hung the saddle to the tree, and he patted her and talked to her for a long while. Then he slipped out of the thicket, and the rangers didn't see him because they were waiting for him to ride out. They waited for three days and finally they crept in and found only the mare and the saddle.

HOW EL TECO SOLD GREGORIO CORTEZ
FOR A *MORRAL* FULL OF SILVER DOLLARS

Gregorio Cortez was gone. While all the armed men were guarding the thicket where the mare was tied, he walked into Cotulla itself. He walked into town and mixed with the Mexicans there. He sat on the station platform and listened to other men while they talked of all the things that Gregorio Cortez had done. Then he went to a store and bought himself new clothes and walked out of the town. He went to the river and took a bath and then swam across, because the bridge was guarded. That sort of man was Gregorio Cortez. They don't make them like him anymore.

He had only three cartridges left, one for one pistol and two for the other, and he had left his rifle with the mare. But he was very near the Rio Grande, and he expected to cross it soon. Still he needed ammunition, so he walked into El Sauz and tried to buy some, but they did not sell cartridges in that town. Then he thought of trying some of the houses, and chose one in which there was a pretty girl at the door because he knew it would be easier if he talked to a girl. There was not a woman that did not like Gregorio Cortez.

The girl was alone, and she invited him into the house. When he asked for ammunition, she told him she had none.

"My father has taken it all," she said. "He is out looking for a man named Gregorio Cortez."

Gregorio Cortez was embarrassed because he could see that the girl knew who he was. But she did not let on and neither did he. He stayed at the house for a while, and when he left she told him how to get to the Rio Grande by the quickest way.

Now all the people along the river knew that Gregorio Cortez was on the border, and that he would soon cross, but no one told the sheriffs what they knew. And Gregorio Cortez walked on, in his new clothes, with his pistols in a *morral,* looking like an ordinary man, but the people he met knew that he was Gregorio Cortez. And he began to talk to people along the way.

Soon he met a man who told him, "You'll be on the other side of the river tonight, Gregorio Cortez."

"I think I will," he said.

"You'll be all right then," said the man.

"I guess so," said Gregorio Cortez.

"But your brother won't," the man said. "He died in the jail last night."

"He was badly wounded," said Gregorio Cortez. "It was his lot to die, but I have avenged his death."

"They beat him before he died," the man said. "The rangers came to the jail and beat him to make him talk."

This was the first news that Gregorio Cortez had heard, and it made him thoughtful.

He walked on, and he met another man who said, "Your mother is in the jail, Gregorio Cortez."

"Why?" said Gregorio Cortez. "Why should the sheriffs do that to her?"

"Because she is your mother," the man said. "That's why. Your wife is there too, and so are your little sons."

Gregorio Cortez thought this over, and he walked on. Pretty soon he met another man who said, "Gregorio Cortez, your own people are suffering, and all because of you."

"Why should my own people suffer?" said Cortez. "What have I done to them?"

"You have killed many sheriffs, Gregorio Cortez," said the man. "The rangers cannot catch you, so they take it out on other people like you. Every man that's given you a glass of water has been beaten and thrown in jail. Every man who has fed you has been hanged from a tree branch, up and down, up and down, to make him tell where you went, and some have died rather than tell. Lots of people have been shot and beaten because they were your people. But you will be safe, Gregorio Cortez; you will cross the river tonight."

"I did not know these things," said Gregorio Cortez.

And he decided to turn back, and to give himself up to the governor of the state so that his own people would not suffer because of him.

He turned and walked back until he came to a place called Goliad, where he met eleven Mexicans, and among them there was one that called himself his friend. This man was a *vaquero* named El Teco, but Judas should have been his name. Gregorio Cortez was thirsty, and he came up to the eleven Mexicans to ask for water, and when El Teco saw Gregorio Cortez he thought how good it would be if he could get the thousand-dollar reward. So he walked up to Cortez and shook his hand and told the others, "Get some water for my friend Gregorio Cortez."

Then El Teco asked Gregorio Cortez to let him see the pistols he had, and that he would get him some ammunition. Gregorio Cortez smiled, because he knew. But he handed over the guns to El Teco, and El Teco looked at them and put them in his own *morral*. Then El Teco called the sheriffs to come and get Gregorio Cortez.

When Gregorio Cortez saw what El Teco had done, he smiled again and said to him, "Teco, a man can only be what God made him. May you enjoy your reward."

But El Teco did not enjoy the reward, though the sheriffs gave him the money, one thousand dollars in silver, more than a *morral* could hold. He did not enjoy it because he could not spend it anywhere. If he went to buy a taco at the marketplace, the taco vender would tell him that tacos were worth two thousand dollars gold that day. People cursed him in the streets and wished that he would be killed or die. So El Teco became very much afraid. He buried the money and never spent it, and he never knew peace until he died.

HOW GREGORIO CORTEZ WENT TO PRISON, BUT NOT FOR KILLING THE SHERIFFS

When the sheriffs came to arrest Gregorio Cortez, he spoke to them and said, "I am not your prisoner yet. I will be the prisoner only of the governor of the state. I was going to the capital to give myself up, and that is where I'll go."

The sheriffs saw that he was in the right, so they went with him all the way to the capital, and Cortez surrendered himself to the governor of the state.

Then they put Cortez in jail, and all the Americans were glad, because they no longer were afraid. They got together, and they tried to lynch him. Three times they tried, but they could not lynch Gregorio Cortez.

And pretty soon all the people began to see that Gregorio Cortez was in the right, and they did not want to lynch him anymore. They brought him gifts to the jail, and one day one of the judges came and shook the hand of Gregorio Cortez and said to him, "I would have done the same."

But Gregorio Cortez had many enemies, for he had killed many men, and they wanted to see him hanged. So they brought him to trial for killing the major sheriff of the county of El Carmen. The lawyer that was against him got up and told the judges that Cortez should die, because he had killed a man. Then Gregorio Cortez got up, and he spoke to them.

"Self-defense is allowed to any man," said Gregorio Cortez. "It is in your own law, and by your own law do I defend myself. I killed the sheriff, and I am not sorry, for he killed my brother. He spilled my brother's blood, which was also my blood. And he tried to kill me too. I killed the major sheriff defending my right."

And Gregorio Cortez talked for a long time to the judges, telling them about their own law. When he finished even the lawyer who was against him at the start was now for him. And all the judges came down from their benches and shook hands with Gregorio Cortez.

The judges said, "We cannot kill this man."

They took Gregorio Cortez all over the state, from town to town, and in each town he was tried before the court for the killing of a man. But in every court it was the same. Gregorio Cortez spoke to the judges, and he told them about the law, and he proved that he had the right. And each time the judges said, "This man was defending his right. Tell the sheriffs to set him free."

And so it was that Gregorio Cortez was not found guilty of any wrong because of the sheriffs he had killed. And he killed many of them, there is no room for doubt. No man has killed more sheriffs than did Gregorio Cortez, and he always fought alone. For that is the way the real men fight, always on their own. There are young men around here today who think that they are brave. Dangerous men they call themselves, and it takes five or six of them to jump a fellow and slash him in the arm. Or they hide in the brush and fill him full of buckshot as he goes by. They are not men. But that was not the way with Gregorio Cortez, for he was a real man.

Now the enemies of Gregorio Cortez got together and said to each other, "What are we going to do? This man is going free after killing so many of our friends. Shall we kill him ourselves? But we would have to catch him asleep, or shoot him in the back, because if we meet him face to face there will be few of us left."

Then one of them thought of the little sorrel mare, and there they had a plan to get Gregorio Cortez. They brought him back to court, and the lawyer who was against him asked, "Gregorio Cortez, do you recognize this mare?"

"I do," said Gregorio Cortez. "And a better little mare there never was."

Then the lawyer asked him, "Have you ridden this mare?"

And Gregorio Cortez answered, "She carried me all the way from El Carmen to the border, a distance of five hundred miles."

Then the lawyer asked him, "Is this mare yours?"

And Gregorio Cortez saw that they had him, but there was nothing he could do, because he was an honest man and he felt that he must tell the truth. He said no, the mare did not belong to him.

Then the judges asked Gregorio Cortez, "Is this true, Gregorio Cortez? Did you take this mare that did not belong to you?"

And Gregorio Cortez had to say that the thing was true.

So they sentenced Gregorio Cortez, but not for killing the sheriffs, as some fools will tell you even now, when they ought to know better. No, not for killing the sheriffs but for stealing the little sorrel mare. The judge sentenced him to ninety-nine years and a day. And the enemies of Gregorio Cortez were happy then, because they thought Cortez would be in prison for the rest of his life.

HOW PRESIDENT LINCOLN'S DAUGHTER
FREED GREGORIO CORTEZ,
AND HOW HE WAS POISONED AND DIED

But Gregorio Cortez did not stay in prison long. Inside of a year he was free, and this is the way it came about. Every year at Christmastime, a pretty girl can come to the governor of the state and ask him to give her a prisoner as a Christmas present. And the governor then has to set the prisoner free and give him to the girl. So it happened to Cortez. One day President Lincoln's daughter visited the prison, and she saw Gregorio Cortez. As soon as she saw him she went up and spoke to him.

"I am in love with you, Gregorio Cortez," President Lincoln's daughter said, "and if you promise to marry me I will go to the governor next Christmas and tell him to give you to me."

Gregorio Cortez looked at President Lincoln's daughter, and he saw how beautiful she was. It made him thoughtful, and he did not know what to say.

"I have many rich farms," President Lincoln's daughter said. "They are all my own. Marry me and we will farm together."

Gregorio Cortez thought about that. He could see himself already like a German, sitting on the gallery, full of ham and beer, and belching and breaking wind while a half-dozen little blond cockroaches played in the yard. And he was tempted. But then he said to himself, "I can't marry a Gringo girl. We would not make a matching pair."

So he decided that President Lincoln's daughter was not the woman for him, and he told her, "I thank you very much, but I cannot marry you at all."

But President Lincoln's daughter would not take his no. She went to the governor and said, "I would like to have a prisoner for Christmas."

And the governor looked at her and saw she was a pretty girl, so he said, "Your wish is granted. What prisoner do you want?"

And President Lincoln's daughter said, "I want Gregorio Cortez."

The governor thought for a little while and then he said, "That's a man you cannot have. He's the best prisoner I got."

But President Lincoln's daughter shook her head and said, "Don't forget that you gave your word."

"So I did," the governor said, "and I cannot go back on it."

Singing the *corrido* of Gregorio Cortez (Salvador Valdez, courtesy of *Nosotros* Magazine)

And that was how Gregorio Cortez got out of prison, where he had been sentenced to ninety-nine years and a day, not for killing the sheriffs, as some fools will tell you, but for stealing the little sorrel mare. Gregorio Cortez kept his word, and he did not marry President Lincoln's daughter, and when at last she lost her hopes she went away to the north.

Still, the enemies of Gregorio Cortez did not give up. When they heard that he was getting out of prison they were scared and angry, and they started thinking of ways to get revenge. They got a lot of money together and gave it to a man who worked in the prison, and this man gave Cortez a slow poison just before Gregorio Cortez got out of jail.

And that was how he came to die, within a year from the day he got out of jail. As soon as he came out and his friends saw him, they said to each other, "This man is sick. This man will not last the year."

And so it was. He did not last the year. He died of the slow poison they gave him just before he was let out, because his enemies did not want to see him free.

And that was how Gregorio Cortez came to die. He's buried in Laredo some place, or maybe it's Brownsville, or Matamoros, or somewhere up above. To tell the truth, I don't know. I don't know the place where he is buried any more than the place where he was born. But he was born and lived and died, that I do know. And a lot of rangers could also tell you that.

So does the *corrido;* it tells about Gregorio Cortez and who he was. They started singing the *corrido* soon after he went to jail, and there was a time when it was forbidden in all the United States, by order of the President himself. Men sometimes got killed or lost their jobs because they sang *El Corrido de Gregorio Cortez.* But everybody sang it just the same, because it spoke about things that were true.

Now it is all right to sing *El Corrido de Gregorio Cortez,* but not everybody knows it anymore. And they don't sing it as it used to be sung. These new singers change all the old songs a lot. But even so, people still remember Gregorio Cortez. And when a good singer sings the song —good and loud and clear—you can feel your neck-feathers rise, and you can see him standing there, with his pistol in his hand.

3 • DAYS IN THE LIVES

Where the Mexican-American odyssey began in point of time is hard to say, for when the Pilgrims arrived in America most of the Indian forebears of Mexican-Americans had already been here on the continent for thousands of years, and their Spanish forebears had been flourishing in such urban centers as Santa Fe for over a quarter of a century and in Mexico City for a much longer period of time. Wherever that odyssey may have begun, the days in the lives of Mexican-Americans have been filled with the pain and the promise of a better life, not for themselves necessarily but for their children.

Indeed, some Mexican-American lives were better than others, especially in those families that adapted quickly and became Americanized rapidly. To achieve the end of Americanization rapidly, Mexican-Americans formed in 1929 the League of United Latin American Citizens, a group that sought also to fight and curb the growing prejudice and discrimination against Mexican-Americans, especially in the Southwest. LULAC members reasoned that perhaps prejudice and discrimination against Mexican-Americans were due in large part to the fact that Mexican-Americans spoke Spanish and were still considered foreigners, even though many of them were already third- and fourth-generation Americans. LULAC thus advocated the primacy of the English language and encouraged special classes in citizenship. Americanization seemed to LULAC members to merit the emphasis. But forty years later the problems of Mexican-Americans were as acute as they had always been.

Mexican-Americans progressed little between World Wars, and in the post-World War II years they were not only forgotten but had reached a point of "invisibility" as the Tucson Conference of the National Education Association pointed out in 1965. The great difficulty for Mexican-Americans has been that they were more often than not considered "Mexicans." And until the Chicano renaissance, there was little attempt on the part of Anglo-Americans to distinguish them otherwise. And to look Mexican is enough to come to the attention of the Immigration Service in its ever-widening search for illegal aliens from Mexico, most commonly identified as "wetbacks" or *"mojados."*

The solution to the problems of Mexican-Americans has been articulated in terms of changing them culturally. The deficiencies of Mexican-Americans could be eliminated simply by absorbing them in the Anglo-American culture, by throwing them into the great American melting pot and boiling out the foreignness in them. But it didn't work out that way.

The tragedy for Mexican-Americans was that even though they responded patriotically to the colors during the war, they were still considered "foreigners" by so many of the Anglo-Americans, many of whom had themselves "recently" arrived from elsewhere, particularly Europe. The irony of the Mexican-American situation was that the first draftee of World War II was Pete Aguilar Despart, a Mexican-American from Los Angeles. Mexican-Americans were to emerge as the American ethnic group having won more Medals of Honor than any other group of Americans except Anglos. Yet at the height of the war, just one month after Private José P. Martínez (U.S. Army) had been killed at the battle of Attu in the Aleutians, an action for which he was awarded the Medal of Honor posthumously, Mexican-Americans were fleeing for their lives in Los Angeles in what came to be known nationally as the Zoot Suit Riots.

The "riots" were sparked innocently enough, but the roots of the incidents lay deep in the strata of American inter-ethnic relations, best exemplified by the statement of Lieutenant Ayres of the Los Angeles County Sheriff's Department. Commenting on the Zoot Suit Riots, Ayres asserted: "The Caucasian, especially the Anglo-Saxon, when engaged in fighting, particularly among youths, resorts to fisticuffs and may at times kick each other, which is considered unsportive, but this Mexican element considers all that to be a sign of weakness and all he knows and feels is a desire to use a knife or some lethal weapon. In other words, his desire is to kill, or at least let blood." Incredibly, Ayres' report was duly endorsed "as an intelligent statement of the psychology of the Mexican people, particularly the youths."

But the war years were to affect Mexican-Americans as no other period in American history had, save the Mexican-American War. While no accurate figures are available as to the number of Mexican-Americans who served in the armed forces, estimates suggest that perhaps as many as half a million Mexican-Americans were in uniform during the war years.

After the war Mexican-Americans moved to assert themselves politically, socially, and economically. At heart, the change in Mexican-American attitudes was brought about by the fact that they felt that having fought to preserve the ideals of American democracy, they would expect nothing less back home than first-class citizenship. However, in the postwar years from 1946 to 1960, Mexican-Americans discovered there were two Americas: Anglo America and the "other America."

The selections in this section reflect a range of attitudes and emotions on the part of Mexican-Americans toward Anglo society.

The quality of Reies López Tijerina's letter from the Santa Fe jail reveals his tenacity of purpose in his struggle to regain the lands Mexican-Americans in New Mexico were cheated out of. Though incarcerated, he continued undaunted his indictment of the Anglo-American system which places more value upon property than upon people.

José Andrés Chacón, on the other hand, is a professional journalist and syndicated columnist who has been bringing the message of Mexican-Americans to the American newspaper public. His portrait of Rubén Salazar, while brief, is nevertheless incisive and to the point. *Message from García* speaks for itself. The title is a play on the title of the well-worn piece "Message to García," which extols the virtues of American determination and individualism.

Armando Rendón

Armando Rendón is a free-lance writer originally from San Antonio, Texas, but presently living in Washington, D.C. He has been affiliated with the U.S. Civil Rights Commission, but is more widely known for his book, *Chicano Manifesto*, from which the following excerpt is taken.

KISS OF DEATH

I nearly fell victim to the Anglo. My childhood was spent in the West Side barrio of San Antonio. I lived in my grandmother's house on Ruiz Street just below Zarzamora Creek. I did well in the elementary grades and learned English quickly.

Spanish was off-limits in school anyway, and teachers and relatives taught me early that my mother tongue would be of no help in making good grades and becoming a success. Yet Spanish was the language I used in playing and arguing with friends. Spanish was the language I spoke with my *abuelita,* my dear grandmother, as I ate *atole* on those cold mornings when I used to wake at dawn to her clattering dishes in the tiny kitchen; or when I would cringe in mock horror at old folk tales she would tell me late at night.

But the lesson took effect anyway. When, at the age of ten, I went with my mother to California, to the San Francisco Bay Area where she found work during the war years, I had my first real opportunity to strip myself completely of my heritage. In California the schools I attended were all Anglo except for this little mexicanito. At least, I never knew anyone who admitted he was Mexican and I

ertainly never thought to ask. When my name was ac-
ented incorrectly, Réndon instead of Rendón, that was
ll right; finally I must have gotten tired of correcting peo-
le or just didn't bother.

I remember a summertime visit home a few years after
ving on the West Coast. At an evening gathering of almost the whole family—uncles, aunts, nephews, nieces,
ny *abuelita*—we sat outdoors through the dusk until the
lark had fully settled. Then the lights were turned on;
omeone brought out a Mexican card game, the Lotería
El Diablito, similar to bingo. But instead of rows of num-
ers on a pasteboard, there were figures of persons, an-
mals, and objects on cards corresponding to figures set in
ows on a pasteboard. We used frijoles (pinto beans) to
mark each figure on our card as the leader went through
he deck one by one. The word for tree was called: *Arbol!*
t completed a row; I had won. Then to check my card I
ad to name each figure again. When I said the word for
ree, it didn't come at all as I wanted it to: AR-BOWL
with the accent on the last syllable and sounding like an
Anglo tourist. There was some all-around kidding of me
nd good-natured laughter over the incident, and it passed.

But if I had not been speaking much Spanish up until
hen, I spoke even less afterward. Even when my mother,
who speaks both Spanish and English fluently, spoke to
ne in Spanish, I would respond in English. By the time I
graduated from high school and prepared to enter college,
he break was nearly complete. Seldom during college did
admit to being a Mexican-American. Only when Latin
American students pressed me about my surname did I
admit my Spanish descent, or when it proved an asset in
meeting coeds from Latin American countries.

My ancestry had become a shadow, fainter and fainter
bout me. I felt no particular allegiance to it, drew no
nspiration from it, and elected generally to let it fade
way. I clicked with the Anglo mind-set in college, mas-
red it, you might say. I even became editor of the cam-
us biweekly newspaper as a junior, and editor of the
iterary magazine as a senior—not bad, now that I look

back, for a tortillas-and-beans Chicano upbringing to bea
the Anglo at his own game.

The point of my "success," of course, was that I had
been assimilated; I had bought the white man's world
After getting my diploma I was set to launch out into a
career in newspaper reporting and writing. There was no
thought in my mind of serving my people, telling their
story, or making anything right for anybody but myself
Instead I had dreams of Pulitzer Prizes, syndicated columns, foreign correspondent assignments, front-page stories—that was for me. Then something happened.

A Catholic weekly newspaper in Sacramento offered me
a position as a reporter and feature writer. I had a job on
a Bay Area daily as a copyboy at the time, with the opportunity to become a reporter. But I'd just been married
and there were a number of other reasons to consider:
there'd be a variety of assignments, Sacramento was the
state capital, it was a good town in which to raise a family
and the other job lacked promise for upward mobility. I
decided to take the offer.

My wife and I moved to Sacramento in the fall of
1961, and in a few weeks the radicalization of this Chicano began. It wasn't a book I read or a great leader
awakening me, for we had no Chávezes or Tijerinas or
Gonzálezes at the time; and it was no revelation from
above. It was my own people who rescued me. There is a
large Chicano population in Sacramento, today one of the
most activist in northern California, but at the time fac-
tionalized and still dependent on the social and church
organizations for identity. But together we found each
other.

My job soon brought me into contact with many Chicanos as well as with the recently immigrated Mexicans
located in the barrios that Sacramento had allocated to the
"Mexicans." I found my people striving to survive in an
alien environment among foreign people. One of the stories
I covered concerned a phenomenon called Cursillos de
Cristiandad (Little Courses in Christianity), intense, three-
day group-sensitivity sessions whose chief objective is the

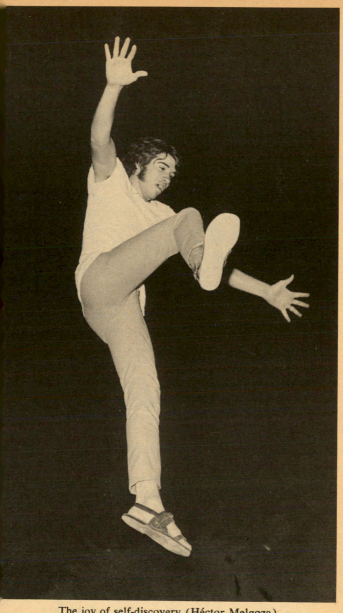

The joy of self-discovery (Héctor Melgoza)

re-Christianization of Catholics. To cover the story properly I talked my editor into letting me make a Cursillo.

Not only was much revealed to me about the phony gilt lining of religion which I had grown up believing was the Church, but there was an added and highly significant side effect—cultural shock! I rediscovered my own people, or perhaps they redeemed me. Within the social dimension of the Cursillo, for the first time in many years I became re-immersed in a tough, *macho ambiente* (an entirely Mexican male environment). Only Spanish was spoken. The effect was shattering. It was as if my tongue, after being struck dumb as a child, had been loosened.

Because we were located in cramped quarters, with limited facilities, and the cooks, lecturers, priests, and participants were men only, the old sense of *machismo* and *camarada* was revived and given new perspective. I was cast in a spiritual setting which was a perfect background for reviving my Chicano soul. Reborn but imperfectly, I still had a lot to learn about myself and my people. But my understanding deepened and renewed itself as the years went by. I visited bracero camps with teams of Chicanos; sometimes with priests taking the sacraments; sometimes only Chicanos, offering advice or assistance with badly needed food and clothing, distributed through a bingo-game technique; and on occasion, music for group singing provided by a phonograph or a guitar. Then there were barrio organization work; migrant worker programs; a rural self-help community development project; and confrontation with antipoverty agencies, with the churches, with government officials, and with cautious Chicanos, too.

In a little San Francisco magazine called *Way*, I wrote in a March, 1966, article discussing "The Other Mexican American":

The Mexican-American must answer at the same time: Who am I? and Who are we? This is to pose then, not merely a dilemma of self-identity, but of self-in-group-identity. . . . Perhaps the answer to developing a total Mexican-American concept must be left in the hands of the artist, the painter, the writer, and the poet, who can abstract the essence of what it is to be Mexican in America. . . . When that understanding comes . . . the Mexican-American will not only have acculturized himself, but he will have acculturized America to him.

If anyone knew what he was talking about when he spoke of the dilemma of who he was and where he belonged, it was this Chicano. I very nearly dropped out, as so many other Mexican-Americans have, under the dragging pressure to be someone else, what most of society wants you to be before it hands out its chrome-plated trophies.

And that mystique—I didn't quite have it at the time, or the right word for it. But no one did until just the last few years when so many of us stopped trying to be someone else and decided that what we want to be and to be called is Chicano.

I owe my life to my Chicano people. They rescued me from the Anglo kiss of death, the monolingual, monocultural, and colorless Gringo society. I no longer face a dilemma of identity or direction. That identity and direction have been charted for me by the Chicano—but to think I came that close to being sucked into the vacuum of the dominant society.

Reies López Tijerina

Reies López Tijerina is best known as the founder of the *Alianza* in New Mexico, a movement dedicated to recovering land grants from the federal government for its members who lost them through a variety of ruses and ploys. His recent efforts have been directed at establishing a National Congress of Land and Culture for securing greater recognition for Chicanos.

On September 22, 1968, Reies López Tijerina went on trial in federal district court in Albuquerque for destruction of federal property (two counts) and assault on a federal officer, Forest Ranger Charles Evans—crimes supposedly committed the previous June 8. He wrote the following letter a few weeks before this trial began.

A LETTER FROM JAIL

Santa Fe Jail, August 15–17

From my cell block in this jail I am writing these reflections. I write them to my people, the Indo-Hispanos, to my friends among the Anglos, to the agents of the federal government, the state of New Mexico, the Southwest, and the entire Indo-Hispano world—"Latin America."

I write to you as one of the clearest victims of the madness and racism in the hearts of our present-day politicians and rulers.

At this time, August 17, I have been in jail for sixty-five days—since June 11, 1968, when my appeal bond from another case was revoked by a federal judge. I am here today because I resisted an assassination attempt led by an agent of the federal government—an agent of all those who do not want anybody to speak out for the poor, all those who do not want Reies López Tijerina to stand in their way as they continue to rob the poor people, all those many rich people from outside the state with their summer homes and ranches here whose pursuit of happiness depends on thievery, all those who have robbed the people of their land and culture for 120 years.

There is nothing new about the assassination attempt against me. Four times my home and office (they are in the same building) have been bombed. Three times, assassins have riddled my home and office with high-powered automatic rifles. One would-be assassin was caught, William Fellion, but he was a former special policeman himself, so he escaped punishment except for performing sixteen hours of hospital work. Another man, an Anglo scientist, is suspected, but the Albuquerque city police refuse to arrest him. Once I was attacked physically when would-be assassins forced my vehicle off the street, two blocks from my office at 2 A.M. The district attorney refused to prosecute them.

The most recent attempt occurred at Coyote on June 8, 1968. And again, instead of prosecuting the would-be assassin, the state moved against me—against the poor people. My appeal bond was revoked by federal judge Howard Bratton on the simple request of a federal agent who attempted to have me killed—and failed. The revocation took place only hours after two eyewitnesses filed affidavits with the district attorney charging federal involvement in the assassination attempt.

The key man involved, James Evans, is the head of the U.S. Forest Service's law enforcement staff in this part of the country. Evans is from the state of Georgia, with a record of being a hater of blacks. According to reliable information, he was transferred from Georgia to New Mexico to escape retaliation from his poor victims. This man Evans is the chosen tool to break the Alianza Federal de los Pueblos Libres and to assassinate the man who is voicing the legitimate claims of the dispossessed people of New Mexico.

There can be no doubt about Evans' intentions. Rees Lloyd, reporter for the *Albuquerque Journal,* testified in federal court that he overheard Evans telling other police officers and agents "I wanted to kill the son-of-a-bitch," referring to me at Coyote on June 8. Even the police themselves stated that everything had been perfectly peaceful and nonviolent before Evans came on the scene that day.

Judge Howard Bratton heard all this as he presided in federal district court in Albuquerque on the move of the U.S. attorney to revoke my bond. He heard enough testimony of the assassination attempt to convince any honest judge, but apparently he was not interested in the truth nor in promoting justice in New Mexico. He and other racist elements still try to sell the public the idea that Reies Tijerina is a violent man. That was the excuse for revoking my bond. So it is clear and on the record that this judge is aware of the attempts on my life—and he has the power to discourage an assassination which, if not avoided, would ruin the Anglo image in the eyes of all "Latin-America." But he chose to do otherwise.

What really happened at Coyote on June 8? Why did the state have ten police officers in the area? Why was James Evans in Coyote when that is not his area of operation? Why did he have so many rangers with high-powered rifles with him? At first, I, like other Indo-Hispano people, intended to keep quiet about the criminal and sinister intent of these federal agents. But then I began to reflect on the consequences that my silence might bring. What if I were assassinated—in jail or out—and the people, especially my people, the poor, are not properly informed? President Kennedy, his brother Robert, and Dr. Martin Luther King never had a chance to tell their people of what they expected, and thus the true criminals (except in the case of Robert Kennedy) had a chance to hide behind the trigger man. If I keep quiet, my silence will no doubt contribute to the plans of these assassins.

Certainly the news media will not inform the people. They prefer to say "Tijerina is a violent man, therefore he deserves legal punishment," but they forget the poor's rights for whom I speak. It is the news media that have a violent mouth—not Tijerina. The news media unlawfully inspire many stupid people to hate me and what I stand for. Even after a jury in a court of law acquitted me last year, they still call me a violent man.

For all these reasons, I have decided to speak out with the truth about what happened at Coyote on June 8.

We must first look back to October 22, 1966, when the officers of the San Joaquin land grant pueblo arrested two forest rangers at Echo Amphitheater, with the support of other pueblos of the Alianza. James Evans was present —mild and meek. He had no high-powered rifles that time. Later, according to reliable witnesses, Evans told another Forest Service officer named Quinter (Quintin? Quentin?) Cole to escalate the pressure on the Indo-Hispanos of San Joaquin— which includes the Coyote area. Cole, a good friend of Evans, was also from the South and also a hater of blacks. It was at this time that Cole, according to witnesses, beat a man named Joe Marfin viciously until some bystanders stopped him. Marfin, a secretarial employee of the Forest Service, was a mild man who had never joined the Alianza but neither did he speak against it. Cole pled guilty, was fined twenty-five dollars, and transferred to Arizona.

We come now to June 8 of this year. The Alianza was having a four-day meeting at Coyote, and state police units had been patrolling the area steadily. They knew that the people of the Alianza were not armed. On June 8, my wife Patsy set fire to a Forest Service sign as a symbol of protest against the robbery of the people's land. She was then arrested by state police, who had witnessed the act. As Evans later testified in the preliminary hearing, he never saw me do anything and no police officer reported to him anything to implicate me. But after my wife was arrested and we were about to leave the area peaceably, suddenly, from the top of the hill where the ranger station stands, there came about fifteen to twenty armed men waving guns, threatening the people, and clearly trying to force the crowd into panic—into making a foolish move. Evans came directly at me.

My first words to Evans and his gunmen, as state policeman Robert Gilliland testified in court, were: "Put those guns away, you are going to provoke this crowd with your foolish threats." He refused. I told him that his attempt to arrest me was unlawful because I had committed no crime in his presence or otherwise. He then leveled his automatic rifle at my chest but, in a split second, ten or twelve people, seeing murder in Evans' face, threw themselves between me and Evans' rifle—this was a spontaneous act.

My wife, already in custody, was very worried about our thirty-month-old child, Isabel. She signaled me to look after our baby, who at the time was crying out loud and alone in the car. Everybody was now telling Evans to put his automatic weapon away, that he was under citizen's arrest (I had placed him under citizen's arrest), and I

Listening to the new imperatives (Donald Pearson, courtesy of *Nosotros* Magazine)

left the scene to go to Isabel. As I put my head into the car where she was sitting, I found myself face to face with death: state policeman Jack Johnson, out of uniform, was aiming his high-powered rifle directly at me—his face ugly and expressing naked murder. I closed my eyes in the same split second that he squeezed the trigger. Even before I expected the BOOM my eardrums went dead. I felt fire in my blood and a lightning going through my whole body. In a cloud of darkness, the cry of my baby suddenly went silent—only the firing pin was heard. An eternity passed in my terrified mind. For the first time in my life, I felt that my entire body was a living brain, without bones or flesh.

In the next second, I moved out of my vehicle and Jack Johnson swung his rifle over my car and aimed again. Again he aimed directly at my head. Again I saw an ugly face full of death—but for some reason this time my body, brain, and eardrums were not shocked as the first time. This time I only felt myself as in a dream, with an electrical numb feeling which gave me the feeling that this was not my day to die. I remember yelling to Evans something to the effect of "Get your trigger men out of here!" I am glad more than one person saw Johnson in his attempt to assassinate me. With twenty men pointing their rifles at the crowd, and in the general confusion, Johnson had all the opportunity in the world to kill me and later claim that I was "escaping."

Johnson was one of two men that Evans had working with him that day. The other was Robert Gilliland, who later testified in court that he hated and wanted to kill me. Both are half-Anglo and half-Mexican, commonly called "coyotes." Such people often refuse to be identified with the Indo-Hispano people. By tradition they are the best tools of the Anglo to perform his dirty work. All the other officers were courteous and well-behaved on that crucial day at Coyote except these two coyotes. I had never seen Jack Johnson before but I had been told many times that the forest rangers were using some coyotes and that eventually a coyote was to assassinate me with the excuse of "Tijerina resisted arrest."

It is very clear that after Evans and his coyotes failed in their assassination attempt, panic overtook them. They know what happens to would-be assassins when their victim escapes—so Evans had no other alternative but to turn to his superiors and ask them to revoke my bond. Evans knows in his conscience that he is a fugitive from justice and that attempting to assassinate the spokesman of the poor people was the mistake of his life. No doubt he will soon be transferred to another state to continue his threats against the peace of the poor. This is typical of the federal agents' Mafia-like machine.

The U.S. forest rangers have become a symbol of organized crime and Hitler-type police state terror. But the conspiracy against the poor does not end with the Forest Service.

Later federal agents took me first to La Tuna federal prison in Texas; then, after a week, they transferred me to the Albuquerque city jail where I am not liked by the Anglo jailers and where two Indo-Hispanos were found hanged at that time. After a week, I was transferred to Santa Fe, then back to La Tuna, then again to Albuquerque, where my wife was not allowed to see me for more than five minutes; then again I was transferred to Santa Fe, and again to La Tuna, and again to the Albuquerque city jail, then to the Bernalillo County jail in Albuquerque, then again to Santa Fe and back to La Tuna, then back to Santa Fe.

It was clear that they did all this to torment my mind and to keep me from adequately preparing my defense. I had told the court that I intended to act as my own attorney and they knew that I had been acquitted on December 13, 1968, in the so-called courthouse raid trial, after conducting my own defense. They were raging mad and tried to force me to accept a court-appointed attorney. I refused twice, so they kept up the pressure and mental torture by denying me all the rights and facilities given to attorneys.

There is no doubt that the federal government is on the WARPATH against me and the rights of the Indo-

Hispanos. Color of law is what the federal agents are using to destroy me.

What is my real crime? As I and the poor people see it, especially the Indo-Hispanos, my only crime is UP-HOLDING OUR RIGHTS AS PROTECTED BY THE TREATY OF GUADALUPE-HIDALGO which ended the so-called Mexican-American War of 1846–1848. My only crime is demanding the respect and protection of our property, which has been confiscated illegally by the federal government. Ever since the treaty was signed in 1848, our people have been asking every elected President of the United States for a redress of grievances. Like the black people, we too have been criminally ignored. Our right to the Spanish land grant pueblos is the real reason why I am in prison at this moment.

Our cause and our claim and our methods are legitimate. Yet even after a jury in a court of law acquitted me last December, they still call me a violent man. But the right to make a citizen's arrest, as I attempted to make that day on Evans, is not a violent right. On the contrary, it is law and order—unless the arrested person resists or flees to avoid prosecution. No honest citizen should avoid a citizen's arrest.

This truth is denied by the conspirators against the poor and by the press which they control. There are also the Silent Contributors. The Jewish people accused the Pope of Rome for keeping silent while Hitler and his machine persecuted the Jews in Germany and other countries. I support the Jews in their right to accuse those who contributed to Hitler's acts by their SILENCE. By the same token, I denounce those in New Mexico who have never opened their mouths at any time to defend or support the thousands who have been killed, robbed, raped of their culture. I don't know of any church or Establishment organization or group of elite intellectuals that has stood up for the Treaty of Guadalupe-Hidalgo. We condemn the silence of these groups and individuals and I am sure that, like the Jewish people, the poor of New Mexico are keeping a record of the silence which con-

Chicanos looking for the better life (Salvador Valdez, courtesy of *Nosotros* Magazine)

tributes to the criminal conspiracy against the Indo-Hispano in New Mexico.

As I sit in my jail cell in Santa Fe, capital of New Mexico, I pray that all the poor people will unite to bring justice to New Mexico. My cell block has no daylight, no ventilation of any kind, no light of any kind. After 9 P.M., we are left in a dungeon of total darkness. Visiting rules allow only fifteen minutes per week on Thursdays from 1 to 4 P.M. so that parents who work cannot visit their sons in jail. Yesterday a twenty-two-year-old boy cut his throat. Today, August 17, two young boys cut their wrists with razor blades and were taken unconscious to the hospital. My cell is dirty and there is nothing to clean it with. The whole cell block is hot and suffocating. All my prison mates complain and show a daily state of anger. But these uncomfortable conditions do not bother me, for I have a divine dream to give me strength: the happiness of my people.

I pray to God that all the Indo-Hispano people will awake to the need for unity and to our heavenly and constitutional responsibility for fighting peacefully to win our rights. Already the rest of the Indo-Hispano world —Latin America—knows of our struggle. It is too late to keep the story of our land struggle from reaching the ears of the Indo-Hispano world. All the universities of Latin America knew about our problems when Rockefeller went there last summer. Will Latin America ignore our cry from here in New Mexico and the Southwest? Times have changed and the spirit of the blood is no longer limited by national or continental boundaries.

The Indo-Hispano world will never trust the United States as long as this government occupies our land illegally. The honest policy of the United States will have to begin at home, before Rockefeller can go to Latin America again to sell good relations and friendship. Our property, freedom, and culture must be respected in New Mexico, in the whole Southwest, before the Anglo can expect to be trusted in South America, Mexico, and Canada.

This government must show its faith to the Indo-Hispano in respect to the Treaty of Guadalupe-Hidalgo and the land question by forming a presidential committee to investigate and hold open hearings on the land question in the northern part of New Mexico. We challenge our own government to bring forth and put all the facts on the conference table. We have the evidence to prove our claims to property as well as to the cultural rights of which we have been deprived. WE ARE RIGHT —and therefore ready and willing to discuss our problems and rights under the treaty with the Anglo federal government in New Mexico or Washington, D.C., directly or through agents.

This government must also reform the whole educational structure in the Southwest before it is too late. It should begin in the northern part of New Mexico, where eighty percent of the population are Indo-Hispanos, as a pilot center. If it works here, then a plan can be developed, based on that experience, in the rest of the state and wherever the Indo-Hispano population requires it.

Because I know WE ARE RIGHT, I have no regrets as I sit in my jail cell. I feel very, very proud and happy to be in jail for the reason that I am. June 8 in Coyote could have been my last day on earth. My life was spared by God, and to be honored by that miracle at Coyote will keep me happy for many years to come. I am sure that not one of my prison days is lost. Not one day has been in vain. While others are free, building their personal empires, I am in jail for defending and fighting for the rights of my people. Only my Indo-Hispano people have influenced me to be what I am. I am what I am, for my brothers.

Reies López Tijerina

José Andrés Chacón

José Andrés Chacón is a New Mexican now living in Washington, D.C. He has served in various capacities with the U.S. government. At present Mr. Chacón is a doctoral candidate at George Washington University, and is the only Chicano syndicated columnist in the United States.

PROFILE: RUBÉN SALAZAR

The first full-scale riot in the city of Los Angeles since the Watts holocaust of 1965 left one man dead, more than 60 injured, 185 jailed, and 178 businesses vandalized or looted. Property damage was estimated at better than a million dollars.

The dead man was Rubén Salazar, a Mexican-American journalist. Salazar died at the Silver Dollar Café on Whittier Boulevard. He was hit in the head by a tear-gas projectile fired by a deputy sheriff. Officers reported they had gone to the café after receiving a report that there was a man inside with a gun. They said they had called for everyone in the café to come out and fired the projectile when no one moved.

The police found no gun, but the deputy sheriff's missile hit the one man in the crowd of 20,000 who, as a journalist, had focused attention on police abuses, one of the prominent issues in East Los Angeles. Salazar's friends claim he was about to expose a pattern of alleged "suicides" of Chicanos in cells at the sheriff's substation in East Los Angeles.

Salazar served on the staff of the *Los Angeles Times* for ten years and earned a reputation as a forthright, objective, and conscientious reporter. President Nixon, on learning of his death, stated, "Through all of the years I knew him and his work, Rubén Salazar exemplified the finest tradition of his craft. He was forthright, honorable, and compassionate. His leadership earned the highest respect and he will be sorely missed."

Salazar was born in Chihuahua, Mexico, in 1928, the son of Salvador and Luz Salazar. When he was age one, his parents moved to El Paso where Rubén attended local schools and then served in the U.S. Army during the Korean conflict. At age twenty-one, he became an American citizen and in 1954 he received the B.A. degree in journalism from the University of Texas at El Paso. While at the university, he worked for the *El Paso Herald Post,* but on graduation, he became a reporter for the *Santa Rosa Press Democrat,* serving until 1957 when he joined the *San Francisco News.*

In 1959, he joined the staff of the *Los Angeles Times.* During the ten-year period he was with the *Times,* he reported from the war zone in Vietnam. He was held by terrorists on a mountain road in Panama. Serving as Mexico City Bureau Chief for two years, he returned to stateside in 1968 where he was assigned to cover the

Mexican-American community, particularly East Los Angeles.

Mexican-Americans constitute approximately 15 percent of the Los Angeles population. This became Salazar's beat. In late 1969, Salazar became news director of KMEX-TV, a Spanish-language television station specializing in coverage of Mexican-American affairs, while at the same time continuing his weekly column on the quality of life for the Chicano in Los Angeles.

The double forum made Salazar a double threat and he became more and more militant as he became more involved in behalf of the city's poor. His frustration continued to grow. The Chicano community had found an articulate spokesman. His essays are classics in the area of Chicano studies.

Authorities and spokesmen for the peaceful Mexican-American antiwar parade and rally that preceded the violence disagreed on how and why the trouble started. Mexican-Americans had come from many states to protest the war and to make public the claim that proportionately more Chicanos were dying in Vietnam than other groups. Chanting "Chicano power" and "Viva la Raza" a cheerful crowd estimated at 20,000 marched three miles on a hot afternoon through the barrios of East Los Angeles.

They had come in peace—now their most respected and articulate spokesman was their martyr. The death of Salazar has not been adequately explained. Mexican-Americans have not accepted Police Chief Edward M. Davis' findings in the death. They do not believe the death was accidental.

Laguna Park, the site of the rally on that fatal day of August 29, 1970, has been renamed Salazar Park. A Salazar scholarship fund in journalism has been established in his honor.

Otis Chandler, publisher of the *Los Angeles Times*, has been quoted as saying, "I liked and admired Rubén. I envy those who knew him better . . . I admired his introspection and perceptive grasp of Mexican-American problems in the community. Rubén made our newspaper

and our community aware of those problems. He had a
basic honesty and was always a fighter."

The Mexican-American community and all America
suffered a great loss in the death of Rubén Salazar.
Whether accidental or not may never be determined. One
thing is certain—the lives of many people have been made
brighter because Rubén Salazar lived.

Philip D. Ortego

Philip D. Ortego is Assistant to the President and Professor of Urban
Affairs at Metropolitan State College in Denver, Colorado. He is best
known for his works on Chicano affairs in such publications as *Saturday Review, The Nation, The Center Magazine, Trans-Action,* and
others. His literary vita includes works in poetry, drama, and fiction.

MESSAGE FROM GARCÍA

It was Saturday afternoon. My friend García, who is
normally not a very talkative man, cornered me in the
lobby of the Cortez Hotel just as the two-day HUD conference on Mexican-American housing was coming to a
close.

"Just what the hell do these *gabachos* think they've
accomplished?" he asked me.

I wasn't really sure if he expected an answer, so I
simply shrugged my shoulders, smiled weakly, and said,
"It's supposed to be part of a follow-up to the Cabinet
Committee Hearings on Mexican-American affairs." Then
I ventured, "You know: the hearings that were held here
with all that hoopla."

"Don't make me laugh," García said, laughing. I was
surprised by García's outburst for, as I said, not only is
he not a very talkative man but he is also a fairly timid

Tenants strike, protesting living conditions (Salvador Valdez, courtesy of *Nosotros* Magazine)

man. But he surprised me even further by saying, "You call this a follow-up?" He seemed to be challenging me. "A foul-up!" he said, getting agitated. *"Eso es lo que es! A foul-up is what I would call it!"*

I could see now how distressed he really was, so I suggested we move to the grill room. García shuffled on his feet a little, shook his head, then finally said, "Naw, man, too many *gabachos* in there. Let's go down to La Morenita."

La Morenita (the brown-skinned female) is a little restaurant in south El Paso that sells good Mexican food and caters to extended conversations. It's the kind of eating place that packs in the tacos, tamales, and tortilla trade. When we got there, Bertha, the owner, put us in one of the back booths and brought us a pot of coffee.

"The fact of the matter," García started right in, "is that the HUD conference has simply *followed* the Cabinet Hearings as part of what is going to be—and mark my words—a string of palliative meetings on Mexican-Americans."

"Oh," I said, weighing his words.

"What d'ya mean, oh?" he said. "You know as well as I do that the Mexican-Americans are *in* this year. Hell, those kids who were distributing leaflets at the conference know what the score is." García produced the leaflet as if from nowhere and slapped it down in front of me. "Look," he said, pointing. García read from the paper: "It's the latest 'fad' to attend meetings about *their* problems." He underscored the word "their."

"All right," I said. "If the HUD conference was *not* a follow-up on the recommendations that grew out of the October hearings for improving the status of the Mexican-American, then what is it?"

"I'll tell ya," he said. "It was purely and simply a gathering to propagandize HUD as a federal agency and, incidentally, to distribute recruiting literature for the department. Did you see that load of junk they had on those display tables?"

I could see that García was getting more agitated the more he talked about the conference. HUD's agenda called for simultaneous workshop sessions, four of them, wherein the moderators, discussion leaders, resource people, and panels moved about while the four audiences just stayed in one place. This distressed García who saw in that arrangement an attempt to divide the conferees.

"Furthermore," he added, "you know those federal people operate under Parkinson's laws: if there's a way to screw up a meeting, they'll find it."

I couldn't help but nod my head, agreeing with García that in retrospect the format for the conference was a little odd. It wasn't really a big conference, like the hearings. So they could have just as easily accommodated all of the conferees in one large auditorium, and simply scheduled the panels consecutively during the day.

García read my thoughts. "And," he said, "did you see

that the moderators of each panel were Mexican-Americans? Pretty conspicuous, don't you think?" I could see him closing in for the kill. "A sop!" he said. "It was an Anglo sop! Did you notice that the discussion leaders were all high-powered Anglo administrators?"

"Hm," I said. "I thought the moderators did a good job, though, considering the purpose of the conference."

"You would," García said. "That's because you think like an Anglo. But it's always sad to see a Mexican-American who *se hace presumido*. You know, who becomes pompous and inflated by his own self-importance. Especially when that importance is bestowed by Anglo leaders."

"You're being a little hard on them, aren't you?" I said.

"Listen," García shot back, "HUD's rhetoric is as soporific as all the rhetoric the Mexican-American has been hearing about the solution to his problems."

"You don't believe it?" I said.

"No!" he said. "Unfortunately, there are still too many Mexican-Americans who lay great store in words, as if the words have a magic all their own, and that somehow the words will effectuate the necessary transformation."

"Then you don't believe in dialogue?"

"Listen, *amigo!* Dialogue is fine. But you soon reach a saturation point with dialogue if it fails to bear fruit."

I nodded, knowing that Mexican-Americans have prayed, and are still praying, for the fruits of the American dream. But when that dream bears only the fruit of the colocynth, then one begins to wonder about the efficacy of prayer, even though the regional administrator for HUD indicated at a news conference that HUD had a responsibility "to match the promises of American opportunity with action in better housing, improved community facilities, and elimination of slums and blight."

"What about Collins' statement that the purpose of the conference was 'to take affirmative action to insure that HUD programs are both understood by and made available to Mexican-Americans'?" I asked García.

He stirred his coffee absently, then after a pause said, "It all sounds good; and it's consistent with the objectives he administration says it's pursuing to help the poor. But when you get down to the nuts and bolts of the various programs it turns out that the Mexican-American lacks the right kind of tools to turn them to his favor or advantage."

"How's that?" I asked.

"Well," García went on, "according to Collins, the conference was supposed to 'give definitive information about how to develop housing for low and moderate income families; what steps are necessary in low-rent public housing under the 'turnkey' method; how nonprofit sponsorship may be used in the production of rent supplement housing; how and where FHA mortgage insurance may be obtained; how neighborhood water and sewer systems and recreational facilities can be improved with HUD assistance; how health, educational, and employment opportunity services can be provided, and how one may apply to HUD for employment.' "

"Those are noble objectives," I said.

"They are," García agreed. "But the conference was not for the *poor* Mexican-Americans; it was for the city fathers and planners who you noticed were not conspicuously present, for nowhere in the intent of the conference—that is, its goals—are the *poor* Mexican-Americans able to participate."

I thought about that, and asked García to elaborate.

"For example," he explained, "Mexican-Americans— the people who actually live in south El Paso—*can't* develop low and moderate income family housing for themselves; they *can't* create low-rent public housing under the 'turnkey' method; they *can't* sponsor rent supplement housing; they're so poor they don't qualify for FHA assistance; they have *no* voice in the installation of water and sewer systems and recreational facilities; they keep looking for health, educational, and employment opportunities, but they're oftentimes so ill-nourished, educationally disadvantaged, and lacking in the necessary employment skills that opportunity is simply a word in a language they're still struggling to cope with. Hell, you said that yourself. And as for employment with HUD: they strike out for lack of experience and education."

"But what about the real heart of the housing problem," I said, "the slums and the ghettoes?"

"HUD's urban renewal concept is *supposed* to take care of eliminating the blighted areas of the American cities," García explained. "But HUD's rationale is that no urban renewal project can be initiated without the approval of the voters." García swore in Spanish. "Before HUD can get into the picture, however, the cities must have an acceptable housing code."

I said, "One would imagine that the cities would be only too eager and anxious to adopt a housing code in order to qualify for HUD money."

"Hijo!" García exclaimed, looking at me incredulously. "You know this isn't the case in many cities where Mexican-Americans live in the most deplorable conditions imaginable."

I smiled sheepishly, realizing the faux pas.

García continued: "El Paso, for example, just this year adopted a housing code. Just this year, mind you. And as you know there is already considerable opposition to it by a faction of the city voters who see it simply as another encroachment of the federal government upon some nebulous rights."

"I know," I said, remembering having seen the almost full-page ad in the *El Paso Times* calling for repeal of the housing code.

"And what about that one discussion leader who kept insisting that HUD programs were available if the people wanted them?" García asked rhetorically. I nodded. "Well, he sure backed into that states' rights defense when challenged by Rodríguez on the grounds that quite often the people who want and need the programs constitute not only an ethnic minority but a political minority as well."

Yes, I thought, corroborating García's words. In many communities where Mexican-Americans are politically ineffective, the Anglo majority effectively denies them the advantages of federal programs. "But an American community is not an enclave," I replied. "It's not an island

eparated from the main. It's part of the American community; and when local governments fail to fulfill their
esponsibility and obligations to *American* citizens, then
's the proper responsibility of the federal government to
orrect inequitable conditions and to provide for the
ommon good of *all* its citizens.''

García clapped loudly. ''Well spoken!'' he said. ''You
ave been brainwashed.''

''But it's true,'' I said.

I could see the anger rising in his face. ''It's true only
* Anglo-America lets it come true.''

''Isn't this what the HUD conference was supposed
o be all about?''

''Right,'' García snapped. ''That's what we had hoped
he El Paso HUD conference was going to be about.
We were hoping that the HUD people would bring word
hat the federal government was going to redeem its word.
'hat the President's message in which he directed the
ecretary of HUD to work out Model Cities programs
nd a program to construct six million new housing units
or low and moderate income families, many of whom are
-panish-speaking, meant what it said.'' García sighed and
ooked away. ''But the HUD program bucks the respon-
ibility back to the cities,'' he went on. ''The cities which
ave done nothing all these years and which may continue
o do nothing for many years to come until the situation
eally becomes explosive. Then everybody asks themselves
ow such a thing could happen.''

''Of course,'' I said, knowing that the Kerner Commis-
ion on Civil Disorders had not issued any profound
ecommendations for solving the problems of American
ninority groups. Any man with common sense could see
hat the recommendations of the Commission represent the
ight thing to do.

''But there are many who will resist the *right* thing for
vhatever reasons they may espouse,'' García cut in, un-
annily reading my thoughts. ''For as the circular of the
issident Mexican-Americans at the HUD conference in-
licated, 'Perhaps it is too much to hope that they would

experience a sense of shame.' The condition of the 'south side' of American cities is the real shame."

"I know," I said. "For most Anglos the 'south side' of El Paso is but a transit zone through which they hurr in their cars; but for the Mexican-American who live there, it's home."

"Tell me," García said, "what did the HUD secretar mean in his prepared statement that the conferees 'in volve themselves in a variety of HUD efforts to improv conditions of urban life'?"

"I suppose he meant we should really get into the thic' of things."

"Really?" García's tone was sarcastic. "One thing i certain," he said; "the conditions of urban life will not b improved with conferences and words alone."

"Nor will they be improved by sneering at such con ferences either," I said.

"Maybe not," García said. "But let me tell you, *amigo* unfortunately there's an element among the liberal Mex ican-American sympathizers, Mexicanologists, if you wil' whose prose is too slick and sentimental. The problems c the Mexican-Americans are all too obvious. They don' need to be slopped up in prose that's *supposed* to reflec Hispanic sentimentalism."

"Listen, García, there are many Mexican-American who are working very hard for the improvement of th Mexican-American's lot. And part of the work involve conferences."

"All right," he said, "but conferences ad nausear simply amplify the existing hostilities. At some time o other, one has to get off the pot. You tell me hov Mexican-Americans can involve themselves in improvin urban life."

"A part of the answer," I said, "comes in politica solidarity."

"True," García replied, "but what about the exploitatio of minority groups by their own members?"

"It must be stopped," I said.

"Yes," García agreed, "but the answer really lies i the attitudes of the *gabacho* majority toward minorit groups." Then he settled back as if pondering a universal problem. "The HUD conference in El Paso has not solved the housing problems of the Mexican-Americans," he said. "For one thing, it didn't even focus on their housing problems. Did you see any of the poor, ill-housed people at the conference? No! They weren't invited to participate in solving their own problems!"

There was a long pause. Neither of us spoke. Finally García looked at me with a disquieting sadness in his eyes, and with great finality said, "Perhaps the conference should have been held in south El Paso among the very conditions HUD says it is trying to eliminate."

"Perhaps," I said, "perhaps."

4 • VOICES AND THE MOVEMENT

Perhaps what best characterized Mexican-American thought in the period from the end of World War II to the close of the 1950s is that Mexican-Americans themselves were divided about the promise of America. For while a sizable number of them had "made it," so to speak, a still significant number of them lived under conditions that had changed little since 1848. In fact, for many Mexican-Americans conditions had grown worse in their transition from an agrarian people to an urban people. By 1960 statistics bore out the fact that almost 80 percent of Mexican-Americans lived in urban environments and were therefore burdened with the additional problems of the urban crisis. Despite some gains, many Mexican-Americans saw the amelioration of their situation as being a long way down the road.

There was little question that in 1960 something was happening in Mexican-American communities. Though the election of 1960 produced little in the way of political patronage, it did provide Mexican-Americans with the expertise to get Edward Roybal elected to the United States House of Representatives in 1962, making him the first Mexican-American ever to be elected to the federal legislature from California. In 1963 Mexican-Americans achieved a singular success in Crystal City, Texas, when they captured the city government.

By 1965 Mexican-American militancy had reached the flash point. No one is quite sure when the Chicano movement per se actually began, although as Alfredo Cuellar has pointed out "there is some evidence that [it] grew out of conferences held at Loyola University in Los Angeles n the summer of 1966." Since then the movement has become extremely heterogeneous, taking in Mexican-Americans from all walks of life. Particularly motivated by the movement and its ideology of *chicanismo*—ethnic brotherhood—were Chicano students and barrio youths no longer looking for America but for themselves.

The miasma of Anglo-American society has been rent asunder by aggressive and militant Mexican-Americans who under various labels of the Chicano renaissance have brought a new sense of purpose and worth to Mexican-Americans. Not all of the voices in this section are voices of the young, but they nevertheless have one point in common: *ya basta!* enough!

Julián Samora

Julián Samora is professor of Sociology at the University of Notre Dame. His works appear in a variety of professional journals. He is editor of *Forgotten Americans,* a collection of essays dealing with the various problems of Chicano existence.

AN INTERVIEW WITH JULIÁN SAMORA

Dr. Samora, you have been observing and interpreting Mexican-American social and political change for a number of years. In your opinion, what are the important strides that have taken place in the last five years or so?

SAMORA: I believe the most important stride, in the last five years, has been the organization of the Mexican-American community. By that I mean, not the total group within the United States but the barrio groups and the local grass roots groups which have really brought about a tremendous change. In other words, I believe the big stride that has taken place is the awakening of the Mexican-American community to the fact that they can *do* something about some of their problems.

Do you see a positive change in the awareness and attitudes of educators regarding Mexican-Americans and their needs? Are they responsive to the needs of Mexican-Americans?

SAMORA: One would think so, although I don't know what has been happening in any particular community. However, with all the pounding that has been done at their doors, one would think that educators would become quite aware of the fact that for years they have not really been doing justice to the education of minority peoples

Mexican-American or others. But let me explain that a little further. In my opinion, the American concept of education is a very simple one—that is, it should be *for* the community. I think we have organized our educational system with the same concept in mind. For example, we have school districts with local school boards, which presumably are the governing and policy-making bodies within the community. The only trouble with the concept is its application. The concept has been interpreted to mean that the school will meet the needs of the *dominant,* or middle class, community, not the minorities or lower classes. If we look at how curricula have been changed and if we look at the teachers who have been hired and where they have been trained, if we look at the whole gamut of education, I think we can clearly see that a very significant part of the community has been left out; namely, the minorities and the poor.

Do you think, then, that the goal of equal educational opportunities for Spanish-speaking Americans is becoming a reality?

SAMORA: I honestly don't know. I think many attempts are being made. I see this in many school districts, in San Antonio, for example. I see some attempts in Los Angeles and some attempts in Denver. But many of these have been *forced* upon the school system, and I am not at all convinced that school systems, school boards, principals, school superintendents, and others really know what they are up to. They may just be responding or reacting to pressure. If this is all that they are doing, then, I would say *no!* This is not the way equal opportunity in education comes about. On the other hand, if they really understand that these people are part of the community and that they may have different educational needs, then, perhaps, the time will come when a minority group will have an equal chance at an education. But at the moment, I think the situation is too much in a state of flux.

What do you think is the responsibility of the local community, as opposed to the federal government, for bringing better education to their community?

SAMORA: Since the whole concept of education in this country is community-based, I feel that most of the responsibility should be in the local community. However, if we look at what the local community has, in fact, done, then I think we can see that local communities are not really going anyplace in terms of equality of education, at least not without the interference of the federal courts. This is particularly true in the South. But the same situation has also been true in the case of bilingual education. I don't know of very many local communities that really got involved in bilingual education before the recent federal support. But there are other problems, especially financial ones. If local communities are strapped with taxation, then no matter how good their intentions, they may not be able to afford bilingual education, or curricular changes, or special materials. And if one looks again at local communities, we see all sorts of gerrymandering. We have seen it in places like Texas, where the major portion of funds go not to the minority schools but to the white schools and to the middle class school. Obviously, this is not equality of opportunity in education.

What is the effect of the Chicano youth movements on Anglo institutions? For example, what direction should the newly established Chicano studies and Third World departments take on the university campus?

SAMORA: That is an important question; it is two questions, actually. The effect of the Mexican-American youth movements on school systems in some areas has been very salutary. I am thinking of the Edgewood School District in San Antonio, for example, where a number of changes were brought about because of pressure from the Mexican-American youth organizations. In most areas, it is the young who have forced the school board and the school establishment to bring about particular changes. In other areas, they have been totally unsuccessful. And yet it seems to me that they have been able to do more in the past two or three years than most of the educators or social scientists who have been writing about the problem for the last twenty or thirty years.

Chicano high school students (Salvador Valdez,
courtesy of *Nosotros* Magazine)

Now, as to the Mexican-American studies programs, there are, to my knowledge, about seventy such programs throughout the Southwest, and a few are beginning in the Midwest and in the East. I must admit that I am somewhat disturbed about some of them. I think there is no question that Mexican-American studies is a legitimate field of pursuit. What has happened, however, is that many of these Mexican-American programs have been established under pressure. In being established under pressure, university administrations have said to those groups, "Begin your own programs, and here's so much money." They say this without really looking at the academic and intellectual problems involved in setting up either a department or a program. I have a feeling, also, that many an administrator has said, "Now I've given you this, so don't bother me anymore." And that is too bad. On the other hand, there are those who have looked at the situation very closely and have then agreed to establish these programs with help from within the academic institution and they have developed some very respectable programs.

One problem, besides money, is personnel. There haven't been that many Mexican-Americans who have pursued a master's degree, or a Ph.D., or who have done research in this field, to staff all the programs that are appearing. This means that in many places there are personnel running programs who are not necessarily qualified to run them. The big qualification is that they be Mexican-Americans. Incidentally, the same thing has occurred among blacks.

By not qualified, do you mean not academically certified or, in fact, not academically qualified to teach?

SAMORA: I have seen some programs in which all the staff must be Mexican-American. They look around for a Ph.D., and they don't find one. They look around for an M.A., and they don't find one. And they look around for a B.A., without regard to his field of specialty. This is what I mean by lack of qualification. And then the person who sets up this program has to fumble around for a good long time before he really knows what he is up to. But the pressure is there to produce something. Now, the person developing that kind of program is going to have a really tough job, because he will have a difficult time getting staff and setting up a curriculum. There are some programs that are now departments, and some that have academically qualified people who have worked in this field for some time. Some of these programs are offering a bachelor's degree and a master's and, they hope, a Ph.D. But it will be a while before these programs really get off the ground and go that far. By then, presumably more and more material will be coming out so that books and articles are available for students to read and research. One of the crying needs for most of these programs seems to be the availability of materials. To be sure, in the past year about ten books about Mexican-Americans appeared. But that is only *ten* books. I hope that in the next five or ten years, more and more researchers will be doing more and more studies that, in turn, will be used by more and more people in Mexican-American programs, as well as in other programs.

Isn't one of the goals of the Mexican-American studies departments to get people with an M.A. degree and a Ph.D. to go back into these departments and teach?

SAMORA: That seems to be one of the goals, and I think it's a laudable one. I suppose as more and more Mexican-Americans get higher degrees, more and more people will be involved in Mexican-American studies. But, presumably, these people will have better qualifications than the group that is running these programs now. Please don't misunderstand me: I am not trying to run these programs down. I think it's just as simple as this: If you have in this country only one hundred Mexican-Americans with Ph.D.'s (and this does not include those in medicine, dentistry, and law, but it does include many with degrees in engineering and the natural sciences), that's all the Ph.D.'s you've got; and you've got seventy Mexican-American programs to staff. It's a matter of arithmetic.

If the systems or administrations of school districts aren't responsive to the immediate needs of Chicano students, do you support a more violent approach?

SAMORA: I personally don't support violence at all. But that's a value judgment on my part. I support peaceful demonstrations. However, there are a number of people who differ in opinion from me. I certainly support change, and to me it is unfortunate that it has to be violent.

Let me put it this way. Do you think that a more aggressive approach by Mexican-Americans has promoted faster change and faster action on the part of the Anglo society?

SAMORA: Absolutely! I think it's a bad premise on which to base change, but, unfortunately, it seems to be the only way minorities can get something done. American society has forced people to demonstrations and violence by not taking care of the needs of these people when they knew that the needs were there. I can cite many instances of this. For example, we have gone to foundations or agencies and asked for particular things, and they have said, "Oh, no, we are too busy with the Negroes. They're rioting everywhere. They are the ones we are helping *now.*" Then the logical question is: "Does this mean that we have to riot, too, in order to get attention?" Then they say, "Oh, no." But that is really what it means. That is why I place the blame right back on society. It has taught us, as it were, that the way to get something done is to speak loudly, be aggressive, demonstrate, even riot and become violent. Then they will pay attention, and this is what I meant when I said that it's a bad premise on which to base changes in a society.

So far this morning, we've been discussing Mexican-Americans almost exclusively. There have been some dissatisfaction and claims of lack of brotherhood from the Puerto Rican community, particularly in New York and on the East Coast. Do you think that Puerto Ricans have been left out of the controversy?

SAMORA: To a certain extent they have. But again, I think we have to look at it in a broader perspective. I think that blacks, Orientals, Indians, Mexican-Americans, poor whites, and Puerto Ricans need to get together on common issues and common goals. I believe there is a commonality of problems here, and I think they would be able to do a lot more, either politically or otherwise, in any particular community if they would get together. The reality of the situation is, however, that many of these groups tend to work alone for what they *think* is their problem. Or, while they recognize that others have similar problems, they are not farsighted enough to see that the black problem is, to an extent, also *their* problem. What one does about this, I don't know. I have seen situations like this in the Midwest, where Mexican-Americans and Puerto Ricans are at odds with each other, when, in fact, they ought to be working together. I have seen situations where coalitions are formed, quite often only on specific issues rather than on the broad problems of a minority. If I were to predict, I would predict that in the years to come there will be more and more of this coalition-forming as we begin to see that we have common problems in many areas. The unfortunate fact at the moment is, however, that there is little bringing together of these groups into a broader organization.

What specifically, in your opinion, needs to be done right now to help elevate the level of education in the Southwest for Mexican-Americans? Are you optimistic, for example, about Title VII or migrant education programs? Which do you think has the most potential at this point?

SAMORA: There is no question in my mind that Title VII will bring about a variety of changes that will be important. As a matter of fact, this is something that a number of us, particularly Dr. Sánchez even thirty years ago, have been talking about for some time, and it is encouraging to know that it has come to be. The question of migrant education is also tremendously important. But it is even more important to get rid of migrancy. But until that happens, migrant education should be given tremendous emphasis, for the simple reason that migrants have tended to get nothing more than a third-grade education over the years, and, obviously, this is closely related to the situation of migrancy itself.

You may know of a very recent study, which I don't think is out for publication yet, by the U.S. Commission on Civil Rights, called the *Mexican-American Education Study*. Its first report just came out last month. It says three things that are important in terms of answering your question. It says that the public school pupils of this ethnic group—Mexican-Americans—are severely isolated by school districts and by schools within individual districts. That obviously means one thing we've touched upon; namely, gerrymandering, the separate but unequal schools that have been part of our history. Now to the extent that this is so—and according to the study, it *is* throughout the Southwest—something has to be done about it immediately. The second thing the study says is that Mexican-Americans are underrepresented in school district professional staffs and on boards of education. I think we have said something about the concept of community education, and this gets right to the point; namely, that schools have not really made an effort to see that all of the community is represented on either school staffs or on school boards. So, obviously, this is a problem which has to be tackled right away. The study's third big conclusion is that the majority of Mexican-American staffs and school board members are found in predominantly Mexican-American schools or districts, which again means the same sort of thing; namely, an educational isolation that should be tackled right away.

What do you think are the basic needs of elementary school principals? What should be brought to their attention? And what can they do to better schools in an area with a high concentration of Mexican-American children, or to make those principals who are not in a highly Mexican-American area more aware of the problem?

SAMORA: I think what they ought to be doing is looking for curriculum changes with the help of the Mexican-American community—teachers, pupils, and parents. I think the other thing they can do is to involve the parents of the Mexican-American community; this goes back to the premise of education serving the community. I think it is a truism that Mexican-Americans don't belong to PTA. It's very obvious to me why they don't: the PTA is meaningless to them and they don't understand it. Even with the best of intentions, it has never been explained to them. However, something like PTA needs to be developed to involve the community. I think, then, these things—bringing about curriculum changes and involving the community—are what principals and superintendents should be doing.

Lydia R. Aguirre

Lydia R. Aguirre has worked in the social work profession for many years. At present Mrs. Aguirre is on the faculty of the University of Texas at El Paso where she teaches courses in the social work program.

THE MEANING
OF THE CHICANO MOVEMENT

Let me start by saying that the Chicano is an extremely diversified "individual." We are as heterogeneous as our history. Without that background of history, it is difficult to understand us. *No somos Mexicanos.* We are citizens of the United States with cultural ties to Mexico and in some instances to Spain, but, within our ties of language and culture, we have developed a culture that is neither Spanish nor Mexican. *Entre nosotros habemos quien habla un español puro, pero también entre nosotros habemos los "batos" que no pueden conseguir "jale" por la razón que sea.*

We are bilingual. We are doctors, university professors, lawyers, and congressmen as well as farm laborers, maids, housewives, plumbers, mailmen, and engineers. There are some Mexican-Americans who are *tío-tacos,* those who ride the fence and *cuando se les aprieta el cinto, nos dan en la torre.* But then, there are some Mexican-Americans who would readily turn Chicano when they are scratched a little. By that I mean when they understand the true value of this our diversified Chicano movement.

About the term "Chicano," I cannot as yet give you a scholarly explanation. From my adolescence in Edinburg, Texas, I remember Chicano as a derogatory term applied *only by us,* who we then insisted should be called Mexican-Americans. We demanded that we be classified as Caucasian. Chicano was a term used self-consciously and degradingly only by ourselves. In his columns in the *Los Angeles Times,* Rubén Salazar attempted to define the term. In one column he wrote, "A Chicano is a Mexican-American with a non-Anglo image of himself . . . actually the word Chicano is as difficult to define as 'soul.'" In another instance, he wrote, "For those who like simplistic answers Chicano can be defined as short for Mexicano. For those who prefer complicated answers it has been suggested that Chicano may have come from the word Chihuahua—the name of a Mexican state bordering on the United States. Getting trickier this version contends that Mexicans who migrated to Texas call themselves Chicanos." In a third reference he said, "Chicanos then are merely fighting to become 'Americans.' Yes, but with a Chicano outlook."

As I understand the word "Chicano" in the Chicano movement, it is this: if there is no lowest of the low and no highest of the high and *each* will wear the label of *Chicano* with pride, he will have personal respect and with it *dignidad y unidad con sus hermanos Chicanos.* He will be proud to assume his heritage guaranteed in the Treaty of Guadalupe-Hidalgo and proud to use the language and customs that are his by heritage, treaty, and *corazon.* Chicano power simply means that in the finding of identity —that is, a right to be *as he is,* not Mexican, not Spanish, not speaking either a "pure" English or a "pure" Spanish, but *as he is,* a product of a Spanish-Mexican-Indian heritage and an Anglo-Saxon (American, or, as Mexico says, *Estado Unidense*) influence—he will unite with his brothers in heritage. As he has pride and unity, so will he lose his self-consciousness and self-degradation and thereby will gain status and power.

Collectively, the Chicano in unity can influence the social systems that have perpetuated social injustices. Some say we are in the midst of a social revolution. I prefer to state that we are in the midst of a renaissance. We challenge the educational system to recognize our "differ-

Labor rally to unionize Chicano workers (Salvador Valdez, courtesy of *Nosotros* Magazine)

entness." We challenge ourselves to be proud of this differentness. We challenge the educational system to teach Hispanic history, to teach bilingually, and to give us adequate schools where students are largely Chicano. We demand not to be segregated. We demand that others recognize our differentness and work within that differentness rather than make the Chicano suppress his Chicanismo and adopt Anglo-Saxon ideals.

We demand that our side of the story be told. From this demand grew the Rubén Salazar Memorial Scholarship Foundation. Rubén Salazar dared to speak the truth. His voice was silenced when he was killed in Los Angeles in the line of duty, covering the 1970 Chicano Moratorium for his paper. Through the mass communications scholarships we are offering, we hope to educate young people in television, radio, and journalism to continue Rubén Salazar's message. Needless to say, the present mass media sometimes distort the truth. What may really be a justified confrontation on a social injustice can be reported as a riotous disruption.

Some of us feel that we need parallel institutions to have real justice. The Rubén Salazar memorial foundation has a long-range goal of establishing or sponsoring a daily newspaper. Later on, who knows—perhaps even Chicano radio and television!

We continue being so terribly diversified, yet we have so many cultural values that unite us. Each area has problems unique to that area. Northern New Mexico is rural and communal. The people there are fighting for their lands and grazing and water rights. Urban areas fight both discrimination and racism. Racism is so difficult to fight because it is so intangible and difficult to pinpoint. Yet it is all around us.

Take, for example, El Paso. People with Spanish surnames number almost half of the population of El Paso. Yet we have very few businessmen proportionately. If we look at executive positions of the major companies, we are lucky to find a sprinkling of Spanish surnames. Many of our educated young people have to leave this community to find jobs. I personally know several young people who looked diligently for jobs for months and either left town or took a menial job. Last week, however, I received a call from an Anglo-Saxon young lady friend of mine who found a good job after only three days of looking in a city strange to her. Were the former just unfortunate incidents and was the latter a fortunate incident?

In approaching the problems facing us, the Chicano uses different methods. Each in his own way is striving to achieve human dignity, self-respect, and just equality. Some Chicanos (and I include myself) attempt to effect change within established systems, and if that does not work, attempt to establish parallel systems. Hence, we have separate newspapers, Chicano conferences, businesses. We attempt to change the educational system to better meet our needs. We demand justice in courts and from police within the established order. Other Chicanos prefer isolationism or brown separatism. These are in the minority. Very few would want a separate nation.

Others, particularly in New Mexico, who brought from Spain and continued the system of an agrarian, communal society into this century, want a return to that system which in that climate and region is almost imperative to survival. It is interesting to note that the Pueblo Indian who lived in that region when the Spaniards arrived had a similar system already in operation.

In our search for identity, we are researching and I feel, perhaps creating, the concept of *Aztlán*. Supposedly, we are descendants, through our Indian heritage, of the native peoples of the Southwest. The Aztlán people had a civilization that is still with us in a modified form through Mexican-Spanish influences. Aztlán lives in any land where a Chicano lives: in his mind and heart and in the land he walks. The emblem used extensively in Chicano circles is a black Aztec eagle on a red background.

Carnalismo, a feeling or an allegiance that permeates the movement, means a type of brotherhood within members of La Raza characterized by depth of feeling and allegiance to other *carnales*. It is the type of feeling and allegiance that many blood relatives have for one another. Once a Chicano is your *carnal,* he will stand with you through thick or thin.

In social work circles (I am a social worker by training), we are looking at the aspects of the Chicano (Mexican-American) family that are conducive to mental health. We are attempting to break the stereotypes associated with the Chicano family and show the Chicano family with its healthful components as well as with its harmful components. We are looking at the extended family and at the social welfare institutions that penalize the Chicano for preserving these family ties. In a sense, our culture has retained the "people orientation" lost to many in our materialistic society.

One of our leaders in the movement has been César Chávez with his organization of farm workers. His is a nonviolent movement. From the frustration of the strikes originated the Teatro Campesino (in Delano, California, in 1965). Out of the need for laughter, the strikers began a fast-paced, almost slapstick style of comedy mimicking those pertinent to the strikers: the patron, the contractor, the scab, and so forth. It is now a tremendously effective mode of showing the problems faced by Chicanos. It is raw; it is realistic; it is life itself!

Reies López Tijerina is another leader. His leadership is primarily in Tierra Amarilla in New Mexico. He is a land-grant spokesman, although presently imprisoned for destroying federal property in one of the national forests. Tijerina is a native of southern Texas. He saw his father run off his land in a most humiliating fashion. He was from humble origins, and he drifted around in farm camps. He was an extremely eloquent, fiery speaker for his *Alianza,* fighting for return of lands to land grantees and communal rights, but, most important, for full recognition of the Treaty of Guadalupe-Hidalgo. Ranchers have distorted laws in this area to suit their needs.

Rodolfo "Corky" González from Colorado has been a leader in the migratory labor area. He is an ex-boxer, lecturer, poet, political activist, and community organizer, as well as a businessman and philanthropist. He is presently president and director of the Crusade for Justice, a Chicano civil rights organization in Denver. His poem, *"Yo Soy Joaquín,"* should be required reading for everyone. Joaquín's first words poignantly describe the anguish of the Chicano who is confused and lost in the Anglo society.

José Angel Gutiérrez of Crystal City, Texas, is a young man who is devoting his most capable energies toward establishing a base of political power in Texas. Chicanos who have become disillusioned with both political parties have created a third party, La Raza Unida.

The Mexican press was a strong ally to the Mexican-Americans who fought injustices during and after World War II. We are still fighting these injustices, but now with a better self-concept, with a sustaining and lasting dedication and determination, and with more sophisticated and greater manpower. The dedication is courageous and contagious. We are fighting the vast racism that is rampant in our country and that seems unable to tolerate differentness. We are fighting for the right to be *as we are*—Chicanos. And within our culture we demand the right to be first-class citizens within this our United States.

Por mi Raza habla el Espiritu.

Armando M. Rodríguez

Armando M. Rodríguez is Assistant Commissioner of Education, HEW. His articles on Mexican-American education have appeared in a variety of journals and magazines.

SPEAK UP, CHICANO

I sat quietly and listened as fifteen Mexican-American citizens who had gathered in a crumbling adobe community center in San Antonio's oldest slum talked about their schools. As director of the U.S. Office of Education's Mexican-American Affairs Unit, I was there to learn what the local citizens and school people felt were their most pressing educational needs.

"We ought to be consulted more about what goes on in our schools," the president of the Mexican-American Community Club said heatedly. "Our high school needs a Mexican-American on the counseling staff. But the school people say they can't find a qualified one to hire. Over 60 percent of the kids are Mexican-Americans and most of them have trouble speaking English. Yet we have only five Spanish-speaking teachers, and not a single person in the school office speaks Spanish. Is it any wonder the kids drop out like flies? The hell with the requirements. Let's take care of these kids' needs, and one of the first is to get somebody who can talk to them."

"Now wait just a minute," interrupted the school district's assistant superintendent. "We have to follow state regulations, you know. You can't put just anybody in the counseling office. You tell us where to find a qualified Mexican-American teacher or counselor and we'll be delighted to hire him."

"At least you could have Mexican-Americans in the school as aides, couldn't you?" asked a neighborhood representative on the community action program board. "But you folks downtown made the requirements so high that none of our people could get a job. Why?"

"We have to have qualified people to work with the youngsters," answered the director of instruction.

"Qualified?" the president broke in. "What could be better qualifications than speaking the language and understanding the kids?"

"Well, we haven't seen much show of interest from the parents," countered a schoolman. "We can't get them out to PTA meetings, can't even get many of them to come to parents' night. We hired a Mexican-American school–community coordinator for some of our schools, but she's finding it an uphill battle getting the parents to take an interest in school matters."

And so it went at meeting after meeting that I attended with Lupe Anguiano and Dean Bistline, my co-workers in the Mexican-American Affairs Unit. We visited seventeen communities on our three-week tour of Arizona, California, Colorado, New Mexico, and Texas. Both Mexican-American community leaders and school people—some seventeen hundred altogether—poured out their frustrations, and we learned a great deal about what the people want and need and in what priority.

In those five states alone, there are more than 5.5 million people of Spanish surname. Eight out of ten live in California or Texas. Their numbers are constantly reinforced by a stream of immigrants from Mexico. Add the 1.5 million other Spanish-speaking people—Cuban, Puerto Rican, Central and South American, and Spanish—who live in Florida and the northeast and midwestern industrial cities, and it becomes apparent that the United States has a substantial second minority group. They are a minority whose historical, cultural, and linguistic characteristics set them apart from the Anglo community as dramatically as the Negro's skin sets him apart. Few people outside the Southwest realize the degree of discrimination this difference has brought about.

For me the introduction to discrimination began thirty-seven years ago when my father brought the family to California from Durango, Mexico. I was nine years old when we settled in San Diego in an extremely poor but well-integrated community of Mexican-Americans, Negroes, and poor Anglos. The trouble was in school. I knew only a dozen words of English, so I just sat around the first few weeks not understanding a thing. I was not allowed to speak Spanish in class. But after school each day I played with neighborhood kids, so I soon picked up enough English to hold my own on the playground. Then I made this smattering of English do in class.

It didn't occur to me or my family to protest. In those days people didn't talk much about ethnic differences or civil rights. The Chicanos (our favorite nickname for fellow Mexican-Americans) pretty much stayed "in their place," working as domestics and laborers in the cities or as wetback stoop laborers in the fields and orchards. Only a few became professionals or businessmen.

I remember being advised by my high school counselor to forget my dreams of going to college and becoming a teacher. "They don't hire Mexican-Americans," he said. Then World War II came along. When I got out of the army in 1944, the GI Bill of Rights saw me through San Diego College. I got a teaching job and eventually became a junior high school principal in San Diego. But my experience was a rare one for the times.

Since then, conditions have changed a good deal. There is spirit in the Mexican-American community now. On my recent trip I saw a pride in the young people that was not so evident when I was growing up. The Chicano today is proud of his role as an American. Many parents, even those who are illiterate, as were mine, are determined that their children will not be like them. And they see education as the means. But along with their determination has come a new impatience. Gone is the meek, long-suffering separateness of the Chicanos. They are beginning to stand up and make their voices heard.

"Head Start is great," said a parent-businessman at one of our meetings. "But it isn't enough. Some of the programs are only for the summer, and our kids need a whole year if they are to have a chance to start out even with the Anglo kids."

"Why can't the schools use more of their government money for food and health services?"

As we listened to their grievances, I realized that our most valuable role at these meetings was as a bouncing board for their ideas. With us present, both school and community leaders found themselves saying things to each other they had heretofore said only within their own group. Inevitably, though, they looked to us, the spokesmen for the government, to "do something." Of course, that was not our role. We were there to help them establish lines of communication and to explain to them the ways in which the U.S. Office of Education can support their efforts. But we had to make clear that it is they, the state and local school people and the community, who must design the programs and carry them out.

Nationally there is a growing amount of concern about Mexican-American affairs that has generated much real help. In evidence is the recent series of conferences at Tucson, Pueblo, and El Paso sponsored by the National Education Association. Also, the federal government created three new agencies with specific responsibilities to the Mexican-American. The Inter-Agency Committee on Mexican-American Affairs assists in development of services that cover the wide range of government activities. The United States–Mexico Commission on Border Development and Friendship is charged with creating programs to improve cooperation on both sides of the border. And the U.S. Office of Education's Mexican-American Affairs Unit seeks to bring some expertise to bear on the education of the bilingual-bicultural citizen and to develop a focus on the effort. This unit is now supported by a newly created Advisory Committee on Mexican-American Education. Still another evidence of concern and help is passage by the United States Congress of the Bilingual Education Act (Title VII of the Elementary and Secondary Education Act). It authorizes funds and support for schools to develop programs in which both English and the native language of the student can be used as teaching tools until a mastery of English has been achieved.

These are a healthy start, as is the rising involvement of the Mexican-American community itself in directing attention to educational issues. Still, some major obstacles remain in the way of the Mexican-American's progress toward educational equality. Of prime consideration is the shortage of teachers qualified to cope with the Mexican-American's particular situation. There are only two thousand bilingual teachers in the elementary and secondary schools today. Equally distressing is the lack of teachers who are even aware of the Chicano's cultural background and recognize his language as an asset. It is a striking contradiction that we spend millions of dollars to encourage schoolchildren to learn a foreign language and, at the same time, frown upon Mexican-American children speaking Spanish in school. The impression they receive is that there must be something inherently bad about their language. This, of course, leads to self-depreciation. To make the situation even more ridiculous, they are often asked to take Spanish as a foreign language later in school.

Only bilingual teachers can correct this situation— teachers who can treat the Chicano's Spanish as an asset while the student is learning English. And that will require a tremendous effort in teacher education. As a starter, the Teacher Corps, cooperating with the Mexican-American Affairs Unit, has set up a high-intensity language training component for a group of interns teaching in schools with a number of Spanish-speaking students. This program lasts six weeks and gives considerable attention to cross-cultural values as well as to language instruction.

A second obstacle to a comprehensive education for the Chicano is the lack of well-integrated curricula. As I toured the Southwest, I saw good programs here and there for preschool youngsters, some good adult basic education going on in one place, a good program to educate the whole migrant family in another. But in no single place did I see a school district whose curriculum and instructional program correlated with the needs of the Mexican-Americans from kindergarten through high school. There were glimpses of hope, though.

In San Antonio, Texas, I was impressed with a program developed by the Southwest Educational Development Laboratory of Austin that used linguistic techniques to improve the fluency of Mexican-American youngsters in oral language as a foundation for reading. Intensive instruction is given in English as a second language, and an identical program of instruction is given in Spanish. The program was started two years ago in nine schools and is in formal operation in the first two grades in San

Chicano children at school (Salvador Valdez, courtesy of *Nosotros* Magazine)

Antonio with plans for continuation in grades three and four. The first group of youngsters in the program are now equaling national norms in reading, and some are even achieving the fifth-grade level. Traditionally Mexican-American boys and girls in southern Texas have lagged at least a year behind the national norms.

San Diego, California, has developed a demonstration center for English as a second language to help school districts create specialized educational programs for students who initially learned a language other than English. One of its bright features has been the large number of parents who worked with the professional staff in designing these programs for non-English-speaking parents and youngsters alike.

The Foreign Language Innovative Curricula Studies at Ann Arbor, Michigan, used funds from Title III of the Elementary and Secondary Education Act to develop a bilingual curriculum program with materials for language arts instruction. The program has been aimed at the Spanish-speaking youngster—both migrant and permanent resident—whose linguistic handicaps severely limit his educational achievement. The program is for the primary grades and stresses the development of materials which are exciting to all youngsters and are suitable for use by teachers with a minimum of specialized training.

By sharing their experiences in these innovative programs, school districts can help one another. And a wealth of good ideas are emerging from conferences such as the one sponsored by the Advisory Committee on Mexican-American Education and the Mexican-American Affairs Unit in Austin, Texas, recently. Here at the Office of Education we have a special task force that works closely with the eight bureaus in considering funding proposals for projects aimed at improving educational opportunities for the Mexican-American.

A third obstacle to the young Chicano's educational success is a lack of models—"heroes," if you will. The school needs to put before him successful Mexican-Americans whom he can emulate as he sets his educational goals. A teacher, a counselor, a principal who is Mexican-

American can do the trick. Discrimination in past generations has, unfortunately, limited the number of such persons. In many heavily Mexican-American schools, there is not a single Mexican-American teacher, let alone a counselor or administrator. Now, however, with the Chicano's education improving and discrimination diminishing, I am hopeful that more and more of today's children will have the career models before them that they need.

If my impression of all this activity and promise is correct, the Mexican-American is about to see the dawning of a new era. He will become a far more productive member of society. His cultural and linguistic heritage will be turned to good use.

Although the Chicano has suffered and lost much in the last one hundred years, he now intends to do what is necessary to win his fight for educational equality. And he will do it today. *Mañana* is too late.

Mario T. García

Mario T. García is Assistant Professor of Chicano Studies and History, California State University, San Diego. He has taught at various colleges and universities and has written many articles on the Chicano movement.

CHICANO YOUTH AND THE
POLITICS OF PROTEST

The question of youth is a very important one to Chicanos. The fact is that the median age of the Mexican population in the United States is about twenty-one years. We are a young population, and this, I believe, is reflected in the vitality of the Chicano movement.

Yet, this vitality and, indeed, radicalization that we see in Chicano youth is not an isolated phenomenon. It is part of a general national and worldwide youth and student radicalization. The decade of the 1960s saw students in this country throw away the so-called apathy of the 1950s and engage in the most momentous student movement in the history of this nation. The "apathetic generation" of the '50s gave way to Mario Savio, Jerry Rubin, Stokely Carmichael, Angela Davis, Los Siete,[1] José Angel Gutiérrez, etc., etc., of the '60s.

Inspired by the courage displayed by blacks—both young and old—in the civil rights movement, young whites began to mobilize not only around civil and human rights issues, but as the war in Southeast Asia was expanded, after the election of the "peace" candidate LBJ in 1964, students began to demonstrate and to demand that the United States stop the killing of Vietnamese and remove the troops from Southeast Asia. Young people by the tens of thousands took to the streets to protest the imperialism of the United States—in the fall of 1969, for example, and, of course, in the historic student strikes of May, 1970, after the invasion of Cambodia by the Nixon Administration. This youth rebellion found outlets, also, in protests against the enslavement and dehumanization of students in our universities, colleges, and high schools; in protests against the destruction of the environment by the profit-oriented industries of this country; and, in the continued struggle of blacks, Chicanos, native Americans, Latinos, Puerto Ricans, Asian-Americans, and women to secure their just and legal rights.

These demands by youth in the United States: to end the war, for student control of their schools, for the rights denied national minorities and women, and for the humanization of an exploitive economic and political system—these demands, and others, are also similar to the demands being raised by young people all over the world, be it France, Czechoslovakia, Mexico, Japan, etc. The

---

[1] A group of seven young Chicano militants arrested in San Jose, California.

Chicano youth at a political rally being entertained by Mariachis (Pat Ellis, courtesy of *Nosotros* Magazine)

outh radicalization of the 1960s, which continues into his decade, despite the attempts of the mass media to nake us believe otherwise, is a worldwide phenomenon. t is the result, not of a generation gap, but of the failure of the capitalist system as well as the bureaucratic workers' tates, to meet the needs of their people, especially the roung. It is this failure that has created the youth and tudent movements of today.

Chicano youth are a part of this movement—they have been influenced by it, but, at the same time, they have contributed to it greatly. The Chicano movement, indeed, as been a youth movement. Look at the faces of those valking picket lines around Safeway and Big Bear;[2] look

[2] These are large chain supermarkets, principally in the West and outhwest.

at the faces of those who marched to Sacramento with
César Chávez; look at the faces of those who attended the
San Jose State Chicano Commencement of 1968, which, in
many respects, began the Chicano movement on the state
college campuses of California; look at the faces around
Corky González at the Crusade for Justice in Denver; look
at the faces of those who marched on August 29, 1970
in the Chicano Moratorium in Los Angeles; look at the
faces of those who assisted in the rise of La Raza Unida
in South Texas, which has led to significant victories in
Crystal City and San Juan; indeed, look at the face o
José Angel Gutiérrez![3] Look at the faces of those who
attended the milestone Chicana Conference in Houston
in May, 1971![4] What do you see? You see the faces o
young Chicanos and Chicanas! There are many who
castigate and downgrade the contribution of our youth
and our students, but they do so out of ignorance, for i
has been the Chicano students and young people, in
general, who have been, and continue to be, in the fore
front of *"El Movimiento"*—it is this segment of our pop
ulation that represents the most radicalized sector of the
Chicano community.

This was not always the case, however. For many years
young Chicanos were alienated and disillusioned, but their
only solutions were to lash out at each other, as seen in
the Pachuco and gang movements of the '40s and '50s
or else, as the novel *Pocho* so well illustrates, young
Chicanos simply joined the army and lashed out at Ger
mans, Japanese, Koreans, and Vietnamese. And if they
did not go to these extremes, they went to other extremes
we joined Viva Kennedy and Viva Johnson clubs!

Yet all this has changed to a considerable degree, and
the Chicano movement is a testimony to this. No cleare

---

[3] Gutiérrez is the founder and organizer of the Raza Unida Part
of South Texas.

[4] This conference dealt with issues that pertain in general to th
women's liberation movement: birth control, abortion, the right o
Chicanas to control their own bodies; this is the first national con
ference of minority women in the U.S. to deal with these issues.

xample of the politicization and radicalization of our
oung *"hermanos y hermanas"* can be given than the
istoric first National Chicano Youth Liberation Confer-
nce in Denver, Colorado, in March, 1969. It was at this
onference, attended by hundreds of young people, that
ie Plan of Aztlán was drawn up.

The Preamble of the Plan points out the increased
wareness of young Chicanos of their national identity
nd of the roots of their exploitation:

In the spirit of a new people that is conscious not only
of its proud historic heritage but also of the brutal
"Gringo" invasion of our territories, we, the Chicano
inhabitants and civilizers of the northern land of Aztlán
from whence came our forefathers, reclaiming the land
of their birth and consecrating the determination of our
people of the sun, *declare* that the call of our blood is
our power, our responsibility, and our inevitable destiny.

We are free and sovereign to determine those tasks
which are justly called for by our house, our land, the
sweat of our brows, and by our hearts. Aztlán belongs
to those who plant the seeds, water the fields, and
gather the crops, and not to the foreign Europeans. We
do not recognize capricious frontiers on the bronze continent.

Brotherhood unites us, and love for our brothers makes
us a people whose time has come and who struggles
against the foreigner *"gabacho"* who exploits our riches
and destroys our culture. With our heart in our hands
and our hands in the soil, we declare the independence of our mestizo nation. We are a bronze people
with a bronze culture. Before the world, before all
of North America, before all of our brothers in the
bronze continent, we are a nation, we are a union of
free pueblos, we are *Aztlán*.

Por la raza todo. Fuera de la raza nada.
(Everything for my people. Without my people nothing.)

The implementation of this nationalist plan for liberatic
is spelled out in six specific points of action:

1. Awareness and distribution of El Plan Espiritual
Aztlán. Presented at every meeting, demonstration,
confrontation, courthouse, institution, administration,
church, school, tree, building, car, and every place of
human existence.

2. September 16, on the birthdate of Mexican independence, a national walkout by all Chicanos of all
colleges and schools to be sustained until the complete
revision of the educational system: its policy-makers,
administration, its curriculum, and its personnel to meet
the needs of our community. [This was widely carried
out in 1969. In San Jose where I was at the time,
10,000 students walked out and demonstrated.]

3. Self-defense against the occupying force of the op-
pressors at every school, every available man, woman,
and child.

4. Community nationalization and organization of all
Chicanos: El Plan Espiritual de Aztlán.

5. Economic program to drive the exploiter out of our
community and a welding together of our people's combined resources to control their own production through
cooperative effort.

6. Creation of an independent local, regional, and national political party.

A nation autonomous and free—culturally, socially,
economically, and politically—will make its own decisions
on the usage of our lands, the taxation of our goods, the
utilization of our bodies for war, the determination of
justice (reward and punishment), and the profit of our
sweat.

El Plan de Aztlán is the plan of liberation![5]

[5] See Antonio Carmejo (ed.), *Chicano Documents* (New York, 1972

The Plan of Aztlán and other pronouncements by Chicano youths, as well as their actions, demonstrate their disillusionment with the "system." Chicano youth—unlike some of our older brothers and sisters, or our *"padres"*— no longer believe in the words of a Kennedy, a Johnson, a McCarthy, a McGovern, a Muskie, and certainly not of a Nixon! Our *"juventud"* realize, as the Plan of Aztlán so graphically puts it, that "the two-party system is the same animal with two heads that feed from the same trough." Our young people realize that both the Democratic and Republican parties do not serve the interests of Chicanos, or of blacks, other national minorities, women, and working people in general; but instead serve the interest of the ruling class of capitalists: the Rockefellers, the Fords, the Vanderbilts, the Kennedys, etc., who run this country.

This disillusionment and awareness has led to the execution of point six under Action of the Plan of Aztlán —the development of Raza Unida parties. The most notable example of this development has been the success of the Raza Unida in South Texas, where, beginning in April of 1970, the Raza Unida has proceeded to gain political control of both Crystal City and San Juan, Texas.[6] A lucid demonstration of what Raza Unida can do was seen this past January when, during a farmworkers' strike near Crystal City, the Raza Unida mobilized all segments of the Chicano community in support of the farmworkers' demands for higher wages. Chicano students and faculty walked out of their schools and joined other Chicanos in picket lines and in a climactic march and rally involving more than 1,800 people. This mass pressure and mobilization led to the farmworkers' demands being met.

In southern California, the significant vote gained in late 1971 by the Raza Unida campaign of Raúl Ruiz in the 48th Assembly District in Los Angeles exemplifies the

---

[6] These are small cities in rural South Texas, where the majority of people are Chicanos.

growing awareness of Chicanos in this part of the South-west of the necessity for an independent Chicano political party that will address itself to the needs of Chicanos an independent party that will organize, mobilize, and politicize the Chicano community 365 days a year, and not just during election time. An example of this is the support the Raza Unida in southern California gave to the March 4, 1972, demonstration in Los Angeles to protest the passage of the Dixon-Arnett Law, which threatens to deport both registered and nonregistered aliens.[7]

The growth of Raza Unida parties is without doubt the most significant development of the Chicano movement for not only is it clearly the vehicle that can unite the Chicano community in our struggle for what is rightfully ours, but it also cuts at the stranglehold the capitalist parties have on our communities. That this significance is likewise, apparent to both the Democrats and Republicans can be seen in their efforts to "woo" the Chicano vote Nixon attempts to do this by appointing "front-store Mexicans," like Señora Bañuelos to federal positions.[8] The Democrats try by creating a Spanish-speaking caucus to direct Chicano political energies back to the Democratic Party, or by going around saying the Raza Unida cannot win, and, therefore, we should support Chicano Democrats or Liberal Democrats like Muskie and McGovern.

These pressures by both parties are increasing, and will continue to increase. The challenge to the Raza Unida parties, and to Chicano young people who are in support of an independent Chicano party, will be whether that independence can be maintained. I believe it can. I believe, certainly for Chicano youth, there is no turning back to the Democrats; the lies, distortions, hypocrisy, etc., of this party over the period of the 1960s are too blatantly obvious

---

[7] Chicanos oppose this law not only on its unconstitutionality, but also on the grounds that no Mexican is "illegal" or "alien" to California; the real "wetbacks" are the Anglos, who crossed the Atlantic and later the Mississippi.

[8] Señora Bañuelos was appointed by President Nixon as the Treasurer of the United States in 1971.

for our young people to ever believe in it again. Much work, however, remains to be done in the development of the Raza Unida, but the first giant steps have been taken, and in the future we will see its continued growth, especially among the vanguard of the Chicano movement— *"nuestra juventud!"*

Part II

THE CREATIVE SPIRIT

5 • POETRY

The fundamental question in any discussion of Chicano poetry must perforce address itself to the relationship between literature and culture. This question assumes *al principio* that a particular culture produces and evolves a particular kind of literature particularized even further by the language and linguistic behavior of that culture. Despite literary correlations such as the novel, the play, the short story, the essay, etc., the Spanish novel is distinctly different from the English novel, just as the French short story is distinctively different from the Russian short story, and so on. These are not just differences in kind we are talking about, but significant differences in structure, tone, atmosphere, etc., all conditioned by the culture and the language communicating that culture to its members. Think then how much more difficult the way to a poem is when that poem is a reflection of a culture other than ours, when the poem is in another language or combination of languages, as is the case with Chicano poetry.

Chicano poetry draws its images and metaphors from the social conditions of Chicano existence which are viewed by Chicano poets as simply extensions of ancient settings and origins. But the metaphor of Chicano existence is woven linguistically into the fabric of the political context in which the Chicano poet finds himself. That is, in order to assert his ethnic identity in a context that seeks to eradicate that identity, the Chicano poet must marshal for us the splendor of our antiquity, and show us how that antiquity bears directly on our present. In "Aztec Angel," for example, Luis Omar Salinas welds the present to the past. He is "an Aztec angel," he tells us, "criminal of a scholarly society" doing favors for whimsical magicians where he pawns his heart for truth and finds his way "through obscure streets of soft-spoken hara-kiris." To sustain the Chicano spirit and soul it is important to know that as Aztec angels we are offspring of a beautiful woman. And this is important when we consider that as Chicanos we are predominantly an Indian people, and that, by and large, in Anglo-American society "Indianness" has not been identified as beautiful any more than black has been.

What Chicano poetry portends, then, is a shift away from mainstream American poetry to a distinctly new poetics that embraces the politics and sociology of poetry as well as new linguistic parameters. Specifically, this new poetics is the result of the Chicano renaissance which placed a conscious emphasis on the Chicano struggle for equality. It is only natural that this kind of shift in poetic perspective conjures up notions of a unique Chicano future in which Anglos play minimal (if any) roles.

An equally important aspect of Chicano poetry to consider is the linguistic aspect. Chicano poets are expressing themselves on the printed page in their Chicano language, evolved from Spanish and English, and their particular experiences in American *barrios, colonias,* and ghettos. Like black English, the Chicano language is at the heart of the Chicano experience; but unlike black English, the Chicano language deals not only with dialects of American English but with dialects of American and Mexican Spanish. Moreover, it has produced a mixture of the two languages resulting in a unique kind of *binary phenomena,* in which the linguistic symbols of two languages are mixed in utterances using either language's syntactic structure.

The works of Chicano poets like Omar Salinas, Abelardo Delgado, and Ricardo Sánchez reflect the existential problems of survival that Chicanos face day-in and day-out. There is anguish and frustration in the vision of Chicano poets, but there is also determination bred from the knowledge of who they are.

The message from Chicano poets for change is loud and clear. There is no mistaking the insistent plea for refornation. Although the spirit of Chicano poetry may be considered revolutionary, its intellectual emphasis, however, is on reason as it attempts to move the hearts and minds of men by appealing to their better natures.

With the exception of the first two poems, all of the other poems have been written since 1960. The poems by Roberto Félix Salazar and José Antonio Navarro are offered as examples of the kinds of poetry Mexican-Americans were writing prior to the Chicano movement, although in "The Other Pioneers" Roberto Salazar touches upon an important contention of the Chicano movement. The impulse to bring together only movement poetry was strong, but it would hardly be representative of the kinds of themes Chicano poets are working with. For they too, like other poets, are observers of the human condition.

Roberto Félix Salazar

Roberto Félix Salazar is an accomplished writer from Laredo, Texas whose poems and articles have been published in *Esquire* and other leading magazines.

THE OTHER PIONEERS

Now I must write
Of those of mine who rode these plains
Long years before the Saxon and the Irish came.
Of those who plowed the land and built the towns
And gave the towns soft-woven Spanish names.
Of those who moved across the Rio Grande
Toward the hiss of Texas snake and Indian yell.
Of men who from the earth made thick-walled homes
And from the earth raised churches to their God.
And of the wives who bore them sons
And smiled with knowing joy.

They saw the Texas sun rise golden-red with
    promised wealth
And saw the Texas sun sink golden yet, with
    wealth unspent.
"Here," they said. "Here to live and here to love."
"Here is the land for our sons and the sons of our
    sons."
And they sang the songs of ancient Spain
And they made new songs to fit new needs.
They cleared the brush and planted the corn
And saw green stalks turn black from lack of rain.
They roamed the plains behind the herds

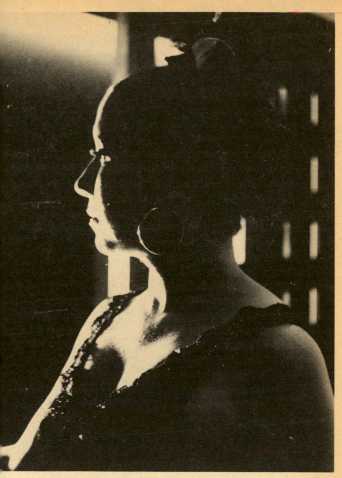

"Gentle mothers left their graces and their arts. . . ."
(Salvador Valdez, courtesy of *Nosotros* Magazine)

And stood the Indian's cruel attacks.
There was dust and there was sweat.
And there were tears and the women prayed.

And the years moved on.
Those who were first placed in graves
Beside the broad mesquite and the tall nopal.
Gentle mothers left their graces and their arts
And stalwart fathers pride and manly strength.
Salinas, de la Garza, Sánchez, García,
Uribe, González, Martínez, de León:
Such were the names of the fathers.
Salinas, de la Garza, Sánchez, García,
Uribe, González, Martínez, de León:
Such are the names of the sons.

José Antonio Navarro

José Antonio Navarro has long been active in the League of Unite
Latin American Citizens, one of the early Mexican-American group
formed to help Mexican-Americans overcome the effects of discrimin
tion.

SALTILLO MOUNTAINS

Dedicated to my friend and brother Knigl
of Columbus, Anastasio P. Sánchez, on ou
visit to the City of Saltillo, Mexico, Augu
30, 1939.

Majestic mountains of a wondrous age,
    Mysterious wonders of a God's design
A challenge to the learned sage,
    The purpose of their being, to define.

Typical scene of American and Mexican high deserts
(Ruth Schensul)

Supremely great, archaic towers of the West
    Serenely stand in grand array,
Unmoved, unchanged, at no time in decay,
    The Omnipotent's creative power to attest.

Like sentries bold, a stranger to apprise,
    These mountains guard a pleasant dale.
To lofty peaks, the heaps of earth arise
    And form a barrier to a fertile vale.

Though barren rocks project from mountain-base
    And rugged peaks enormous heights attain,

Ingenious man a winding course did trace
 Along an endless, jagged mountain-chain.

At yonder crag of legendary fame,
 Burst forth a gentle streaming waterfall;
From whence Saltillo Mountains take their name
 And thus the story reads in ancient scrawl.

What strange phenomena on mountain range prevail!
 By day, the nimbus clouds the ridge surmount,
Bright raindrops falling weave ethereal veil
 That screens from view a giant mount.

How soon the mountains prominence regain!
 (Imperial mountains rule by right)
A balmy breeze dispels the precious rain
 And mountain peaks appear in sight.

Beyond the ridge, so distant seeming,
 A sinking sun descends in flight.
O'er mountaintops and sun rays gleaming
 The heavens tinge with crimson light.

At dawn, an outline of dark mountain-towers
 The skyline borders in the twilight hours.
O'er mountains high the sun ascends in view
 And turns a murky sky to heaven's blue.

A weary rambler set on his retreat,
 Makes no attempt to climb the mountain peak
Content is he to see a striking sight,
 The grandeur of Saltillo Mountains' height.

Nephtalí De León

Nephtalí De León wrote poetry "amidst the suffocating rows of cotton" in the Big Valley of Texas. For a time he published *La Voz de los Llanos,* a Chicano newspaper in the Texas Panhandle. His most recent book is *Chicanos: Our Background and Our Pride.*

This is an epic poem written for an interpretative dance. The basis of the poem is the Aztecs' belief of the need to nurture their sun God through human sacrifice.

OF BRONZE THE SACRIFICE

Oh! The dead leaves are fallen.

As ill butterflies they crash
Upon the fiery ground.

And a frigid ice wind sweeps
     sweeps from the blue mountain.

Now the sky of silver weeps
     weeps many cold teardrops . . .

     The maiden,
     The jewel,
Flower of the Aztec kingdom
More beautiful than cold moons,
By the night-stars envied . . .
Weeps, weeps in her troubled sleep.

155

Atlantean figure of Mexico's mysterious past (Charles Schensul)

So still is all,
       but in silence weeps in its troubled sleep.

Oh Tenochtitlán!
       Cradle of the Gods
       Cradle of Bronze warriors
       Turn your eyes into silver—
       Turn your heart into stone.

              The maiden
              The jewel,
The virgin bloom of the land,
From the jungles and the plains,
The virgin of spirit pure,
              as clean as the white snow
              from Ixtaccihuatl the bloom
              faithful and true in love.
              The maiden
the sweet sacrificial flower
weeps and sings of her deep pain.

This night, night of Tlaloc
She of the black strands
                     blacker than the feathers
                     of the sacred serpent,
She of the tiger looks,
She of the astute limbs
Faster than eagle wings
Quicker than fish fins
—Her blood she must see it run!

Oh Tenochtitlán! Cradle of the Gods,
Cradle of Bronze warriors,
Turn your eyes into silver
Turn your heart into stone!

              The maiden
              The jewel,
       She knows it all,
Her body flies in dark anguish

Gyrating toward the stars,
Like frightened desperate arrows,
     arrows of anguish,
     arrows of fear,
Falling like a bird,
     a ravaged beast,
     or the hypnotic song
of fiery Netzahualcóyotl.

     The maiden
     The jewel,
   She knows it all,
Her pure body with no blemish
Her sad and beautiful spirit
Must tonight be broken,
Must tonight be ravaged
As the tiger tears the bodies
When he breaks the eyes
When he steps on spiders.

Oh! She must die
The empire's jewel
For the golden Gods
For the Gods of fire—
Quetzalcóatl, Huitzilipochtli,
Gods of life, Gods of fire.

   But now! The child knows,
She must tell us of the fiery story,
She must tell us of her blood and glory
     that will give oceans,
     that will give life
   to the god of suns,
      and to the Goddess
        Coatlique.

Oh! Dance, Autumn-night Dance
Night of the cold teardrops
That fall as the dead leaves fell

When with horror the warrior saw—
        his love!
With tears and green screams torn.

II

The sky of silver weeps,
      weeps many cold teardrops.

Huitzilipochtli is dead.

III

From the land of fires roared Quetzalcóatl,
    the God of life, of the fire feathers,
        savage the warrior,
           of fury,
           of fire,
           of ice.

Black armies with hatred looked—
The night and its dark forces . . .
—anxiously spied the skies
Searching the God of life
        the valiant,
        the heroic
Quetzalcóatl Coatlique.

With cries of a tiger he battled—
Oh! Glorious the fight, of fire and blood
Cutting the dark forces—
        the night,
        the fog,
        and the cold.

To far-away corners all shadows ran,
fleeing from the god of war—
the god whose eyes shone

with triumph and fire,
which gave life—
       to the wheat,
       to the corn,
       to the men.

But oh! costly the victory.
Quetzalcóatl Coatlique bleeded in cascades
Of cruel wounds who wailed in red voices,
And it came, oh it came,
       the evening gray
       and the young warrior
       suffered white hair.

And the God Quetzalcóatl dying
    gave light to the warrior
      the valiant,
      the martyr,
    Huitzilipochtli.

Oh valiant warrior!
Even though weakened and white in his hair,
With fury he fought the forces of darkness,
Lost was the battle, now all was in vain,
      now all was foreseen
      the loss and the glory
      were already seen.

Huitzilipochtli is dead.

The black wings of the night now fall,
      and fall,
Drowning our faithful warrior,
Whose blood flies out in rays
Like many anxious arrows.
Redder than the quetzal feathers
    or the altar stone
    turns the horizon.

IV

Oh Tenochtitlán!
Cradle of the Gods
Cradle of Bronze warriors
Turn your eyes into silver—
Turn your heart into stone!

And do not weep, bold warrior
Forget your love now sacrificed.
Your eyes are deep caverns
Where never the sun shone.

     The maiden,
     The jewel,
She must now die—
That with her blood she may give life
      to the bold,
      to the brave
      Quetzalcóatl,

Teotihuacán, Pyramid of the Sun

Whose ferocious arms, whose ferocious eyes,
Will roar from the East with new life,
And pushing the shadows that the night nestles
    his hands will give light and life
        to the wheat,
        to the corn,
        to the men . . .

Oh! Tenochtitlán!
Cradle of valiant men
Hide your bronze heart
    that you carry in your hand,
Never let your furious arms
    forget your destiny and glory.

            v

Ay! The dead leaves are fallen.

As ill butterflies they crash
Upon the fiery ground.

And a frigid wind sweeps
    sweeps from the blue mountain.

And the sky of silver weeps
    weeps many a teardrop.

Luis Omar Salinas

Luis Omar Salinas has lived a patchwork existence reflected in his poetry. His poetry appears in various publications. He has taught at Fresno State College in California.

AZTEC ANGEL

I

I am an Aztec angel
    criminal
        of a scholarly
          society
I do favors
        for whimsical
          magicians
where I pawn
        my heart
          for truth
and find
        my way
through obscure
        streets
of soft-spoken
           hara-kiris

II

I am an Aztec angel
    forlorn passenger

163

on a train
of chicken farmers
and happy children

III

I am the Aztec angel
fraternal partner
of an orthodox
society
where pachuco children
hurl stones
through poetry rooms
and end up in a cop car

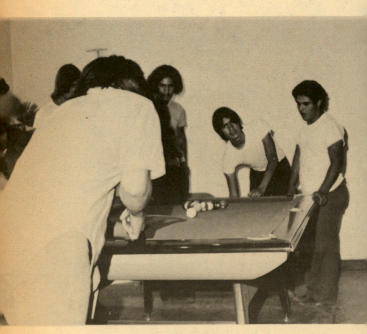

"Aztec Angels" (Salvador Valdez,
courtesy of *Nosotros* Magazine)

their bones itching
and their hearts
busted from malnutrition

IV

I am the Aztec angel
    who frequents bars
spends evenings
    with literary circles
and socializes
    with spiks
niggers and wops
    and collapses on his way
    to funerals

V

Drunk
    lonely
        bespectacled
    the sky
            opens my veins
            like rain
    clouds go berserk
            around me
        my Mexican ancestors
            chew my fingernails
    I am an Aztec angel
            offspring
        of a woman
            who was beautiful

CRAZY GYPSY

I am Omar
   the crazy gypsy
      nimble-footed
         and carefree

     I write poems
        on walls
           that crumble
             and fall

     I talk to shadows
        that sleep
           and go away
             crying

     I meet fearless girls
        who tell me
           their troubles
             my loneliness
                bottled up in their
                tummy.

II

I am Omar
   the crazy gypsy
      I write songs
         to my dead mother
           hurl stones
             at fat policemen
                and walk on seaweed
                  in my dreams.

I walk away from despair
   like a horse walks away
     from his master
       end up in jail
          eating powdered eggs
         for breakfast.

III

My spine shakes
  to the songs
   of women

I am heartless and lonely
   and I whistle a tune
     out of one of my dreams
       where the world
         babbles out loud
           and Mexican hat-check girls
          do the Salinas Shuffle
         a dance composed
        by me in one
          of my nightmares
         and sold
        for a bottle
         of tequila.

IV

I am Omar
  the crazy gypsy
    I waltz through avenues
      of roses
   to the song
     of mariachis

V

I am Omar
   the Mexican gypsy
         . . .
      I speak of love
         as something
      whimsical and aloof
         as something
      naked and cruel

I speak of death
         as something inhabiting
               the sea
            awkward and removed

I speak of hate
         as something
            nibbling my ear. . . .

vier Honda is an El Pasoan whose poetry has appeared in numerous blications. He is presently an intern with the Teacher Corps at the niversity of Texas at El Paso.

NAG'S HEAD, CAPE HATTERAS

Etched against a leaden sky,
Birds delicately fly
Frozen in the motion of their flight.
The clouds, motionless,
Are permanently fixed, without relief,
Varying shades of gray.

At a distance
The restless dunes,
Lonely, desolate, beckon
With their straggly reeds
Given motion
By the endless winds.
The roaring waves
Crash blindly
On the jetty
"Closed until the summer."
There is no other sign of life.

The night is velvet ebony.
There is only dark.
There is no beginning: there is no end:
Only the waves in their incessant crashing.
All is suspended in timelessness.

The wind rises
Then subsides, then rises again.

Rafael Jesús González

Rafael Jesús González is chairman of the Latin American Studi
Department at Laney College, Oakland, California. He is one of t
leading Chicano poets, although he is best known for his scholar
works on the life and literature of Pre-Columbian Mexico.

TO AN OLD WOMAN

Come, mother—
    Your rebozo trails a black web
    And your hem catches on your heels
You lean the burden of your years
On shaky cane, and palsied hand pushes
    Sweat-grimed pennies on the counter.
Can you still see, old woman,
The darting color-trailed needle of your trade?
    The flowers you embroider
    With three-for-a-dime threads
Cannot fade as quickly as the leaves of time.
    What things do you remember?
Your mouth seems to be forever tasting
The residue of nectar-hearted years.
Where are the sons you bore?
    Do they speak only English now
    And say they're Spanish?
One day I know you will not come
And ask for me to pick
The colors you can no longer see.
    I know I'll wait in vain
For your toothless benediction.
    I'll look into the dusty street
    Made cool by pigeons' wings
    Until a dirty child will nudge me and say:
      "Señor, how much ees thees?"

THE OYSTER OF THE GREEN GAZE

You are the sea.
    And God.
The spume-plumed crests
Billow in your pain-blue eyes—
   And God has your feet.
    And I worship you with silence.
   (Is it kindness
     Or is it cowardice?)
Must I sacrifice myself to my belief?
   Or should I sacrifice my belief to myself?
    (And what does it really matter?)

I love you—
    Enough.
 Tomorrow when we meet
 You shall question me
 With a hurt-blue glance
And my laughter will answer:
   "Take this silence."
You shall take it
   (awkwardly)
    not knowing what it is.
Thank me for my silence.
Each word I do not speak is a blue pearl.
   And like the precocious oyster
   I shall die
   From bearing much too many pearls.

HOMAGE TO THE GREEK

Theotocopulos—
Grays—
In the temper of a soul
Toledo lies in the seethe of a boiling sky—
St. Francis adores

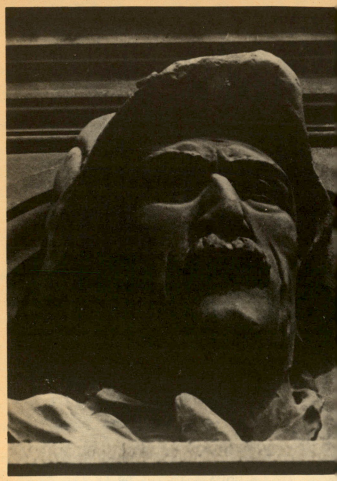
"Homage to the Greek" (Héctor Melgoza)

In the grays of a lonely ecstasy—
And I?
Greek—
Shall I speak to you?
What do these people know of you
(*Tú—griego*)
As they pass your oil-smeared canvas
In the replica of a soul?
Enigma—I would know you
And macerate my loneliness
In that spirituality of grays that is your speech.
Speech—silence—
But no matter—we are one—
For the moment—you and I.
Between my words and the absurd mysticism
Of your brush lie eons—
And yet—
I understand you.

Your grays
Could have been dipped from my soul
And your elongated hands molded
From the figments of my affections—
So man is immortal—
If proof could be had I would believe you.
But you paint
Too much like me to believe you.
The phantasm of your verse
absurd indelible gray—
And a gray that extends
Tenaciously toward black
And then again to white—
Genius or fool—
I do not know—
But gray—always gray.
A gray not of mediocrity but spiritual
And withered away
By too much passion
And too much fast—

Young with an oldness
        That superseded your birth—
I understand you—but my anchor
        Is sunk too deep in mire—
I love you but these wings
        Are much too weak for flight
And I stand in awe
        Not daring more than this.

Jane Limón

Jane Limón is a teacher in El Paso. Her poetry has appeared in various publications.

incongruity

old beggar woman outside the church
stained-glass windows and golden altar

scraps of paper and cigarette butts
in the rushing, gushing, silver-blue fountain

the blood on the cape and the fallen horse
along with the grace and moment of death

the ugly, poor, pitiful, and perverse
alongside the beautiful, honorable, and honest.

Leo Romero

Leo Romero grew up in Las Vegas, New Mexico, and has been a student for the last three years at the University of New Mexico in Albuquerque. On beautiful days he rides his bicycle "searching for poems."

I TOO, AMERICA

America
blue eyes and blond hair
America from England
Protestant America
pilgrims
Dutch New York
America of George Washington
on every dollar
and Lincoln
on every penny
America of shells
exploding in the air
and in every elementary school
from the Atlantic to the Pacific
children are taught
about Daniel Boone
and Davy Crockett
remember the Alamo
kill the dirty Mexicans
America of North
and South
marching into Santa Fe
in the name

of the United States of America
we are taking away your land
we respect your quaint customs
and picturesque
way of living
but if you oppose us
you will be hung
America of Thoreau
in New England
pleading civil disobedience
while the American army
marches into Mexico City

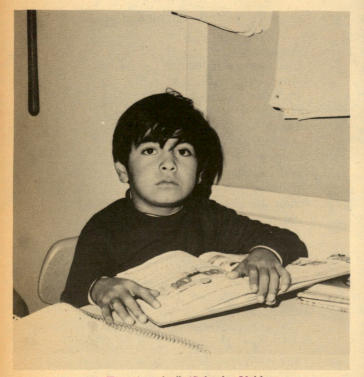

"I, Too, America" (Salvador Valdez,
courtesy of *Nosotros* Magazine)

and children throw themselves
from Aztec pyramids
against the invading Americanos
their pulsating hearts
in their hands
the heroes of Mexico
and President Polk
smiling wryly
at a freshly painted map
of an expanded America
remember the *Maine*
charging over San Juan hill
Theodore Roosevelt
the Rough Riders
Castro coming down
from the mountains
is cheered by the populace
and America of the CIA
and the Bay of Pigs
wants him shot
America who made a
martyr of Che
America of Vice-President
Nixon in South America
being stoned
America of United Rubber
Shell and Coca-Cola
America sending Rockefeller
on a goodwill tour of South America
as a representative
of the capitalistic-enterprise system
so that the sandaled peasants
will gawk at him
and want to be Americanos
Viva Americanos
Hell no
Yankee Go Home
Yankee Go Home
Yankee Go Home
and take Coca-Cola with you

and take your blood men with you
who have been bleeding us
like monstrous mosquitoes
who have been like leeches
take them away
or we will handle them our own way
America that imprisons
César Chávez
because of grapes and lettuce
America that wants cheap labor
America of profit
at the expense of others
America who imprisoned Reies Tijerina
for attempting to lawfully
secure wrongly taken lands
America who drugs
the giant of Mexican-Americans
and steals
their gold-laying chicken
their lands of uranium
and forests and oil
America I too
live on this continent
and in this country
I too am an American
and my eyes are brown and my hair
obsidian black
America from Spain
Catholic America
conquistadores
Sur América
mestizo Méjico
Simón Bolívar los Incas
los Aztecas
Juárez y Villa y Zapata

Elvira Gómez

Elvira Gómez has taught for a number of years with the El Paso schools. She writes poetry for various publications.

OPEN

A sign will hang
(If hanging signs are possible)
With words
(Which I presume will be
In all the languages
There've been)
—And what if there be some
Who cannot read?
But anyway, on high
There'll be a sign
And it must really
Be way high.
Where?
      Where the road curves
And the pilgrim's
Shoes wear out
And his bones ache
Artificially awake
From walking
And his eyes are watery
And his hair is strung
Long and loose
And his clothes with patches
And dirt hide him.
This sign

Which only
One can hang
Will say
In front of heaven
Since heaven is a place
Like a neon which luminously glows
Open—if it reads so—or closed

Georgia Cobos

Georgia Cobos has written poetry since childhood. Her first poem, written at the age of eleven, was published in the *San Diego Tribune*. She lives with her husband in Del Rio, Texas, where she teaches sixth grade.

SUFFER LITTLE CHILDREN

Pride runs cold down my street
As passion gasps for its need upon an empty belly.
Love here is oft' relegated to a place
Where time continually denies it.
Pride runs cold as *they* run down the streets at night;
Wild!
Wild but free?—NEVER!
Wild and chained to grunts and curses,
To hate, superstition,
To cold and hunger.

Wild and chained to an evil sort of barter: You're so
    pretty,
Give me . . .

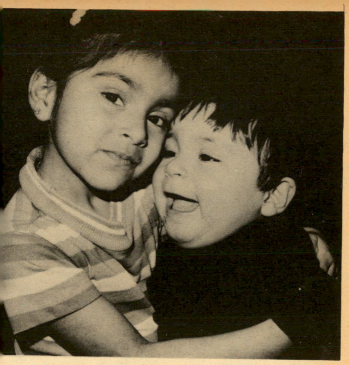

Innocence of youth (Salvador Valdez,
courtesy of *Nosotros* Magazine)

And love is oft' relegated to distant hills and prettiness
When
     Manuel smells;
     Victor wisecracks,
     And Sofia purses her lips and smiles
     At the little boys she knows will be around
     In a couple of years.

Pride and love are lost within the yellow cumulative
    folder—
That one which limits and relegates my boys to hoods and
    slaves,
And my girls to early ugliness and pain.

Pride is gone forever from a well-equipped science lab—
When the young scientist cannot read;
From a geography shelf, from a globe, a map, a bowl of
    flowers
When their only purpose is destruction
And the consequence—a silent and unexplained punish-
    ment.

Pride runs cold as Andrés scribbles their names
Upon a wall with a broken window.
    THEY BROKE IT!
    ONCE IN THEY WROTE THE CRY:
    "KNOW ME. I AM SOMEONE!"

Pride runs cold as Armida utters obscenities perfectly at
Those who love her with her poor cleft-palate.
She cannot stand being loved.

Pride is pilfered from a teacher told:
    "Make haste.
      Keep 'em busy."   or asked
    "Will they be ready? No? Push 'em up!
    New books for them?"

Pride runs cold when Julia screams to me each welcome
    Monday,
"My mother says to whip me," and then bemoans the fact
    that I don't.

Pride runs cold when
    EACH VERDICT GIVEN BY *THEM*,
    EACH JUDGMENT SOLICITED FROM *THEM*
    EACH IDEA OF JUSTICE AND LOVE AND
    AFFECTION TO *THEM*

is a swat
a slap
a denial of love;
and horror takes its place when a teacher knows that—
it's really all they know.

Pride is denied and love is lost
As children stumble through a maze of English
To hate and deny it.

Pride is lost
As the glories of the Spanish
And the brilliance of Cristóbal Colón's Indians
Are lost to their children.

Pride becomes shame
As the tones of a mother tongue
Learned from a lullaby or a *consejo*
Are wrested and snatched
From babes who would use them.

Pride *does* run cold at the sight of

      Generations of injustice,
      A slough of meaningless lives
      And unused and unwanted abilities.

Tomás Rivera

Tomás Rivera is professor of Modern Languages at the University of Texas at San Antonio. In 1970 he was recipient of the Quinto Sol prize for literature. His poetry, prose, and fiction have been widely published.

SOUNDLESS WORDS

Words without sound
how terribly deaf.
What if I were to remain
here
in the words
forever?

WHEN LOVE TO BE?

When love to be?
when
leaves warmly cover
protectingly from
sun and snow and wind
and feet
everyone will walk toward me
not away
when
love to be
comes
now, no one listens

I've been ready for so long

since many times
of leaves covering
warmly to protect
yet dying
from sun and snow and wind
and feet

I've been ready for so long

when love to be
will everyone walk toward me
and stay?

PAST POSSESSIONS

A piece of string
A broken top
A crooked kite
A wooden gun
A mop . . .

Quiet . . . Noise

A long thin weed a lance
A few large cans a dance
Boxes
for cars and houses

Such trivial things

"The Eyes of a Child" (Ed Lettau)

THE EYES OF A CHILD

First, the color,
then the comprehension
of a limitless love.

The eyes of a child
must surely touch.
Its color

Unknown comprehension
open to be shut
open to create.

Color, form, limitless eyes
of a limitless love.

The eyes of a child can touch
The eyes of a child can feel
The eyes of a child can be.

Do they know that we know?

Tino Villanueva

Tino Villanueva, born in San Marcos, Texas, is presently a doctoral candidate and Teaching Fellow at Boston University's Department of Foreign Languages and Literatures. His poetry has appeared in *Caribbean Review*, *El Grito*, and others.

MY CERTAIN BURN TOWARD PALE ASHES

My certain burn
    toward pale ashes is told by the
    hand that whirls the sun; each
    driving breath beats with the quick
    pulsing face.

My falling stride
    like sand toward decision,
    drains heavy with fixed age; each
    ghostly grain a step in time that
    measures tongues

My ruddy sea
    that streams to dryness, bares
    bewildered its clay bone; each
    vessel's roar at God's speed drowns
    by force.

My waking light
    began when the fertile lips spun
    my pulse; and I, with muted tongue,
    was drawn destroyed from the making-
    mouth into this mass.

And held below
    by nature, the sweeping hand now
    turns my dust-bound youth; tell the
    world that I was struck by the
    sun's grave plot.

CHICANO IS AN ACT OF DEFIANCE

In memory of Rubén Salazar

> How simple death is: how simple,
> yet how unjustly violent!
> She refuses to go about slowly, and slashes
> when you least expect her wicked slash.
> Miguel Hernández

On your tongue— the flowing of
accentuated ink: a challenge
for those who stereotype.

Chicano is an act of defiance— you'd say.

Your last day,
laid out in protest.
In the rifles (hidden) waits
compact
death.

The accuracy of triggers/Senseless confrontation.
La Raza prays— breathing is a risk.
Blasts.
Random shots—
       La Raza prays.
Parafascist blasts
paramilitary blasts
blasts that kill pupils and
persistent throats.
The *Silver Dollar Cafe* is only for eating.

Cesar Chavez leading boycott march (Wide World Photos)

Someone didn't bother reading intents.
Three die.

In the wind

you left your indelible, committed cry.
Perspectives went spreading through the streets.

One can decipher
a well-articulated cry.

Jaime Calvillo

Jaime Calvillo is a Texas poet whose works appear in various journals and magazines.

LIFE OF A BRACERO
WHEN COTTON IS IN SEASON

You started out at six A.M.,
    had your breakfast, cotton
sack in hand, and at seven
    piled into the trucks that pulled
out and drove you to the fields.

There, bent double all the day,
    down endless rows you worked,
reaping patiently their white fruit;
    you filled the sack, packed it down,
gathering all you could, and when
    you brought it to the trucks, it
was with a reluctance vaguely understood.
    Empty, flat, out of shape, the
sack was handed back and back you
    went to fill it as before.

At noon you ate your lunch beneath
    the trucks, pillowed on the borrowed
cotton; you took a rest then walked
    once more into the fields, bending
down to serious work flowering on
    every plant.

Braceros in the fields (Wide World Photos)

About six P.M., when late afternoon hung
    heavy in the air, you set aside
your work and, sack bundled beneath
    your arm, pulled yourself into the
truck that drove you back to camp.

As darkness turns to dark, you have
    your evening meal and after
thinking some, fall down to sleep,
    bedded on your cotton sack.

Raúl Salinas

Raúl Salinas has published poetry in a variety of journals and anthologies. He is currently very much interested in the activities of La Raza Unida political party.

LOS CAUDILLOS (THE LEADERS)

Stifling
      Crystal City
                  heat
rouses Texas sleepers
      the long siesta finally over
at last, at long, long last
      Politics wrested from
tyrannical usurpers' clutches
      fires are stoked
                  flames are fanned
Conflagrating flames
      of socio-political awareness
Rich Dago vineyards
      Chávez doing his pacifist thing
          "Lift that crate
             & pick them grapes"
stoop labor's awright—with God on your side
      Califas gold not ours to spend, baby
Small wonder David Sánchez
      impatient & enraged in East L. A.
dons a beret, its color symbolizing
      Urgent Brown

Voices raised in unison
    in northern New Mexico hills,
        "¡esta tierra es nuestra!"
cached clutter: invalid grants—unrecognized treaties
their tongues are forked,
    Tijerina,
their decks are marked
    Indo-Hispano
      you're our man
Denver's Corky boxing lackeys' ears back
    let them live in the Bottoms for a while
      see how they like a garbage dump
for a next-door neighbor
José Angel Gutiérrez: MAYO's fiery vocal cat
    the world does not love energetic noisemakers
      or so says papa henry b. (the savior of San
      Anto)
        who only saved himself

In eastern Spanish ghettos
    Portorro street gangs do
      Humanity
Young Lords: (Cha-Cha, Fi & Yoruba)
    burglarize rich folks' antibiotics
      rip off X-ray mobile units/hospital
    —become medics for the poor—
ghetto children must not die
    of lead poisoning & TB
Latin Kings: (Watusi Valez & the rest)
    if you're doing social service
    how can you be on
terrorizing sprees (with priest accompanist)
    in near Northside Chicago?
      Ubiquitous? We're everywhere!
Arise! Bronze people,
    the wagon-wheels gather momentum . . .

A TRIP THROUGH THE MIND JAIL

for Eldridge (Cleaver)

LA LOMA
Neighborhood of my youth
    demolished, erased forever from
    the universe.
    You live on, captive, in the lonely
    cellblocks of my mind.
Neighborhood of endless hills
    muddied streets—all chuckhole-lined—
    that never drank of asphalt.
    Kids barefoot/snotty-nosed
    playing marbles, munching on bean tacos
    (the kind you'll never find in a café)
    2 peaceful generations removed from
    their *abuelos'* revolution.
Neighborhood of dilapidated community hall
    —Salón Cinco de Mayo—
    yearly (May 5/Sept. 16)[1] gathering
    of the *familias*. Re-asserting pride
    on those two significant days.
    Speeches by the elders
    patriarchs with evidence of oppression
    distinctly etched upon mestizo faces.
    "Sons of the Independence!"
    Emphasis on allegiance to the *tri-color*[2]
    obscure names: Juárez & Hidalgo
    their heroic deeds. Nostalgic tales of war
    years under Villa's command. No one listened,
    no one seemed to really care.
    Afterwards, the dance. Modest Mexican
    maidens dancing polkas together
    across splintered wooden floor.

---

[1] May 5, French driven from Mexico; September 16, Mexican
Independence from Spain
[2] *tri-color* = Mexican flag

They never deigned to dance with boys!
The careful scrutiny by curbstone sex-perts
8 & 9 years old. "Minga's bow-legged,
so we know she's done it, huh?"
Neighborhood of Sunday night *jamaicas*
at Guadalupe Church.
Fiestas for any occasion
holidays   holy days   happy days
'round and 'round the promenade
eating snow-cones—raspas—& tamales
the games—bingo   cake walk   spin the wheel
making eyes at girls from cleaner neighborhoods
the unobtainables
who responded all giggles and excitement.
Neighborhood of forays down to Buena Vista—
Santa Rita Courts—Los projects—friendly neighborhood
cops 'n' robbers on the rooftops, sneaking peeks
in people's private nighttime bedrooms
bearing gifts of Juicy Fruit gum for
the Projects girls/chasing them in adolescent heat
causing skinned knees & being run off for the night
disenchanted walking home affections spurned
stopping stay-out-late chicks in search of
Modern Romance lovers, who always stood them up
unable to leave their world in the magazine's pages.
Angry fingers grabbing, squeezing, feeling,
french kisses imposed; close bodily contact, thigh &
belly rubbings under shadows of Cristo Rey Church.
Neighborhood that never saw a school bus
the crosstown walks were much more fun
embarrassed when acquaintances or friends or relatives
were sent home excused from class
for having cooties in their hair!
Did only Mexicans have cooties in their hair?
    ¡—Qué gacho!
Neighborhood of Zaragoza Park
Where scary stories interspersed with
inherited superstitions were exchanged
waiting for midnight and the haunting
lament of La Llorona—the weeping lady

of our myths & folklore—who wept nightly,
along the banks of Boggy Creek,
for the children she'd lost or drowned
in some river (depending on the version).
i think i heard her once
and cried
out of sadness and fear
running all the way home nape hairs at attention
swallow a pinch of table salt and
make the sign of the cross
sure cure for frightened Mexican boys.
Neighborhood of Spanish Town Café
   first grown-up (13) hangout
   Andrés,
   tolerant manager, proprietor, cook
   victim of bungling baby burglars
   your loss: Fritos 'n' Pepsi-Colas—was our gain
you put up with us and still survived!
You, too, are granted immortality.
Neighborhood of groups and clusters
  sniffing gas, drinking muscatel
  solidarity   cement hardening
  the clan   the family   the neighborhood   the gang
    ¡Nomas!
  Restless innocents tattoo'd crosses on their hands
  "just doing things different"
  "From now on, all troublemaking mex kids will
  be sent to Gatesville for 9 months."
  Henry home from *la corre*
  khakis worn too low—below the waist
  the stomps, the *greña* with duck-tail
    -Pachuco Yo-
Neighborhood of could-be artists
  who plied their talents on the pool's
  bath-house walls/intricately adorned
  with esoteric symbols of their cult
  the art form of our slums
  more meaningful & significant
  than Egypt's finest hieroglyphics.

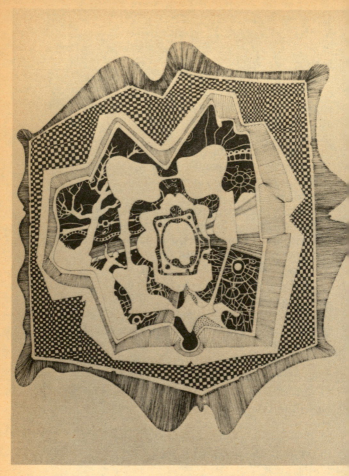

"A Trip Through the Mind Jail" (Salvador Valdez,
courtesy of *Nosotros* Magazine)

Neighborhood where purple clouds of *Yesca*
   smoke one day descended & embraced us all
   Skulls uncapped—Rhythm 'n' Blues
      Chale's 7th St. Club
   loud Negro music-wine spodee-odees[3]-barbecue-grass
   our very own connection man: big black Johnny B——.
Neighborhood of Reyes' Bar
   where Lalo shotgunned
   Pete Evans to death because of
   an unintentional stare,
   and because he was *escuadra,*
   only to end his life neatly sliced
   by prison barber's razor.
   Duran's grocery & gas station
   Güero drunkenly stabbed Julio
   arguing over who'd drive home
   and got 55 years for his crime.
   Raton: 20 years for a matchbox of weed. Is that cold?
   No lawyer no jury no trial i'm guilty.
      Aren't we all guilty?
   Indian mothers, too, so unaware
   of courtroom tragi-comedies
   folded arms across their bosoms
   saying, *"Sea por Dios."*
Neighborhood of my childhood
   neighborhood that no longer exists
   some died young—fortunate—some rot in prisons
   the rest drifted away to be conjured up
   in minds of others like them.
   For me: only the NOW of THIS journey is REAL!
Neighborhood of my adolescence
   neighborhood that is no more
   YOU ARE TORN PIECES OF MY FLESH!!!
   Therefore, you ARE.
LA LOMA—AUSTIN—MI BARRIO—
      i bear you no grudge

---

[3] Wine spodee-odees = drinking wine spodee-odees (spondee liba-
tions: music used to accompany drinking; ode: lyric poetry marked
by exaltation of feeling and style). Louis Jordon made "Drinkin'
Wine Spodee-Odee" famous in the '30s. Spo(r)ty-(r)ode is part of
the black vocabulary.

i needed you then . . . identity . . . a sense of belonging.
i need you now.
So essential to adult days of imprisonment,
you keep me away from INSANITY'S hungry jaws;
     Smiling/Laughing/Crying.
i respect your having been:
  My Loma of Austin
  my Rose Hill of Los Angeles
  my West Side of San Anto
  my Quinto of Houston
  my Jackson of San Jo
  my Segundo of El Paso
  my Barelas of Alburque
  my Westside of Denver
Flats, Los Marcos, Maravilla, Calle Guadalupe, Magnolia,
Buena Vista, Mateo, La Seis, Chiquis, El Sur and all
    Chicano neighborhoods that now exist and once
    existed; somewhere . . . someone remembers. . . .

Raymundo Pérez

Raymundo Pérez was born in Laredo, Texas, toward the end of the
pachuco era. He is nicknamed "Tigre" because of the fighting spirit
he exhibited as the shortest member of his high school football team.
He is presently pursuing a law degree at the University of Colorado
at Boulder.

HASTA LA VICTORIA SIEMPRE

The train runs down the tracks,
A dying child lies on his back.
Brother, oh brother of mine, who lives in dark.
As you listen to the beat, listen,

Chicano flag of freedom (Salvador Valdez,
courtesy of *Nosotros* Magazine)

I hear my heart beat my life away.
My eyes are completely dry.
You tell me I'm high.
You know and I know it's a lie.
Yet you point your finger.
Brother, oh brother *vendido*
You are hollow inside.
What lies will you tell your child?
How do you sleep at night?
You know that I'm right.
La Causa is your child, mine, *de todos de nosotros.*
Hasta La Victoria Siempre....

Ricardo Sánchez

Ricardo Sánchez writes more than poetry; his works project the harsh realities of Chicano life as he sees it and as he has experienced it. His book *Canto y Grito mi Liberación* is soon to be released by Doubleday.

to a child

social enigmas fill us
with hope, a desperate hope.

living in el barrio
hurts sometimes,
when medication is a privilege
not a right,
when we view our being
like a castigation
and we cry in anguish
when a child hurts ...

"To a Child" (Héctor Melgoza)

it is not understandable,
but pain is enigmatic confusion.

and we run madly and amok,
howling out
soul-seared duelos,
searching for a way,
a way out to alleviate,
our steps hesitant,
we view social phenomena
hoping for godliness,
                a torch to light the way . . .

child, oh, child,
with eyes that mirror,
a smile that questions,
a countenance that quavers—
you have a right to live;
a right to stand tall,
a right to carve your destiny
out of more than just the hope
two huddled grandparents wish for
each time you cry your hurts . . .

little girl, providence is real
i want to shout, yet,
it is unreal that you must feel
hurt lashing at your being;
you are young,
                understand not,
and your muted questions
go unanswered . . .
but
    you shall live,
    you shall thrive,
and
    your tomorrows
        shall be beacons for my searching eyes . . .

EL PASO

Death stalks leisurely
wearing a broad-brimmed straw hat

    (with scalps brown, black-wilted
    on the fire-engine-red band
    like flies and fish hooks or
    totems symbolizing manhood),
and
the sun beats down
    children baked like earth.

El Paso
    resonator of flapping tortillas,
    wobbly with beer and diluted alcohol
    in eastside, southside alley ways,
    home of legends—
    el largo con/safo 1959,
    or the mad song
    of contraband carriers,
    outpost for any angry puffer
    marijuana can cull . . .

El Paso
    West Texas tip
    dry-hot
and your people take pride
and call you the international city:
    "A taco stand on one side of town,
    A hamburger haven on the other—
    and pancho dealing pot
    for a hebe in between."

El Paso—
    you stand haughty
    and denigrate all else
    boasting of a unique flavor
    (unadulterated poverty?);

Last night
mariachi music flooded my brain
and I saw multitudes swaying
and the mariachis were checkerboardlike,
　　　　the *gritos* became finger snappings
and I no longer understood
　　　　my real culture.

I ran your streets barefooted
and brown with a simple smile
　　　　and uttering sing-song phrases . . .
Nights are lonely upstairs
　　　　at Overland and Kansas streets;
the keys clang out a weird symphony
keeping time with the neon lights
Juarez is . . . in the distance—

　　　　The river is sand,
　　　　the mountains bleak—
and Saturday night always
　　　　strays about looking for something to happen.

Yes, desolate, flat-painted el paso
even the thought of *mañana* tires you,
for bustle could not become you . . .
It is always afternoon siesta time for you—
　　　　　it is
　　　　because you are
　　　　　　　　el paso!

vision

man talked, indian man
proud
of past
when continent was bronze
and buffalo throve,
fruit was good,

chemistry a natural process
          of the universe . . .

i visibly froze thoughts,
    land is not my question,
only the morality of the situation
involves me . . .

    the land is there
    for those who work it,
    for those whose sweat
                    & blood
                    & love
                    & realness
          have drenched it . . .

i hear my indian brothers,
their questions move me,
and my sanity returns

          i am more than just a person,
          i reside in nature,
            a bronze-flecked man
            caught in the realness of my people . . .

mestizo, son of providence
          merging indio with hispano,
beginning of the cosmic process,
universal man precursor,

that, my brothers, is my vision. . . .

Margarita Virginia Sánchez

Margarita Virginia Sánchez was thirteen years old when she wrote "Escape." She now lives in California and continues to write poetry.

ESCAPE

Last week,
I had been white
    . . . we were friends

Yesterday,
I was Spanish
    . . . we talked . . .
        once in a while.

Today,
I am Chicano
    . . . you do not know me.

Tomorrow,
I rise to fight
    . . . and we are enemies.

el alma

LA RAZA

yesterday, today,
today and tomorrow,
tomorrow, and again tomorrow;
Why . . . wait!!

Yesterday, today, and tomorrow (Pat Ellis,
courtesy of *Nosotros* Magazine)

. . . i have come home,
i wait no more.
. . . yesterday,
i broke my shackles:
of those shackles,
i forge a knife.

i hold my new strong knife
stabbing the spirit of injustice
. . . brought against me.
i am . . . La Raza;
my heart, my breath . . .
. . . my blood.

i am La Raza

i am . . . Chicano
i . . . stand straight and proud.
yes . . . i . . . stand—
. . . till my heart refuses . . . breath,
. . . till my blood sees no more,
till . . . i know no life.

　　　　still . . .

. . . i remain—
　　　　MY SOUL IS CHICANO.

　　　　　el alma

Pedro Contreras

Pedro Contreras is a young Californian poet who is presently workin
on a volume of Chicano poetry.

BROWN-EYED CHILDREN OF THE SUN

Up to California from Mexico you come,
to the Sacramento Valley to toil in the sun.
Your wife and seven children, they're workin', every one
and what will you be givin' to your brown-eyed childre
    of the sun?

Your face is lined and wrinkled and your age is forty-on
Your back is bent from picking, like your dying time ha
    come.

"Brown-Eyed Children of the Sun"

Your children's eyes are smiling, their life is just begun;
and what will you be givin' to your brown-eyed children
of the sun?

You are bending and you're picking with your back and
arms in pain.
Your wife and seven children, they never do complain.
"Oh, Jesus, can't you help us, can't you shade us from
this sun?"
And what will you be givin' to your brown-eyed children
of the sun?

Your hands can feel the soil as you're working in the fields.
You can feel the richness in it, you can see the crops it
yields.
You're tired and you're hungry and your day is almost
done;

and what will you be givin' to your brown-eyed children
    of the sun?

You have marched on Easter Sunday, to the capitol you've
    come;
and you've fought for union wages and your fight has just
    begun.
You are proud men and you're free men and this heritage
    is one
that you can be givin' to your brown-eyed children of the
    sun.

José Angel Gutiérrez

José Angel Gutiérrez is the founder of La Raza Unida political party
which offers political alternatives to Chicanos. In addition to his
political activities he is a doctoral candidate in Political Science at
the University of Texas at Austin.

22 MILES

From 22 I see my first 8 weren't.
    Around the 9th, I was called "meskin."
      By the 10th, I knew and believed I was.
        I found out what it meant to know, to believe . . .
          before my 13th.

Through brown eyes, seeing only brown colors and feeling
    only
brown feelings . . . I saw . . . I felt . . . I hated . . . I cried
    . . . I tried
. . . I didn't understand during these 4.
              I rested by just giving up.

While, on the side . . . I realized I BELIEVED in
 white as pretty,
    my being governor,
      blond blue-eyed baby Jesus,
        cokes and hamburgers,
          equality for all regardless of race, creed, or color,
            Mr. Williams, our banker.
            I had to!
        That was all I had.
      Beams and communism were bad.
                        Past the weeds, atop the hill, I looked back.

Pretty people, combed and squeaky clean, on arrowlike
    roads.
Pregnant girls, ragged brats, swarthy *machos,* rosary beads,
and friends waddle clumsily over and across hills, each
    other,
mud, cold, and woods on caliche ruts.
At the 19th mile, I fought blindly at everything and
    anything.
 Not knowing, Not caring about WHY, WHEN, or FOR
    WHAT
  I fought. And fought.
    By the 21st, I was tired and tried.

              But now . . .
I've been told that I am dangerous.
That is because I am good at not being a Mexican.
That is because I know now that I have been cheated.
That is because I hate circumstances and love choices.

  You know . . . chorizo tacos y tortillas ARE good, even
    at school.
  Speaking Spanish is a talent.
Being Mexican IS as good as Rainbo bread.
And without looking back, I know that there are still too
    many . . .
    brown babies,

pregnant girls,
  old 25-year-old women,
    drunks,
      who should have lived but didn't,
        on those caliche ruts.

  It is tragic that my problems during these past 21
          miles
    were/are/might be . . .
      looking into blue eyes,
      wanting to touch a Grinquita,
    ashamed of being Mexican,
  believing I could not make it at college,
pretending that I liked my side of town,

    remembering the Alamo,
  speaking Spanish in school bathrooms only,

My side of town (Salvador Valdez,
courtesy of *Nosotros* Magazine)

and knowing that Mexico's prostitutes like Americans
  better.

At 22, my problems are still the same but now I know I
am your problem.
That farm boys, Mexicans and Negro boys are in Vietnam
is but one thing I think about:
                 Crystal City, Texas 78839
                 The migrant worker;
                 The good Gringo:

Staying Mexican enough;
Helping;
Looking at the world from the back of a truck.

The stoop labor with high school rings on their fingers;
The Anglo cemetery,
Joe the different Mexican,

                 Damn.
                 Damn.
                 Damn.

Abelardo Delgado

Abelardo Delgado is the poet laureate of Aztlán. His poem "Stupid America" has been widely reproduced in posters and anthologies. He is presently director of the Special Services Program at the University of Texas at El Paso.

STUPID AMERICA

stupid america, see that chicano
with a big knife
on his steady hand
he doesn't want to knife you
he wants to sit on a bench
and carve christfigures
but you won't let him.
stupid america, hear that chicano
shouting curses on the street
he is a poet
without paper and pencil
and since he cannot write
he will explode.
stupid america, remember that chicanito
flunking math and english
he is the picasso
of your western states
but he will die
with one thousand masterpieces
hanging only from his mind.

The Chicano has emerged from Indo-Hispano roots
(José Medina)

LA RAZA

no longer content with merely shouting vivas
or wearing bright *sarape* and big sombrero,
we are coming in as if the world will receive us
as humans and not as pinto bean amoebas.

raza evolving, ever stronger, ever one,
filling the Spaniard olive merging shadow
and kneeling with the indian worshipping the sun
and fighting revolutions with a rusty gun.

we, raced or razed mestizos shouldering conquest
and enduring the harsh whip upon our *cuero*
having had our sacred origin need no quest
to find identity or set our souls at rest.

though *mejico* is *la madre patria* we go
the world over seeking only greener meadow;
poetic, sentimental, proud, copper ego
serving as an emblem to a dream's *testigo*.

identified by a last name or a language
full of *picardía, raza* placed *primero,*
raza placed to serve as paste to close the wedge
between the human and the divinely alleged.

raza which fortunately includes the many
who in the midst of poverty build a grotto;
unfortunately, *vendidos* for a penny,
agringados who think macho is uncanny.

the national, green carder, U.S. citizen,
the *pocho,* the *manito* and the bracero,
the Mex-Tex, what's the difference?   *olvidensen,*
it's the milk, *raza,* that an indian's chichi sent.

LA TIERRA

la tierra is *la raza*'s kissing cousin,
she's the patient mother who will listen
to the sun-baked lament of the one who toils,
she's playmate to the growing dozen.

she's the sweetheart of young chicano dreamers
decorating those dreams with live green streamers,
she's the woman with the perfumed sexy soils,
her somber existence through yonder glimmers.

she is the banner of the revolution
and wide battlefield and source of its solution,
nourishment of men or mirror of turmoils,
womb of all that starts, tomb of all conclusion.

mejico got some of you back . . . how dismal,
new mexicans reclaim you . . . odds abysmal
and texans wash their hands with your spat-out oils,
while californians sing from your gold hymnal.

men love you, hate you, regulate you,
they sell you, trade you and speculate you,
they build, they plant, they mine and from your despoils
bring life . . . comfort, riches, and glamour anew.

while the arabs and jews over you dispute
the price of your foot an anglo will compute,
but only the soul of one, like a snake recoils.
soul chicano which unison it can't repute.

look . . . a chicano's skin is adobe-vented,
his wrinkles are *surcos* that time itself planted,
the mud that in his veins passionately boils,
and his soul something that *la tierra* invented.

LA CAUSA

what moves you, chicano, to stop being polite?
nice chicano could be patted on the head and wouldn't
bite
and now, how dare you tell your boss, "Go fly a kite"?
    es la causa, hermano, which has made me a new man.

what is this *causa* which disturbs your steady hand,
could it be an inherited love of land
or the indian impudence called pride that I can't
understand?
    this *causa, hermano,* is charcoaled abuse ready to burn.

what nonsense this brown power that you claim,
what stupid demands erupt from wills untamed,
what of your poetic submissiveness that brought you fame?
    es la causa, hermano, which leaves no one untouched.

delano awaits the verdict of the nation,
del río and justice dance in wild anticipation,
el paso and *la causa* will be good for the duration
  es la causa, hermano, raping apathy with flair.

san antonio cannot sleep another night,
los angeles cannot forfeit another fight,
denver cannot hide from us its burning light,
  es la causa, hermano, don't let our heroes feel betrayed.

albuquerque trembles with the blast of sacrifice
y todo el valle carries life at a cheap price,
los barrios y los campos become a symphony of cries,
  es la causa de la raza an anthill upon your chest.

la causa for all those blindly involved who do not know
is the planting of *mañanas* which will grow
permitting the faceless chicanos of that day to go
  like eagles, as high as they can, as high as they want to.

6 • DRAMA

There is little in the way of Mexican-American drama save for occasional plays like *Los Comanches* and *Los Tejanos,* plays of the nineteenth century written specifically to commemorate important events. What may properly pass for Mexican-American drama are *actos* and *mitos* currently performed and staged by the various Chicano theater groups. One such group, El Teatro Campesino, the Chicano migrant theater that grew out of the *Huelga* at Delano in 1965, has transformed the ancient Aztec myths for the *campesino* stage to Chicano relevancy. In one magnificent *acto* entitled "Bernabe," the Chicano link to the ancient Indian heritage is strengthened and articulated masterfully. This message is being carried everywhere in the United States (and abroad) by El Teatro Campesino in its various annual tours. Luis Valdez, director of the company, describes Chicano theater as "beautiful, *rasquachi,* human, cosmic, broad, deep, tragic, comic, as the life of *la raza* itself." The consequence of El Teatro Campesino has been the creation of similar theatrical companies elsewhere, including universities with as few as a dozen Chicano students.

The distinctive character of Chicano theater lies in its seeming "artlessness." There is no attempt to create setting or atmosphere or character. Valdez, for example, employs *calavera* (skull) masks to create the illusion of temporality. All the skull masks are identical. Only the actions, dress, and voices of the actors differentiate them as characters. The end result is a kind of stylized theater resembling the Japanese Kabuki theater or the Greek mask plays.

Lest my comments be misunderstood to mean that Mexican-Americans have no dramatic tradition, let me hasten to point out that folk drama has been immensely popular among Mexican-Americans who annually stage the old plays in much the same fashion as the early English folk dramatists staged their plays in town squares, churches, and courtyards. In the Mexican Southwest, liturgical pastorals depicting the creation and fall of man and of Christ's resurrection evolved into "cycle plays" similar to those of Spain. As early as 1598 religious plays like *Los Moros y los Cristianos, Los Pastores,* and *Los Tres Magos* were acted in New Mexico. Still extant and acted today are such religious plays as the *Comedia de Adan y Eva, Los Tres Reyes,* and *Auto del Santo Nino.* Aurora Lucero credits the survival of these plays to the "fervor" with which the soldiers of the crown and the soldiers of the cross recited Spain's prayers, retold her stories, and sang her songs. The result, she asserts, was "a tradition that was to take roots in the soil—roots that flowered into a pattern that has constituted the basis for living in the Hispanic New World, and a tradition that still endures."

Plays like *Los Pastores* which have been staged in the New World for over four hundred years have widely affected the populace of the Southwest. Through the Christmas season, especially, *Los Pastores* is reenacted in halls or *salas* to commemorate the nativity of Christ. There was a time when the play was staged in the nave or atrium of a church, and in those villages or towns too small or too poor to afford a priest *Los Pastores* was presented in lieu of midnight mass on Christmas eve. Eventually, however, the nativity play was taken out of its religious context and became more of an entertainment than an instruction. And as *Los Pastores* became earthier the representation was broadened with theatrical comic touches.

To be sure, there were plays written in Spanish by Mexican-Americans, but drama in English has received the least impetus. This may be due in part, perhaps, to the fact that a play, unlike fiction or poetry, needs a stage, a setting, and an audience to bring it to life. Nevertheless, only recently have Mexican-Americans turned their attention to drama seriously, intent on fitting it into the fabric of the American dramatic tradition. One such Mexican-American playwright is Estela Portillo, whose play *The Day of the Swallows* is a deft portrayal of Mexican-American existence.

Estela Portillo

Estela Portillo lives in El Paso, Texas, with her husband and children, and teaches in the El Paso public schools. She hosts a local
television program dealing with Chicano cultural affairs. Her works
appear in various publications.

THE DAY OF THE SWALLOWS

A Drama in Three Acts

THE CHARACTERS

In Order of Appearance

ALYSEA	EDUARDO
CLEMENCIA	CLARA
JOSEFA	DON ESQUINAS
TOMÁS	FATHER PRADO

The tierra *of Lago de San Lorenzo is within memory of
mountain-sweet pine. Then the maguey thickens with the
ferocity of chaotic existence; here the desert yawns. Here
it drinks the sun in madness.*

*The village of Lago de San Lorenzo is a stepchild; it is
a stepchild to the Esquinas hacienda, for the hacienda has
been a frugal mother and a demanding father. Its name
comes from the yearly ritual of the saint-day of San Lorenzo when all the young women gather around the lake to
wash their hair and bathe in promise of a future husband.
The tempo of life, unbroken, conditioned, flavors its heart-
beat with dreams and myths. The hacienda is the fiber
upon which existence hangs. The church, the fluid rose,*

224

assures the future promise of Elysian fields. No one dares ask for life.

What is this footfall beyond ritual, beyond livelihood? What is this faint unknown ache in the heart? It's more than just the rasp of hope. . . . The young know this; and they go to the spring with lyrical intimacy. By the lake, eyes burn and feet dig the mud of the spring; someone traces mountain against sky and gulf expands, drowning, drowning. The obligation is remembered back in the village; the toll of the church bell offering sanctuary is a relief; the lake becomes too much for them.

At daybreak the fiesta day is sanctified with a misa at sunrise; the choir rejoices the promise of day. A holy procession is led by the priest and an "honored member" of the church. Offerings to the patron saint are generous amidst frugality. The animals are blessed; the people are blessed; all is washed clean.

Perhaps secretly each villager senses the werewolf moon inside him; the bite into passions will be hard and fierce after sunset.

On the day of San Lorenzo, in the heat of July, everybody goes to the lake; this day the lake is invaded by village life. When the church bells toll eleven in the sun, the late morning is the sole witness to the bathing of the virgins. The lake becomes a sacred temple. The high priestesses talk of hopes, lovers, and promises. In earnest belief, they wash their hair in spring water to insure future marriages in heaven. It is true, no one has seen a marriage made in heaven, but each girl hugs the private truth that hers will be the one.

Two hundred years before the Esquinas family had settled in Lago de San Lorenzo on a Spanish grant of fifty thousand acres, the Indians were pushed out further into the desert. This was the way of the bearded gachupín, with his hot grasp and his hot looks. Their greedy vitality was a wonder to the Indian. It was also death.

But now the barrio clustered itself around the hacienda. The conquered conquered the conquerors.

There is a house, the only house close to the edge of the lake. Here our story begins. . . .

Beautiful old Mexican house (New York Public Library)

ACT I—Scene 1

Josefa's sitting room; it is an unusually beautiful room, thoroughly feminine and in good taste; the profusion of lace everywhere gives the room a safe, homey look. The lace pieces are lovely, needlepoint, hairpin, limerick, the work of patience and love. Upstage left is a large French window; from it one can view a large tree. On the tree is a freshly painted tree house of unusual size and shape. It is an orb that accommodates a great number of birds. The room faces south, so it is flooded with light; the light, the lace, the open window all add to the beauty of the room, a storybook beauty of serenity. To the right is a door leading to the kitchen; there is another door leading to a bedroom; downstage left there is a door leading to the outside.

Alysea is sitting on the floor when the curtain rises. It is before dawn; but a few minutes after the curtain rises, light begins to fill the room. Alysea is cleaning the sitting room carpet, an unusual task for this hour. Next to her is a pail; she uses a piece of cloth with quick, frantic movements, rinses, and continues the scrubbing. After a while she looks at the cloth in her hand intently, as in realization of what she is doing. Suddenly she drops it, seemingly in horror. She looks helpless and lost. Still sitting on the floor she leans her head against a chair and cries silently, staring up into the now streaming light from the window. There is the sound of the milk bell. It is Clemencia delivering. When she hears it, Alysea jumps up, wipes away traces of tears with her apron, then opens the French window and looks out.

ALYSEA: She'll come right in if I'm not at the door to pay her.

She looks around the room. Her eyes fall on a small side table next to the couch. She goes to the table and stares at a long kitchen knife with traces of blood on it. Hurriedly, she picks up the cleaning cloth, and uses it to pick up the knife gingerly. She wraps the cloth

*around the knife and places it in a side table drawer.
During this interval, Clemencia's noisy arrival is heard.
The kitchen door is opened; there is a tug of milk can,
then a pouring of milk. Several sighs and ejaculations
about hard work are heard. Alysea looks around the
room one last time as Clemencia walks in.*

CLEMENCIA: Josefa! Alysea! My centavos for the week
are not on the kitchen table. *Hombre . . .* do I have to
beg for my money? *Oye . . . ¿dónde están?*

ALYSEA: *Buenos días,* Clemencia . . . early?

CLEMENCIA *(staring at Alysea)*: *Que horror!* What is the
matter? You look terrible. Have you been up all
night?

ALYSEA *(smooths her hair; looks at her hands guiltily)*:
Yes . . . I stayed up late. A new pattern in lace.

CLEMENCIA: You work hard to please Josefa, don't you?
(She notices Alysea looking at her hands.) What's the
matter with your hands? Not rheumatism . . . you're
just a girl. . . . Look at mine! Life has eaten them
up. . . . I feel pain . . . ay! . . . it is my destiny to
suffer. . . . You owe me seven pesos.

ALYSEA: Yes, of course. *(She goes to the household
money box, takes a set of keys from her apron pocket
and opens it. She counts out the money.)* Cinco . . .
seis . . . siete.

CLEMENCIA: *Gracias . . . (Looks at Alysea again and
shakes her head)* Rest in the afternoon . . . you look
all in. You can in this house. There is beautiful peace
here.

ALYSEA: Yes . . . here it stretches itself out to breathe. . . .

CLEMENCIA: You begin to talk like Josefa now . . . you
like her . . . eh? She doesn't want you to work yourself to death . . . she is too kind.

ALYSEA: The most considerate of persons . . . but there is
so much to do.

CLEMENCIA: Of course, San Lorenzo . . . *mañana . . .*
Josefa will be so grand leading the procession with the
Father to the church . . . a happy day for the barrio . . .

we all share Josefa's honor like we have shared her goodness . . . a great lady.

ALYSEA: I had forgotten . . . the procession tomorrow.

CLEMENCIA: What's the matter with you? Forgotten?

ALYSEA: Don't mind me. . . . I'm not myself today . . . Clemencia.

CLEMENCIA: Doña Josefa is an angel. All her life, she goes around . . . with that walking stick of hers . . . always she goes . . . like an avenging angel . . . helping . . . what a sight she must be . . . pounding with her stick on those evil people. . . . One, two . . . that's for wickedness! (*She makes motions of one pounding away.*) She takes care of the devil all right . . . eh? Yes . . . she saved you from the sickness. . . .

ALYSEA: Saved me . . . from the sickness . . . what is shadow? What is sickness?

CLEMENCIA: Talk sense, child! . . . you need rest. (*She looks at lace work on table.*) My . . . you are making lace as beautiful as Josefa's! You are lucky.

ALYSEA: Lucky? (*She goes to the window.*) This room is beautiful . . . isn't it? I'm lucky to be here . . . aren't I? (*Pause*) Appearances . . . they are very funny! Tomorrow the church will honor Josefa . . . how very funny! (*She begins to laugh; then the laugh is eventually lost in sobbing.*) Oh, God!

CLEMENCIA: What is the matter? (*She looks around.*) Where is Josefa . . . . Josefa! (*She goes to Alysea and feels her forehead.*) Are you feverish?

At this point, Josefa enters. She is a tall, regal woman about thirty-five. Her bones are Indian's; her coloring is Aryan. She wears her hair back severely. Her movements are graceful and quiet. The cuffs and collar of her dress are of exquisite lace. She walks up to Alysea and puts her arm around her.

JOSEFA: Alysea, quiet! (*She turns to Clemencia.*) She's not feeling well, I suppose.

CLEMENCIA: She worked all night.

JOSEFA: Oh?

CLEMENCIA: You must make her rest.

JOSEFA: You're right, of course . . . .

CLEMENCIA: Well . . . I must be going. . . . I'm late on
my rounds . . . (*She sighs.*) I wish I could stay here.
(*She looks around.*) What heavenly peace . . .

JOSEFA (*smiling*): You are welcome . . . this is your
home . . .

CLEMENCIA: Doña Josefa . . . you are an angel!

JOSEFA: No . . . just happy! . . . Did you get your money?

*Josefa escorts Clemencia to the door. Clemencia gives
a last anxious look at Alysea.*

CLEMENCIA: She'll be all right in your hands, Josefa.

JOSEFA: I'll see that she rests.

*Clemencia leaves through the kitchen door. Josefa
remains silent as the sounds of departure from the
kitchen are heard.*

JOSEFA: You should rest. . . . Clemencia's right.

Alysea shakes her head.

JOSEFA: Do you think it's wise? . . .

ALYSEA: Wise! the way you word it . . . wise!

JOSEFA: Very well, I'll put it another way . . . is this the
time to break down? Beautiful days demand our
strength. . . . We must be faithful to loveliness.

ALYSEA (*incredulously*): You believe that? (*She walks
up to Josefa almost menacingly.*) How can you justify
in that way? You!

JOSEFA (*softly*): There are things we must do . . . to
keep a sanity . . . to make the moment clear. (*Pause*)
Any signs of the swallows? Isn't the tree lovely?

ALYSEA: Have you forgotten? . . . how can you! . . . Josefa,
last night. . . .

*Alysea is overwhelmed with the memory; she runs out
of the room. Josefa looks for a moment after her; then
she touches the lace curtains on the window.*

JOSEFA: We pattern our lives for one beautiful moment . . .
like this lace . . . little bits and pieces come together . . .

to make all this . . . my world . . . a crystal thing of light; Alysea must understand . . . she must!

There is a knock at the door leading outside. Josefa goes to the door; she opens it; it is Tomás, her shiftless uncle.

TOMÁS: Oh . . . it is you, Josefa! You're not at the hacienda this morning.

JOSEFA: What are you doing here?

TOMÁS: The pump . . .

JOSEFA: You fixed that already. . . . I've told you not to come around here at this time of day. . . .

TOMÁS: You do not appreciate . . . always suspicious. . . .

JOSEFA: I don't want you bothering Alysea . . . ever. . . .

TOMÁS: It is like you . . . to think the worst of me.

JOSEFA (*with resignation*): How are the children? Your wife Anita?

TOMÁS: They manage better than me . . . thanks to you . . . . There is little steady work . . . . I need a few centavos . . . Josefa . . . . you're rich!

JOSEFA: What for . . . tequila?

TOMÁS: Just a little money . . . look, my hands . . . they shake . . . . I need it, Josefa . . . please!

JOSEFA: Don't beg!

TOMÁS: You let Clara have all she wants. . . .

JOSEFA: That is none of your business.

TOMÁS (*noticing the pail*): Eh . . . what's this? Looks like blood!

JOSEFA: Go to the kitchen . . . help yourself to meal and beans . . . for the family.

Tomás is still staring at the pail.

JOSEFA: Did you hear me?

TOMÁS: Yes . . . yes, Doña Perfecta . . . Doña Perfecta . . . so charitable . . . ha! ha!

JOSEFA: I'm not in the mood for your sarcasm.

TOMÁS: You will lead the procession tomorrow like the queen of the world . . . eh? You can spare a few centavos? a bottle? Do you keep some in the house when you get it for Clara?

JOSEFA: You're not getting any money.

TOMÁS (*starting to leave*): What's in that pail?

JOSEFA (*indignant*): I don't have to satisfy your curiosity.

TOMÁS: *Cálmate.* . . . I was just asking. . . .

Josefa turns her back to him; he leaves through the kitchen door; his grumbling is heard as he helps himself to the food offered by Josefa. Josefa stares at the contents of the pail; she looks away and touches her temples with her fingertips. She sits in a rocking chair, leans back, closes her eyes, and grips the arms of the chair. She rocks back and forth.

JOSEFA: There is no desert here . . . only light . . . to live each day with nothing . . . to sink . . . (*She closes her eyes and rocks.*) The lonely, lonely struggle . . . then to emerge . . . to find the light . . . I have so much now . . . I want to give so much now . . . Alysea must understand! We must keep this world of light at all costs. . . .

She rises and walks to the window and stands absorbing the light; one can sense an obvious union between the light and Josefa.

JOSEFA (*softly*): How moist your lips, my light. . . Through me . . . through me . . . you live. (*She comes back from her intimate world and looks at the birdhouse with pleasure.*) The long flight . . . how tired they will be; how thirsty after the desert . . . here my swallows will find peace . . . home. (*As she looks at the tree, Tomás comes through the patio outside the window. He has a sack over his shoulder. Josefa does not seem to be mindful of him. Tomás calls.*)

TOMÁS: Hey, Josefa! Are you casting a spell . . . so early? You don't scare me . . . I know you, *querida* . . . I know many things . . . you burn inside. . . .

Josefa stares at him unbelievingly, as if he has destroyed a beauty; then she turns away from the window.

TOMÁS: Hey, Josefa . . . don't run away . . . the great Doña Perfecta runs away from her good-for-nothing uncle . . . that's funny . . . ha, ha!

JOSEFA (*firmly, but in an ominous tone*): Go home, Tomás, go home.

She closes the window and walks to an unfinished damask close to the window. She sits down, unhooks the needle, and begins to work on it. Her concentration is a fiery intensity; this is obvious in her finger movements. Alysea comes back into the room; she is now composed and refreshed; she has put on a pretty dress. She sees the pail and removes it, taking it into the kitchen; all this time Josefa remains absorbed in the damask. Alysea comes back. Josefa looks up.

JOSEFA: You look so nice! Every morning now . . . you look like the garden. . . .

ALYSEA: Nothing is as beautiful as your garden . . . paradise must look like that.

JOSEFA: A garden of light . . . perhaps it has a sense of paradise. . . .

ALYSEA: Tomás was here?

JOSEFA: Sneaking around as usual . . . (*Pause*) the pretty dress . . . for Eduardo again?

ALYSEA: Yes . . . I'll bring in the morning coffee . . . scones?

JOSEFA: Fine . . . and honey . . . suddenly I'm hungry . . . (*She leaves the damask and begins to clear the coffee table.*) By the way . . . ask Eduardo to have some morning coffee with us today . . . don't run off for your usual morning walk.

ALYSEA: May I? Thank you . . . he's been coaxing me . . . he's absolutely fascinated by you.

JOSEFA: Do invite him.

Alysea seems to be holding back tears, although she has pretended calm through the conversation.

JOSEFA: What's the matter?

Alysea is not able to answer; she just shakes her head. Josefa walks up to her. Alysea stands still and helpless. Josefa takes Alysea's face in her hands.

JOSEFA: You are so dear to me . . . I don't like to see you

like this . . . Alysea, don't dwell on what happened . . . things will be all right. Haven't I always made things all right?

Alysea still doesn't answer.

JOSEFA: The tragic things in my life taught me one thing . . . calm. The waiting . . . that is harder than struggle. . . . Alysea, learn how . . . to find a strength . . . this loveliness here . . . our world . . . isn't it worth it?

Alysea begins to cry gently. Josefa comforts her. Alysea becomes limp; she places her head on Josefa's shoulder like a child. Josefa strokes her hair.

JOSEFA: Your hair . . . your beautiful hair . . . here, let me comb it. . . .

Suddenly Alysea breaks away. She seems at a loss, then remembers the coffee.

ALYSEA: I'll get things started in the kitchen . . . Eduardo will be here any moment now.

JOSEFA: About last night, Alysea . . . we must have a story.

ALYSEA (*she seems to shiver*): Story?

JOSEFA: When I took David to the hospital . . . the doctors . . . everyone was sympathetic . . . I told them someone had broken in . . .

ALYSEA: And David?

JOSEFA: He will be all right.

ALYSEA: I can never believe that. . . .

JOSEFA: I will take care of him always. . . .

ALYSEA: You killed him!

JOSEFA: Don't! He'll be back with us in a few weeks . . . I will make a fine life for him always. . . .

ALYSEA: He'll never . . . he'll never . . .

She is overcome by emotion; she walks out of the room into the kitchen. Josefa looks after her. She remains standing for a moment; then she picks up a book of poetry from the lamp table.

JOSEFA: Santa Teresita . . .

> *"El hombre toma . . . toma y hiere,*
> *La flor desnuda . . . temblorosa . . ."*
> ("Man takes . . . he takes and wounds
> The tremulous . . . naked flower")

In her world of God . . . she saw what I see . . . she knew the light . . . beauty . . . truth . . . yes . . . in a cloister.

She looks around the room. Then she walks up to a workbasket and picks up a piece of lace. She holds it to the light and intently traces the pattern.

JOSEFA: The web . . . the beautiful web we weave! Anything . . . anything is worth this!

ACT I—Scene 2

A few minutes later; Alysea comes from the kitchen with a morning tray; coffee, scones, juice. She places the tray on the coffee table. There is a knock. Alysea goes to the door. It is Eduardo.

EDUARDO (*a young man of mixed heritage*): I came through the path. . . .

ALYSEA (*drawing him in*): I'm glad. Josefa wants you to have morning coffee . . . in here . . . with her. You always come for me in such a hurry . . . you hadn't seen this room . . . had you?

EDUARDO: No . . . never! (*Looking around*) Well . . . you were right . . . what a room! . . . for women.

ALYSEA: What do you mean?

EDUARDO: It is a dream of gentleness . . . peace; it is not a man's room . . . but it is beautiful.

ALYSEA: You're right . . . Josefa made this haven . . . away from the world of men.

EDUARDO (*looking at her quizzically*): You like that?

ALYSEA: After what I've lived through . . . yes; this was

heaven . . . when she brought me here. Sit down . . . she'll be here any moment.

Eduardo watches Alysea as she arranges napkins, spoons.

EDUARDO: Have you told her . . . about our plans?

ALYSEA: No . . . she suspects something between us.

EDUARDO: And?

ALYSEA: It is hard to understand her feelings . . . there is a stillness in her.

EDUARDO: She dotes on you . . . I don't think she will be pleased . . . after all, I'm taking you away to a wilderness . . . mountain, pines. My squaw . . . living and loving in the open.

He goes to her, gathers her in his arms; they kiss, Alysea clings to him.

EDUARDO: It won't be like this . . . you know!

ALYSEA: I'll be with you . . . isn't that everything?

EDUARDO: And the gentle life you love?

ALYSEA: What you will share with me . . . will be so much more.

They embrace again.

EDUARDO: Say! Have you seen the morning? It is a conspiracy . . . sun, clouds, green fields . . . and the pines from the distance . . . I can hardly wait. Let's leave right now . . . pack the horses . . . . take the mountain trail past the lake . . . the way of my people.

ALYSEA: Not now . . . you crazy Indian!

EDUARDO: We'll find a clearing . . . plow . . . build a cabin . . . have babies. . . .

ALYSEA: Sometimes I think you have to be out in the open . . . no matter what . . .

EDUARDO: That's where my God is.

Eduardo sits down; Alysea stands behind his chair and gently traces his cheek.

ALYSEA: Your world! A beautiful God exists . . . in your

world . . . when you talk . . . He is free . . . green . . . open. You know something?

EDUARDO (*catching her hand and kissing it*): What?

ALYSEA: Father Prado understands your God too. At confession . . . I told him about not attending mass because we go exploring . . . to find the tallest pines . . . I told him about your God . . . he smiled and told me I had found a holier temple.

EDUARDO: Let's take him with us.

ALYSEA (*laughing*): You know better . . . his life is the barrio . . . the people.

EDUARDO: He will marry us . . . before we leave. . . .

ALYSEA (*pulling away*): No . . . we must wait . . .

EDUARDO: Why? Listen, woman . . . no one in her right mind turns down a marriage proposal. . . .

ALYSEA: I want you to be sure . . . after a while . . . after we have shared. . . .

EDUARDO (*in jest*): You shameless hussy . . . you wish to live in sin, eh?

ALYSEA: Don't jest . . . . there was so much ugliness . . . before Josefa brought me here . . . I remember . . . they brought a bunch of us from the country . . . they promised jobs as seamstresses; my barrio was poor . . . we went hungry . . . so I came . . . the city was a nightmare . . . they locked us up in an old house . . . they gave us disgusting soiled dresses to wear . . . then we found out.

EDUARDO: Stop torturing yourself.

ALYSEA: No . . . let me finish . . . I've never told you . . . I hid in the closet of the room; an ugly man with fat hands asked the girls where I was . . . they didn't know . . . he cursed; I was trembling underneath a pile of dirty dresses suffering with the sweat of lust . . . I closed my eyes. Then, I decided to run . . . I simply got up . . . and ran . . . down the stairs . . . into an open hall . . . where men . . . men with hard, dead looks stared . . . no one expected me to try and escape through the front door . . . but I did . . . I got as far as the street . . . then he caught up with me; his hands were at my throat. . . .

EDUARDO: That's enough. . . .

ALYSEA: All of a sudden . . . Josefa appeared . . . with her walking stick. She raised it over her head and beat the man . . . he cried out in pain . . . she never faltered . . . then she brought me to this world of light . . .

EDUARDO: We shall marry tomorrow night . . . that's it!

ALYSEA: No . . . no . . . there's something else . . . (*She becomes very agitated.*) Eduardo . . . last night . . . *Josefa enters.*

JOSEFA: Good morning . . . am I late? Is the coffee cold?

ALYSEA: No . . . no . . . you are just in time.

EDUARDO (*drawing out a chair for her*): Our great lady! *Alysea becomes busy with the food.*

ALYSEA (*to Josefa*): Juice?

JOSEFA: Yes . . . thank you. Eduardo, what are you up to . . . charming the women so early in the morning?

EDUARDO: What better time?

JOSEFA: You are different! Alysea . . . give Eduardo . . . some of this orange . . . it's delicious . . .

EDUARDO: No! No! just coffee . . . and what's this? (*He picks up a scone, tastes it.*) Wonderful! I had heard about all your wonders . . . but . . . cooking too!

JOSEFA: Alysea baked them . . . from an old recipe of mine . . . .

Alysea hands Eduardo some coffee.

EDUARDO: Thank you, *linda* . . . .

Alysea serves herself. Josefa looks intently from one to the other.

JOSEFA: All these walks you two take . . . into forbidden country . . .

EDUARDO: How can beauty be forbidden? . . .

JOSEFA: I feel the same way . . . but the desert mind forbids it . . . many times.

ALYSEA: It won't be forbidden tomorrow . . . all the young girls will bathe in the lake at noontime . . . the promise of a perfect love . . . .

EDUARDO: I hear it is your year, Josefa . . . you will lead the church procession . . .

JOSEFA: My people enjoy planning for it . . .

ALYSEA: Josefa is as bad as Father Prado about the barrio people . . . all is to please them . . . .

EDUARDO: And what pleases you, Josefa?

JOSEFA: To make them happy!

EDUARDO: I can see why they talk of you with awe . . . .

JOSEFA: I am Indian, you know . . . yet not of desert, not of them, in a way. Yet . . . totally theirs.

ALYSEA (*rising*): Well . . . I shall leave you for a few moments; Josefa . . . the lace for the capitol . . . must make the morning express . . . excuse me.

Alysea leaves. Eduardo finishes his coffee.

JOSEFA: She's falling in love with you . . .

EDUARDO: It's mutual . . . .

JOSEFA: For how long, Eduardo?

EDUARDO (*stands, hands in pockets, somewhat ill-at-ease*): Love is not timed.

JOSEFA: Isn't it?

EDUARDO: What do you mean?

JOSEFA: Clara.

EDUARDO: You know?

JOSEFA: She has described to me . . . your every mood . . . your every gesture . . . in love . . . .

EDUARDO: I don't know what to say!

JOSEFA: Guilt?

EDUARDO: Ridiculous . . . there's no guilt in love!

JOSEFA (*laughing as if to herself*): The way you men justify . . . the word "love" doesn't it really mean . . . take? . . . destroy?

EDUARDO: It isn't that . . . .

JOSEFA: Of course not! Disguised in a man's words . . . in a man's promises . . . . oh, I know, you make a dream of your deadly game.

EDUARDO: Alysea's happy.

JOSEFA: Is she? For how long . . . until you find another fancy?

EDUARDO: What I feel for her is different . . . .

JOSEFA: I remember Clara telling me the same things

about you and her . . . how easily you put her out of your life.

EDUARDO: Clara understands.

JOSEFA: No, Eduardo . . . she just accepts . . . she knows nothing else.

EDUARDO: You make me feel guilty . . . why?

JOSEFA: I'll tell you why . . . Alysea has love here; she is happy . . . she has found her place in the world . . . safe with me . . . there is a constancy here . . .

EDUARDO: All right! I don't think one should have conditions . . . I know I love her now . . . I want to love her forever . . . but it is not for me to know . . . .

JOSEFA: She belongs here . . . with me . . . You men explain away all your indiscretions, so easily . . . after all, you make the rules and enjoy the abuses!

EDUARDO: That's not fair . . .

JOSEFA: That's funny . . . . When has a man been fair to . . . women?

EDUARDO: You are distorting . . . .

JOSEFA: What I offer her is not a violence. . . . Man's love is always a violence.

EDUARDO: I'm sorry.

JOSEFA: For what . . . the evil in the world?

EDUARDO: I love Alysea.

JOSEFA: Oh, yes . . . you love, he loves, they love . . . how convenient the word "love!"

Eduardo remains silent. Josefa suddenly realizes he is a guest.

JOSEFA (*in an even, pleasant voice*): Come, Eduardo, you must forgive me for such an outburst. . . . What a terrible hostess I am! Don't mind me, when there is concern for the people you love . . . Here, let me refill your cup! (*She pours him some coffee and hands it to him.*) There is a special happiness in this house, you know. . . .

EDUARDO (*reassured*): I know . . . it is the soaring sea in you.

JOSEFA: What?

EDUARDO: You carry things, people with you . . . wher

your strength is washed away . . . you leave beauty behind.

JOSEFA: How lovely . . . you are easy to fall in love with. . . .

EDUARDO: So are you . . . if a man is brave enough.

JOSEFA: Brave?

EDUARDO: You are a whirlwind. . . .

JOSEFA: I have always sought the calm. . . .

EDUARDO: Ah . . . but your depths! Josefa, I sense them . . . you are not the barrio.

JOSEFA (*amused*): Such discernment! . . . but then, you are right. . . . I am of the lake.

EDUARDO: I've heard . . . I hear you dare the lake alone . . . in solitude. . . .

JOSEFA: The barrio stories are myth . . . primitive fears . . . what most of the people fear is instinctive. . . .

EDUARDO: In what way?

JOSEFA: Out in the lake . . . out in the pines . . . they see themselves too well . . . they have become the desert . . . it is too much to accept . . . so monsters are created . . . . but for me . . . ah . . . for me!

EDUARDO: Tell me. . . .

JOSEFA: When I was young . . . when I refused to go bathe on San Lorenzo's day, when I chose the moonlight in any season . . . it was defiance . . .

EDUARDO: What did you defy?

JOSEFA: What defied me . . . the world! Yes, I would go . . . to defy . . . then . . . but it became something else.

EDUARDO (*looking at her intently*): Why didn't you ever marry? No one good enough?

JOSEFA (*shrugs it off*): I never saw the dream . . . I never felt the hope . . . there was always too much clarity for me . . . (*Pause*) . . . Do you think me beautiful?

EDUARDO: Yes . . . very . . . mixed in with a dangerous excitement. . . .

JOSEFA: You are making love to me . . .

EDUARDO: I make love to all things beautiful . . . don't you?

JOSEFA (*in a whisper*): Yes . . . oh, yes. . . .

Alysea comes in breathless.

ALYSEA: Well . . . you two . . . that wasn't long was it? (*Looks at both of them.*) You two must have found marvelous things to talk about . . . it shows!

JOSEFA: I tell you, Eduardo . . . this girl has possibilities. . . .

EDUARDO: I know. . . .

ALYSEA: Did she tell you about her magicians?

EDUARDO: She was about to . . . when you came.

JOSEFA (*looking at him intently*): How did you know . . . I was about to?

EDUARDO: The light in your eyes . . . the sudden magic in you. . . .

ALYSEA: I know what you mean, Eduardo . . . such a mystical thing. . . .

JOSEFA: You have laid the setting . . . so kindly. (*She walks to the window and looks out with her eyes closed as she speaks.*)

JOSEFA: The magicians are real, you know! I found them . . . long ago . . . the night of the Festival of San Lorenzo. The virgins had bathed by the noon-day sun . . . I . . . I went after the Rosary bell . . . I went when they were all celebrating; the silence was perfumed . . . desire was heavy . . . painful. Does it surprise you that I speak of desire? Oh, yes . . . I felt it . . . to my fingertips . . . it was so real, the beautiful need . . . the lights of the barrio were far off in another world . . . this always affected me . . . I became another being far from my kind . . . even my desire was a special suffering. . . .

EDUARDO: You still did not marry.

JOSEFA: What does that have to do with desire? My desire . . . like my being . . . became a purer grain. It was more than someone to see or touch . . . or embrace . . . it was a need for a pouring of self . . . a gentleness . . . a faith. I did not want the callous Indian youth . . . with hot breath and awkward hands . . . a taking without feeling . . . no, not that! I wanted so much more. . . .

Josefa turns to look at Alysea and Eduardo, caught in her spell.

JOSEFA: Look at you . . . children . . . listening to fairy tales. . . .

EDUARDO: Children believe. . . .

JOSEFA: So do I! . . . isn't it funny?

EDUARDO: No . . . it is like that with some people.

JOSEFA: For me . . . it came true! . . . the wonder was my magicians. That night at the lake there was a different music . . . the stillness sung inside me . . . the moonlight grew in me . . . it became my lover . . . There by the lake, I felt the light finding its way among the pines . . . to me . . . It took me . . . then . . . perhaps it was my imagination . . . it said to me . . . "We are one . . . make your beauty . . . make your truth." Deep, I felt a burning spiral . . . it roared in my ears . . . my heart . . . (*Pause*) It was too much to bear . . . so I ran and ran and ran until I fell . . . not knowing where; I lay there in utter quiet . . . then I opened my eyes and found myself calmly looking up at the stars . . . sisters of my love! The moon had followed me; it lay a lake around me, on the grass. . . .

EDUARDO: Were you afraid?

JOSEFA: Afraid? There was no room . . . the joy was too great. I had the secret of the magicians . . . the wine of love . . . the light was me; I knew that I would bear the children of light . . . the moon . . . the burning lake.

ALYSEA (*in a whisper*): I believe her . . . look around you, the children of light . . . her garden . . . the lace . . . her love for the barrio people . . . her bright, bright calm. . . .

EDUARDO (*taking up the pace*): Her person. . . .

JOSEFA: Hush . . . you two . . . don't go on so!

The voice of Tomás from the outside window breaks the spell.

TOMÁS: Josefa! . . . David's horse! . . . I found it out in the pasture . . . without a bridle . . . Josefa!

JOSEFA (*goes to the window*): David's horse?

EDUARDO (*going to the window*): Need any help?

JOSEFA: He didn't hear you . . . he's coming in. . . .

Alysea all of a sudden loses all her brightness; she seems frightened and lost. She looks at Josefa's every move; Josefa shows no reaction; she calmly begins to pick up cups, napkins.

JOSEFA: It is getting late . . . my! The morning has flown . . . such a wonderful time . . . I hope it isn't too late for you two to go for your walk.

EDUARDO: No . . . no . . . there's plenty of time.

Tomás comes in through the kitchen door.

TOMÁS: He must have broken out from the stable . . . I thought I would tell you before I took him back to the hacienda. . . .

JOSEFA: Yes . . . take him back . . . horses will do that.

Eduardo takes Alysea by the hands. He looks at her intently.

EDUARDO: What on earth is the matter? You need some morning air . . . I'll tell you what . . . I'll take you to a place where I can trace the path of the swallows any day now. . . .

Alysea doesn't seem to be listening to him; Josefa notices this and promptly suggests.

JOSEFA: Yes . . . I insist on it . . . take her; right now . . . enjoy this lovely day. . . .

Eduardo takes Alysea by the shoulder.

EDUARDO: Come on. . . .

He stirs her to the door; Alysea does not resist. They exit.

TOMÁS (*slyly*): I guess she feels bad about David . . . what happened last night. . . .

JOSEFA: What?

TOMÁS: I heard the talk in the barrio . . . someone broke into the house . . . that is . . . that is what you claim.

JOSEFA: What do you mean?

TOMÁS: You didn't tell me earlier. . . .

JOSEFA: Tell you? Why should I tell you anything?

TOMÁS: The blood in the pail . . . you didn't tell me anything about that either . . .

JOSEFA: So?

TOMÁS: Well . . . I remember . . . all those times . . . you save the poor, innocent, helpless ones . . . you never say anything . . . it's always the barrio who puts the story together . . . you are clever. . . .

JOSEFA: Don't be ridiculous. . . .

TOMÁS: Yes . . . people have no idea how clever you really are . . . la Doña Perfecta! You saved Alysea from the evil man . . . you saved David from a drunken father, the barrio tells the story of an angel . . . but it's funny . . . somehow . . . they never remember to tell that you crippled one man and the other died on the road where you left him. . . .

JOSEFA: You are pitiful . . . like those two men . . . destructive and pitiful. . . .

TOMÁS: Perhaps you'll get your hands on me too.

JOSEFA (*calmly, with disdain*): Hadn't you better see about that horse?

TOMÁS: Now the town is busy making you out a heroine . . . an intruder? That's hard to believe . . . the girl looked too guilty a while ago . . . (*He studies Josefa who is straightening up.*) But you . . . it's amazing! . . . such grace . . . such pious silence . . . yes . . . you are a dangerous one, all right!

JOSEFA: All this . . . this foolishness, I know, is leading up to some sort of blackmail . . . you want money . . . don't you?

TOMÁS: You know me so well! . . . after all, I'm on your side . . . we are of the same blood. . . .

JOSEFA: Get out of here . . . and be careful about what you say . . . you clown! . . . who's going to believe anything you say? Be careful . . . or I may let you starve.

TOMÁS: Didn't work . . . eh? No money?

JOSEFA: You've tried my patience long enough . . . I have

better things to do with my time . . . go and see about that horse. . . .

Josefa picks up the tray and starts toward the kitchen.

TOMÁS: Not even a few pesos?

Josefa looks at him contemptuously and walks out into the kitchen without a word.

TOMÁS: She'll break! She'll break . . . once I lay all my cards on the table . . . stupid women! . . . (*He looks around the room.*) I know they keep the household money somewhere around here . . . yes.

He begins to look in the drawers.

ACT I—Scene 3

Later the same morning. The room is empty, full of light, when Clara enters. She is the wife of Don Esquinas, owner of the hacienda. She has the grace and elegance of good living. But, at closer scrutiny, one can see that this once beautiful woman is dissipated. Her blond beauty, although meticulously enhanced by great care, has the flavor of fading youth. She carries a knitting bag. Although she has been in this room many times, she is each time overwhelmed by the unusual light. She walks up to the table, lays her bag on it, opens it, searches for a cigarette; she finds one, lights it, and draws its flavor leisurely. She catches sight of Josefa's workbasket; she also sees the damask; she traces the design; then she picks up a piece of lace from the workbasket and examines it admiringly.

CLARA: Angel filigree . . . how lovely . . . it's unearthly. . . .

As she examines the lace, Alysea walks into the room breathlessly. Her arms are full of freshly cut flowers. She glances at Doña Clara apologetically.

ALYSEA: Doña Clara . . . am I late?

CLARA: No, no . . . I just got here.

ALYSEA (*going to the vase and setting the flowers next to it*): I always linger too long in the garden. . . .

CLARA: What a garden . . . what incantations does Josefa use?

ALYSEA: It's marvelous, the way she does it . . .

CLARA: She talks to the flowers. . . .

ALYSEA: She talks to all living things. . . .

CLARA (*looking at Alysea as she arranges the flowers in the vase*): You too . . . how you have blossomed in this house.

ALYSEA: Me?

CLARA (*in a deliberately contained voice*): Of course, this time it could be Eduardo . . . I hear he loves you.

ALYSEA: Love does that . . . doesn't it?

CLARA: It's true then! . . . and you love him too?

ALYSEA: Yes.

CLARA: Well . . . (*She puts out her cigarette.*) That's that! . . . where is my dress?

ALYSEA (*coming out of her reverie*): Oh, I'm sorry . . . of course, your fitting.

Alysea goes to a wardrobe and takes out a simple gown. She hands it to Clara. Clara goes behind the screen.

CLARA: I suppose you'll go away with him?

ALYSEA: He wants me to . . . I haven't quite decided. . . .

CLARA: About love?

ALYSEA: Am I good enough for him? I have to use reason. . . .

CLARA (*almost impatiently*): You don't have to reason love . . . my God!

ALYSEA: Will it be fair to him!

CLARA: What love there is . . . you take . . . don't reason it away . . . take it!

She comes from around the screen and gives her back to Alysea so Alysea will fasten the dress. Both are facing the mirror. Clara looks Alysea directly in the eyes.

CLARA: Love is always fair just because it is. (*She can't look in the mirror any longer.*) What's the matter with me . . . look at me . . . an expert on love . . . ha! (*She bites her lip.*)

ALYSEA: You are beautiful and wise. (*Clara doesn't answer; she deliberately becomes absorbed with the gown. She surveys herself in the mirror.*)

CLARA: It seems to lack something . . . Alysea . . . what do you think?

ALYSEA: Of course . . . Josefa made something very special for it . . . (*She looks around.*) Where is it? Oh, yes . . . I'll be back in a minute.

Alysea goes through the bedroom door. Clara goes to the mirror and traces the lines on her face. She then walks up to her knitting bag, takes a flask, opens it.

CLARA (*bitterly*): Here's to youth! (*She drinks long draughts. She does it three times; then she puts the flask away. She walks up to the mirror again.*)

CLARA: Well, my girl . . . what's in store for you? He's left you . . . you always knew he would leave you . . . what is there now, my girl . . . except time? . . . (*She covers her face with her hands.*)

Alysea comes in from the bedroom with a beautiful lace shawl. Clara quickly recovers and looks at the shawl.

ALYSEA: Look . . . isn't it beautiful . . . a *duende* design.

CLARA: Andalusian?

ALYSEA: Yes . . . Josefa copied it!

CLARA: Superb!

Alysea drapes it over one shoulder and claps it on Clara's waist.

CLARA: Oh, thank you . . . but . . . these days I need the right lights . . . not all things are kind to me anymore. . . . Yes, it is beautiful. . . .

She turns and contemplates Alysea.

CLARA: Look at you . . . you are so young . . . your beauty so sharp . . . only yesterday, my dear, only yesterday, I was young like you . . . mark that well!

Josefa comes in through the outside door. Clara sees her. She goes to Josefa and kisses her cheek.

CLARA: I missed you this morning . . . you didn't come.

JOSEFA: Didn't I tell you? . . . there's a million things to do before tomorrow.

CLARA: The shawl . . . it's beautiful . . . only Josefa!

JOSEFA (*surveying her handiwork*): The design . . . the delicacy against the dark dress . . . it is impressive . . . you wear it well.

Josefa notices that Clara is somewhat too gay; a little bit unsteady.

ALYSEA: Shall I get the combs?

CLARA: Combs?

JOSEFA: Mantilla combs . . . made by the gypsies. . . .

CLARA: To go with the gown.

ALYSEA: I'll get them.

She walks back to the bedroom. Josefa looks at Clara realizing what the matter is.

JOSEFA: You must have started early . . .

CLARA: What? (*She busies herself at the mirror.*) You worry too much . . . just a little courage . . . I needed a little courage . . .

JOSEFA: Eduardo?

CLARA (*turns and faces Josefa; pain in her eyes*): He loves her.

JOSEFA: I know. . . .

CLARA: You see . . . I needed a little courage this morning.

JOSEFA: If you start again . . . promise me you won't!

CLARA (*with false gaiety*): I promise. (*She closes her eyes.*) I wish . . . I wish I were young for one day . . . just one day . . . so he would love me the way I love him.

JOSEFA: Men don't love . . . they take . . . haven't you learned that by now?

CLARA: Oh, Josefa . . . you are wrong . . . you are wrong . . . a woman was made to love a man . . . to love is

enough for a woman . . . if only they would let us love
them without negating, without negating. . . .

JOSEFA: Why, Clara? Why must you give . . . so easily?
Not to them . . . Clara . . . not to men!

CLARA (*shrugs*): My downfall? (*In a whisper*) My life?

JOSEFA: Here . . . enough of that . . . there are beautiful
things to love . . .

*Alysea returns with the combs. She hands them to
Josefa who goes to Clara and expertly places them in
her hair.*

CLARA: Without mantilla?

JOSEFA: It would be too much with the shawl. . . .

CLARA: Yes . . . of course . . . you're right . . . a gypsy
with majesty!

ALYSEA: Yes . . . That's what you look like . . . a gypsy
queen.

JOSEFA: *El espíritu duende.* . . .

CLARA: Like your magicians?

JOSEFA: Perhaps. . . .

*The church bell rings midday; suddenly two swallows
are seen outside the window.*

ALYSEA: Look!

JOSEFA: They're coming . . . the advance guard . . . every
year.

CLARA: You love them . . . don't you? . . . your magicians
let you find so many things to love . . . lucky . . . lucky
Josefa.

JOSEFA: The swallows are safe here . . . after the long,
long, lonely flight. . . .

CLARA: Lonely? . . . they come in droves. . . .

*The three look outside the window for a minute. Choir
practice begins.*

JOSEFA: Look at the lake . . . it shimmers with love . . .
(*Turns to Clara*) I said lonely, Clara, because finding
direction . . . is lonely . . . it is too personal a thing. . . .

CLARA: I see what you mean . . . Josefa (*Looks out the window pensively*), why don't I see the love shimmering in your lake?

Josefa smiles.

ALYSEA: Her magicians . . . isn't it, Josefa?
JOSEFA: Yes . . . my magicians.

ACT II

It is early afternoon of the same day. Josefa comes through the outside door. There is a small injured bird in her hands. She cradles it gently and examines it.

JOSEFA: You poor little thing . . . a broken wing . . . don't worry, you'll be fine in a little while . . . (*She puts the soft piece of life against her cheek.*) There will be no second pain . . . Alysea!
ALYSEA (*comes in through the kitchen door*): Yes?
JOSEFA: Look . . . I found it in the garden . . . it lay there . . . . small, helpless . . . look, he's thirsty . . . quick, get some water and an eye-dropper.

Alysea goes into the bedroom. Josefa sits in her rocking chair and places the bird gently on her lap . . . . Alysea comes back with a cup and an eye-dropper. Josefa picks up the bird, fills the eye-dropper, and patiently feeds the bird water. The bird drinks.

JOSEFA: See . . . oh, he has life . . . this one!
ALYSEA: Just a baby . . . let us set the wing . . . I'll get some small twigs and a bandage. . . .

She leaves again; Josefa continues feeding the bird.

JOSEFA: How did you find the birdhouse . . . eh? My magicians must have led you here . . . before the others . . . every year . . . the sky is black with their wings . . .

here they rest . . . and eat . . . you will be safe . . . until you join your brothers and sisters . . . yes. . . .

Alysea comes back; together they carefully set the small wing.

JOSEFA: There!

ALYSEA: Let's put him in the birdhouse . . . he's tired . . .

Josefa kisses the bird; then both of them go to the window, lean out to the tree, and place the bird in the tree house. Satisfied, Josefa and Alysea look at each other. Josefa reaches out and begins to stroke Alysea's hair.

JOSEFA (*softly*): We share so much . . . just wait . . . the magicians will come to you . . . I know. . . .

ALYSEA: What?

JOSEFA: Remember how much you wished for the magicians?

ALYSEA: No . . . no . . . I don't want them anymore. . . .

JOSEFA: But. . . .

ALYSEA: When you brought me here . . . all that's happened . . . it is so unreal . . . a year of mists and deep sinking dreams . . . but not anymore!

JOSEFA: Hush . . . you're just upset . . . that's all . . . .

ALYSEA: No . . . last night . . . no . . . never again. . . .

JOSEFA: Poor little girl . . . you've tired yourself out all morning . . . I forgot . . . I don't know why . . . but I just forgot about . . . about last night.

ALYSEA (*looking at her with horror*): Josefa . . . no! Forgot? How could you?

JOSEFA (*becoming slightly agitated*): Habit . . . to keep strong . . . since I was little . . . to keep strong . . . I put ugliness away.

ALYSEA: Where? Where?

JOSEFA: What do you mean?

ALYSEA: If you have a conscience . . . where could you put it away?

JOSEFA: There will be atonement. . . .

ALYSEA: No . . . that's impossible . . . you think . . . it will . . . disappear? The blood . . . the knife . . . (*She*

runs to the table where she had placed the knife.) Look
. . . I'll show you . . . you make it disappear! (*She opens
the drawer and stares unbelievingly.*)

ALYSEA: The knife . . . it's gone!

She begins to look frantically everywhere.

ALYSEA: Did you hear me?

Josefa seems almost unaware of Alysea's frenzy.

JOSEFA: Yes . . . of course. . . .

*Alysea begins to look again and this time finds the mon-
ey box gone.*

ALYSEA: The money box . . . it's gone too.
JOSEFA: Tomás . . . of course . . . he took the money and
the knife.

*Alysea collapses into a chair and covers her face with
her hands. Tomás' voice is heard singing a barrio love
song; Alysea looks up in fright. Josefa goes to the door
of the kitchen and calls out into the patio behind the
kitchen.*

JOSEFA: Tomás! Come in here. . . .

*Tomás comes into the kitchen still singing. He walks
into the room. Josefa watches him warily, Alysea in
terror.*

TOMÁS: Well . . . well . . . Did you call me, *querida?* (*He
strokes Josefa's arm intimately. She breaks away.*)
JOSEFA: Don't you ever put your hands on me!
TOMÁS: Ha! ha! ha! . . . Doña Perfecta . . . (*He looks
around the room.*) You know . . . I think I'll move over
here . . . I like this house . . . ah! . . . it is time I had a
little elegance in my life . . . yes. (*He sprawls out in a
chair.*)
JOSEFA: You've been drinking. . . .
TOMÁS: Yes . . . I have been drinking . . . and I shall drink
some more . . . you can afford it. . . .

Alysea begins to cry.

Tomás: What's the matter with her?

Josefa: She is tired . . . and I . . . have had enough of your insolence. . . .

Tomás: *Que maravilla* . . . How long . . . Josefa . . . how long . . . can you keep it up? (*He paces in front of her; she remains calm.*)

Tomás (*practically shouting in her face*): I took the knife! Do you understand . . . I took the knife! . . . aren't you afraid, Josefa?

Alysea begins to cry desperately. Josefa goes to her. She tries to comfort her.

Josefa: Don't, Alysea . . . remember . . . it's late . . . we have to pack for David . . . he'll need his things in the hospital . . . compose yourself . . . Why don't you go and start packing . . . I'll talk to Tomás.

Alysea nods her head in agreement; she rises and leaves as if she wanted escape.

Josefa (*turns and faces Tomás*): Have you ever . . . have you ever . . . done anything kind for anybody?

Tomás (*sarcastically*): No . . . just you . . . *querida* . . . you are the angel . . .

Josefa: All right . . . what do you intend to do?

Tomás: Nothing . . . you see . . . we . . . you and I . . . must have a clearer understanding . . . I know much more than you think . . . about you and (*nods toward bedroom*) her!

Josefa stiffens.

Josefa: All right . . . you win . . . I'll give you money. . . .

Tomás: No more crumbs . . . dear niece . . . I call the play . . . from now on.

Josefa: You're bluffing . . . lying . . . as usual.

Tomás: Am I?

There is a knock at the door; with alacrity Tomás springs up and goes to the door and opens it. It is Don Esquinas, Clara's husband.

TOMÁS: Ah . . . Don Esquinas, won't you come in?
Don Esquinas brushes past Tomás, totally ignoring him.
Tomás makes a mock gesture of humility.

DON ESQUINAS: Josefa . . . the worst has happened . . . .
I warned you!

JOSEFA (*placing her hands on her heart*): Clara . . . let
me go to her. (*She starts to go; Don Esquinas stops
her.*)

DON ESQUINAS: It's too late. . . .

JOSEFA (*savagely*): It isn't . . . I can take care of her.

DON ESQUINAS: How? By giving her more drink . . . you've
done enough harm. . . .

JOSEFA: Harm? I have been her sole companion for years
. . . I have suffered with her . . . nursed her . . . Harm?

DON ESQUINAS: Do you know how I found my wife this
afternoon when I got home? She was lying in bed . . .
stark naked . . . screaming about crawling . . . crawling,
dark . . . she slashed everything in sight . . . broke the
mirror . . . there were bottles . . . everywhere. . . .

JOSEFA: My poor, poor darling. . . .

DON ESQUINAS: I . . . the servants . . . we were helpless
. . . it was dreadful . . . she kept screaming and sobbing
that your magicians had . . . had no faces. . . .

JOSEFA: She's so alone. . . .

DON ESQUINAS: Your lies . . . the liquor and your lies . . .
both supplied by you! I'm taking her to the sanitori-
um . . . this time for good.

JOSEFA: She is so alone. . . .

DON ESQUINAS: Stop saying that! You . . . . you supplied
her with liquor. . . .

JOSEFA: All that unhappiness . . . . she is so lost . . . there
was nothing else . . . She promised me this afternoon.

DON ESQUINAS: Promised? You stupid woman . . . you
knew she wouldn't keep the promise. . . .

JOSEFA (*suddenly in anger*): I tell you . . . you won't
listen . . . . you men never listen . . . all she had was
hopelessness. . . .

DON ESQUINAS: You don't know what you are talking
about . . . . She always had everything . . . since the day

she was born . . . never, never, did she have to lift a
finger . . . anything she desires. . . .

JOSEFA: Except her husband!

DON ESQUINAS: What in damnation?

JOSEFA: She wanted you to love her. . . .

DON ESQUINAS: Love her? You women are insane! I
married her . . . didn't I?

JOSEFA: She knew all about your . . . your women. . . .

DON ESQUINAS: That is a man's way! You have no right
to question . . . Tell me, how much liquor did you give
her? When did you give it to her?

Josefa remains silent.

DON ESQUINAS: Well?

JOSEFA: She wanted a baby . . . .

DON ESQUINAS: Nonsense! We settled that long ago . .
that was past and forgotten. . . .

JOSEFA: No . . . it was never forgotten . . . she cried every
night. . . .

DON ESQUINAS: Silly tears of a drunken woman . . . adopt
a baby . . . a baby not of the Esquinas blood? For my
heir? absurd!

JOSEFA (*bitterly*): Which of your bastards are you going
to choose as your heir?

DON ESQUINAS: You ungrateful peasant . . . let me tell
you . . . you influenced her too much . . . this is probably all your fault . . . I don't want you around the
hacienda now that she is gone . . . do you hear?

*Josefa turns her back on him; Don Esquinas is some-
what at a loss. Her calm toward his anger is disconcert-
ing. He stands for a moment, then he walks out of the
room. On his way out, Tomás follows him, still assum-
ing a pose of mock humility.*

TOMÁS: It is terrible, Don Esquinas, what my niece has
done . . . if I can make up for it in any way . . . please
call on me. . . .

*Don Esquinas ignores him and leaves. Tomás turns to
Josefa.*

Tomás: See what you have done to your friend . . . the wife of our Don?

Josefa too ignores him. Tomás' attitude of humility is now gone. His attitude is again cunning and sly. He walks up to Josefa.

Tomás: Tch, tch, tch, . . . Doña Perfecta is not perfecta . . . eh?

Josefa (*not listening to him*): She's gone . . . the light of my magicians never came to her . . . poor, poor lost child.

Tomás: You are insane about those magicians. (*Josefa walks away from him; Tomás grabs her arm angrily.*) I'm sick and tired of you ignoring me! You think I'm scum? I don't matter . . . do I? Well, you listen, Doña Perfecta, you listen to me!

Josefa waits silently for him to let go of her arm. When he does, she touches her temples with her fingertips.

Josefa: I have a headache. . . .

Tomás: None of your tricks . . . listen to me! I saw you . . . do you hear . . . I saw you. Last San Lorenzo's day, I remember. I left the fiesta . . . I was too drunk; I walked toward the lake . . . I remember, it was a clear, clear night; the moon lighted everything . . . as I came near the lake past the back of this house . . . I saw two figures come from the water's edge . . . they ran . . . one caught up with the other!

Tomás watches her maliciously and intently, wishing to get a reaction. Her surface is still calm as he scrutinizes her face.

Josefa: What are you trying to do?

Tomás (*laughing slyly and triumphantly*): It was you and the girl . . . you and the girl . . . wasn't it? Now . . . I begin to put things together . . . it all fits!

Josefa: Your drunken hallucinations. . . .

Tomás: I know better, *reina del barrio* . . . you are a. . . .

Josefa: If you have nothing else to threaten me with. . . .

(*She walks away from him with disdain.*)

TOMÁS (*practically screaming with exasperation*): You think you can always win, with your calm; you're not made of stone . . . you'll break, milady . . . I'll be back. Inside you're trembling with fear. . . .

She turns abruptly and faces him haughtily. Tomás falters first; he turns and leaves. As Josefa looks after him, Alysea comes from the bedroom wearing street clothes.

JOSEFA (*turns and sees her*): Finished?

ALYSEA: Yes, I'm ready.

Josefa walks up to her and puts her arm around her.

JOSEFA: The ride will do you good; after you come back from the hospital . . . after you see my little David, we'll have supper here . . . then, we can have one of our little chats.

ALYSEA (*gently breaks away from Josefa*): I'm not coming back.

JOSEFA: Not coming back?

ALYSEA: I meant to tell you earlier . . . I'm going away with Eduardo.

JOSEFA: Because of what happened last night?

ALYSEA: Many reasons, but mostly because I want to be with him.

JOSEFA: You are like all the rest . . . you insist on being a useless, empty sacrifice!

ALYSEA: I love him.

JOSEFA: Love him? Tell me, how long will your precious Eduardo love you? (*Pause*) You know who was here? Don Esquinas! Clara drank herself insane because your Eduardo left her. What do you think he'll do to you?

ALYSEA: I can't believe that . . . there's more to love.

JOSEFA (*ironically and bitterly*): Love! remember the brothel? No different . . . you choose darkness . . . all your pains are still to come! Haven't I taught you anything?

ALYSEA: It all fell apart . . . last night. All I can remember are David's eyes. (*She breaks down sobbing.*)

JOSEFA: He'll be all right . . . I'll take care of my little love . . . as long as he lives . . .

ALYSEA: His eyes told me. You and I were all the terror in the world.

JOSEFA: No . . . the terror is in the world out there . . . don't say that!

ALYSEA: The violence . . . the useless violence. . . .

JOSEFA: I forbid you to go on like this.

She walks to the window and reaches into the birdhouse until she finds the crippled bird. She picks him up, fondles him, and holds him against her cheek.

JOSEFA (*with eyes closed*): Remember how he came . . . crippled, starved, half dead?

ALYSEA: The way I came?

JOSEFA: It will be safe here and happy. You have always been safe and happy! We have so much, Alysea.

Alysea remains silent.

JOSEFA: You know why I built the birdhouse?

She seems to be remembering something painful. She goes to the rocking chair, places the bird on her lap, and strokes it gently.

JOSEFA: When I was seven . . . the swallows came . . . they came one hot dry dawn . . . and continued all day . . . on the edge of the desert that still hotter afternoon . . . I saw noisy boys with desert time on their hands . . . playing . . . I watched the playing become a violence . . . they were catching birds . . . now it became a killing . . . they stoned them . . . plucked them . . . laughing with a fearful joy . . . the sand was a sea of dead birds . . . I . . . I . . . couldn't stand it . . . I ran . . . I hit them . . . I said, "Stop! Stop!" (*Pause*) They laughed; then for a joke . . . for a joke they said . . . they held me down, the burning sand against my back . . . . In spite of all my terror, I opened my eyes . . . a boy . . . a big boy . . . held a swallow over me; he took a knife . . . cut the bird . . . Oh, God! so much blood . . . all that blood. (*Josefa strokes the bird*

gently and shakes her head, closes her eyes.) It spilled
. . . spilled into my face . . . ran into my mouth . . .
warm . . . warm . . . salt warm . . . was it my tears?
the blood?

*She stands and goes to the window still with the bird;
she caresses the bird with her cheek and places it gently
in the birdhouse. The Rosary bell begins to toll. It is
sunset. Josefa looks out in silence.*

JOSEFA: Alysea, . . . look, the lake is screaming with life
. . . look . . . the colors of love . . . then . . . the day
went . . . (*She turns to Alysea.*) Out there . . . the
beauty is lost in fears . . . what do you expect out there?
Stay with the radiance . . . Alysea, stay with me!

ALYSEA: I won't be coming back.

*Alysea turns and leaves, going into the bedroom; Josefa
looks after her for a moment, seems to start after Alysea, then changes her mind. She turns to the unfinished
damask. She unhooks the needle and begins to work on
it in deep concentration. Alysea returns with a suitcase. Josefa does not look up although she is aware of
Alysea. Alysea comes close to Josefa rather hesitantly.
Josefa looks up and smiles.*

JOSEFA (*in a casual tone*): Look . . . do you think I ought
to give the design a name? I saw it in a dream the other
night . . . so vivid! perhaps I should call it "Swallow
Song." What do you think?

ALYSEA (*looking intently at the design over Josefa's shoulder*): It looks like flowing grain . . . with . . . with a
streak of lightning . . . so well intermingled . . . how
strange! . . . beauty and terror as one . . . see? (*She
traces the pattern with her finger.*)

JOSEFA: How foolish of you . . . that is not lightning . .
it is . . . it is sweet rain.

Alysea looks intently at the pattern, then at Josefa.

ALYSEA (*softly*): Lovely Josefa . . . no, no . . . you
could never see the lightning . . . only your gentle lights

(*She picks up her suitcase and starts to leave.*) Good-
bye, sweet lady of light!

*Josefa looks up but does not answer. Alysea moves
toward the outside door.*

JOSEFA (*as if in afterthought*): Alysea?
ALYSEA: Yes?
JOSEFA: On the way . . . please stop by the rectory . . .
will you? Tell Father Prado I cannot make Rosary
tonight. Tell him . . . if he would be so kind . . . to come
later this evening. . . .
ALYSEA: Of course. (*She hesitates for a moment, as if at a
loss for words. Then with one last look of love for
Josefa and the room, she departs. After Alysea leaves,
Josefa continues putting the final stitches on the
damask.*)
JOSEFA: There! Finished . . . another birth of light!

*She stands and stretches as if very tired. She rubs the
back of her neck and breathes deep. She goes to the
window again. It is now dark.*

JOSEFA: My lover! You look morning crystal in the water
. . . so still . . . so deep . . . I ache for you so! you
beckon me shamelessly . . .

*She stands at the window as the curtain drops for Act
II.*

ACT III

*Late the same evening. The church bells are announcing
the end of Rosary. Josefa is sitting in her rocking chair
saying her prayer beads. Every so often she pauses in
thought. There is a knock at the door. Josefa rises and
goes to the door. Father Prado enters.*

FATHER PRADO (*kissing her on the cheek*): My dear . . .
how are you this evening? We missed you at Rosary

. . . you always lead prayer with the confidence of an angel . . . a hundred things to do before tomorrow . . . eh?

JOSEFA: It's good to see you! (*She leads him by the arm to a settee.*)

FATHER PRADO: Tell me . . . can I help with anything?

JOSEFA: You are here . . . that is more than enough.

FATHER PRADO: You must give me a chance . . . you do so much for the church, for me . . . now let me do something for you.

JOSEFA: Father . . . you are my kindred spirit . . . the oasis in the middle of the desert.

FATHER PRADO: You spoil me. . . .

JOSEFA: I finished the boys' surplices for tomorrow. . . .

FATHER PRADO: See what I mean? Your lovely little hands (*Kisses them*) produce such lovely wondrous things for us . . . (*Looks around*) And this place! A sanctuary . . . who would think? To find such a place as this in our desert barrio? Ah . . . all things and all people here are too mindful of the desert . . . except you.

JOSEFA: My magicians, Father!

FATHER PRADO (*in jest*): Of course, your magicians!

JOSEFA: I wonder if you take me seriously? Come . . . would you like some coffee? Tea?

FATHER PRADO: No . . . no, it is late; I ate too much at supper . . . I tell myself every night it seems . . . but I go on eating just the same.

JOSEFA: The way you work for the barrio people! Every church festival is such a chore for you . . . you work yourself to death. . . .

FATHER PRADO: So do you!

JOSEFA: We can't help it . . . can we, Father? You love the people as much as I do.

FATHER PRADO: It means so much to them . . . these festivals . . . they are just ritual to you . . . aren't they?

JOSEFA: Maybe . . . but what blossoms from the barrio people because of the festival . . . that is not ritual . . . there is a rebirth . . . they come to life for a little while

FATHER PRADO: Tomorrow will be very special for them . . . a day to honor their Josefa. Such a legend you are

JOSEFA: If it makes them happy.

Father Prado looks at her intently.

FATHER PRADO: Are you feeling all right? You look a little pale . . . of course! How stupid of me . . . so many things have been happening today . . . even in the rectory life seeps in . . . .

JOSEFA: You know about Clara?

FATHER PRADO: Unfortunate . . . *pobrecita* . . . such a beautiful child.

JOSEFA: She won't be coming back this time.

Josefa begins to cry softly. She brushes a tear from her cheek.

FATHER PRADO: There . . . there, don't cry! (*Comforts her*) I know how you feel . . . you two were so close . . . she depended on you so!

JOSEFA: When life is a farce . . .

FATHER PRADO: In her own way . . . there was so much meaning . . . Alysea has found something special too . . . she and Eduardo stopped by the rectory.

JOSEFA: One by one . . . like leaves from a tree . . .

FATHER PRADO: I know! Then . . . the terrible thing . . . I heard in the village . . . the terrible thing that happened to David . . . I hope they catch——

Josefa interrupts violently.

JOSEFA: Father!

FATHER PRADO: What is it, child?

JOSEFA: May I have confession now?

FATHER PRADO (*puzzled*): Here?

JOSEFA: Please, Father!

FATHER PRADO: Of course, if that's what you want. . . .

He comes near her; as he does, she falls to her knees and leans her head against his body.

FATHER PRADO: What is wrong?

JOSEFA: Forgive me, Father, for I have sinned . . . . (*Father remains silent.*) I have sinned . . . I have sinned. . . .

FATHER PRADO: God forgives. . . .

JOSEFA: Oh, Father . . . I'm lost! I'm lost. . . .

FATHER PRADO: All of us . . . at one time . . .

JOSEFA: I am guilty of grievous sins . . . they are beyond forgiveness . . . people will judge them so! Father . . before I tell you . . . you must know . . . I do not feel sorry . . . I want . . . I need . . . the calm . . . to keep things as they are.

Father simply nods his head.

JOSEFA: David was hurt last night . . . I lied about the intruder. There was no intruder . . . I was the one.

FATHER PRADO (*incredulously*): You . . . did that to David?

JOSEFA: Yes . . . (*She braces herself as if to accept the fact.*) I did that to David.

FATHER PRADO: I can't believe it . . . you! Not you!

JOSEFA: Me, Father, me!

FATHER PRADO: It was inhuman. . . .

JOSEFA: Oh, Father! I . . . I don't know . . . why? why?

FATHER PRADO: Tell me, my child, there must have been a reason . . .

JOSEFA: Last night . . . last night . . . after supper . . David helped Alysea and me put the last touches on the birdhouse. David was so excited . . . (*Pause*) The moon . . . the reflection of diamonds in the lake . . life . . . all were too much for me . . . I was overflowing . . . I felt the sweetness of the night with every fiber . . every fiber . . . (*Lost in memory; then she resumes her story.*) David didn't want to go to bed . . . he insisted on staying up all night to wait for the swallows . . . Of course I said "No!" He left for bed reluctantly . . (*Pause*) Father?

FATHER PRADO: Yes?

JOSEFA: Have you ever felt as if you were one total yearning . . . it roars and spills. . . .

Father Prado remains silent.

JOSEFA: Alysea and I are lovers.

FATHER PRADO: What?

OSEFA: A year ago tonight we became lovers . . . if you remember she had been with me for some months before San Lorenzo's day . . . she was something new in my life . . . she felt and responded to my every mood . . . my every act . . . Oh! To have someone in your life! I had repulsed all the men in the barrio . . . the coarseness! The taking! No . . . no . . . I could never surrender to that . . . but when she came, she filled my life in so many ways . . . so many ways . . . it was natural that the yearning grow for more . . . the body too is master. . . .

ATHER PRADO: Yes, my child, of course it is!

OSEFA: A year ago I took Alysea to the lake on the eve of San Lorenzo . . . She had heard about the Bathing of the Virgins at noon the next day . . . Could she go . . . she asked! I was angry . . . I knew all the hope . . . all the dreams of those girls would turn to jagged violence . . . it was a lie . . . The whole ritual is a lie!

ATHER PRADO: No . . . no, Josefa . . . to those girls the dream of a perfect love is true as long as it gives meaning to their lives. . . .

OSEFA: I know what men are!

Father Prado remains silent.

OSEFA: I told her . . . go with me when the moon comes out . . . when the lake waits for just me . . . it is my lover! (*Pause*) She believed me . . . It is true, Father . . . the lake is my lover. . . .

ATHER PRADO: Oh, my child!

OSEFA: We bathed . . . and then . . . it happened . . . (*Pause*) Last night, after David went to bed . . . I felt the nymph magic . . . I took Alysea . . . Suddenly . . . there was David . . . in the middle of the room. The horror in his eyes . . . Why? why? There was horror in his eyes. . . .

ATHER PRADO: He did not understand. . . .

OSEFA: Oh, Father! Now . . . I can see why . . . now! But . . . last night . . . it was not the Josefa he loved that David saw . . . I could not stand what he saw! I could not!

FATHER PRADO: God forgive you!

JOSEFA: Something happened in me . . . I don't know wha
it was . . . I ran . . . I ran into the kitchen and foun
a kitchen knife . . . Somehow . . . somehow I knev
David would tell . . . the barrio people would look a
me that way too. . . .

FATHER PRADO: I never thought you would care abou
what people . . .

JOSEFA: Oh, Father . . . until last night I never knew m
fears . . . I went back to where Alysea was holding th
frightened child . . . then . . . then I made Alysea hol
him tight . . . Father, it was not her fault! there hav
been so many furies in her life . . . she drowned in m
agony . . . she trusted me . . . what else could she do
(*She goes to the window, looks out at the lake for*
moment.) Father . . . look . . . come look at the lak
. . . maybe you can understand the power it has ove
me . . . Look . . .

Father Prado goes somewhat reluctantly to the window
He also looks out, but remains silent.

JOSEFA: I took the knife and cut David's tongue. . . .

FATHER PRADO: *Jesucristo, perdona a tu hija.* . . .

JOSEFA: I was silencing the world from reprimand . . .
knew I had to silence the world from reprimand . . .
felt no guilt . . . all I knew . . . the life I had . . . th
faith of the barrio people . . . this house of light . .
must be preserved . . . I silenced all reprimand wit
my terrible deed . . . (*She covers her face for a m*
ment. Then she gathers strength and continues talking.
With the light of day . . . I knew better . . . others ha
not my eyes . . . others had not my eyes . . . others ha
not my reasons . . . or my magicians . . . (*She looks*
Father Prado intently.) Can you ever understand?

FATHER PRADO (*as if talking to himself*): I don't unde
stand . . . I don't understand why I didn't see . . . dete
what was happening to you . . . .

JOSEFA (*puzzled*): Happening to me?

FATHER PRADO: All your beauty . . . your calm . . . you
giving was . . . your talent . . . what a splendid cano

for the twisted fears of so many years . . . so many years . . . I'm an old fool . . . forgive me, my daughter, I have never really seen you . . . I pride myself in knowing you so well . . . I claimed I loved you . . . how blind . . . how blind . . .

JOSEFA: Don't blame yourself, Father . . . I am what you see . . . that is really what I am . . . Not what you discovered this moment. . . .

FATHER PRADO: My poor, poor child. . . .

JOSEFA: No . . . Father . . . don't pity me . . . anything but that! That is one thing I shall never suffer. . . .

FATHER PRADO: I have never seen you cry . . . Josefa . . . until tonight . . .

JOSEFA: The past . . . the dark gnawing . . . such hungers! I must not be a desert . . . now they are harmless ghosts. . . .

FATHER PRADO: Are they?

JOSEFA: You don't understand . . . do you?

FATHER PRADO: I want to. . . .

JOSEFA: The magicians created "me!" . . . the blight of meniality never touched me . . . The magicians gave me the purity of light . . . and the wisp of beauties at my fingertips . . . so . . . I really am . . . what you always thought I was. . . .

FATHER PRADO: There is so much God in you! . . .

JOSEFA: God in me? . . . no, Father . . . no . . . I failed goodness . . . I wanted, I prayed . . . to save my soul as the church instructed . . . as your faith believed. . . .

FATHER PRADO (*somewhat taken aback*): But . . . you are the most pious . . . the most constant . . . in the barrio . . . Faith shines in you . . . all the beauty you create. . . .

JOSEFA: Faith? Oh, no, Father . . . no . . . It was not faith, it was the light of my magicians . . . I bear the children of light! I am its high priestess. . . .

FATHER PRADO: I . . . I . . .

He can't go on; he sits down and places his head in his hands. Josefa looks at him and is full of concern. goes to comfort him.

JOSEFA (*she says this as if she does not believe it herself*):
Don't grieve for me, Father . . . for what I have done,
I am willing to atone . . . David will be my whole life
. . . I will create beauty for him . . . for you . . . for the
barrio people . . . longings will fade away with com-
mitment . . . . Father . . . Father (*She kneels in front of
him.*) Forgive me, Father, for I have sinned . . . I have
grievously sinned.

*With tears in his eyes, Father Prado strokes her hair in
silence.*

Final Scene

*Dawn the next morning; the sitting room is a pastel
paradise; there is life in the birdhouse, a roar of bird
sounds; Josefa comes from the bedroom with a white gown
over her arm. It is the gown to be worn at the procession.
She goes to the window and looks at the tree with great
happiness.*

JOSEFA: I waited for you . . . before dawn I heard the
flurry of the sea . . . oh, what a sight you were over my
burning lake . . . straight . . . straight . . . you came to
me . . . to this temple of peace . . . no more songs of
pain for you. . . .

*Church bells sound morning vigil. The procession will
follow in the freshness of the early morning. Josefa remembers the barrio world.*

JOSEFA: My day . . . my day . . . but, oh my people! . . .
it was not meant to be shared with you . . . my day was
planned by my magicians . . . long before you planned
this one for me . . . I must get ready. . . .

*She goes behind the screen, puts on her gown, comes
ack and looks in the mirror. Her dress is white. She
oks unusually young and beautiful. All of a sudden*

she touches her rather severe hairdo. Then she lets down her hair.

JOSEFA (*looking at herself intently in the mirror*): Yes . . . yes . . . this way . . . there is a wildness in me . . . (*She laughs in joyous delirium.*)

Then she becomes the usual Josefa for a moment. She remembers the boys' surplices. She goes to the wardrobe and takes them out. She lays them carefully over a chair.

JOSEFA: There . . . something of me will be at the procession . . . yes, even that . . . the boys will find them here. . . .

She takes a final look in the mirror, then she goes to the window and looks out to the lake.

JOSEFA: So still your water . . . but I know your passions underneath . . . deep . . . deep . . . for all time . . . Hush! I'm coming. . . .

As she turns to leave, she touches the lace, the damask now finished, the fresh flowers on the table . . . with love . . . with a tender regret . . . but a secret within her . . .

JOSEFA: My magicians will let me come back as light . . . yes, yes!

She goes to the door and gives the room one final glance.

JOSEFA (*in a whisper*): Wait for me. . . .

Church bells begin to toll for the gathering of the procession. Voices are heard outside the window.

VOICES: "Here! the starting will be here . . . in front of Josefa's garden." "Has anyone seen Josefa this morning?"

The sitting room seems alive even without people; the two boys enter. They have come for the surplices.

1st Boy: Hey . . . look . . . they're over there. (*Each of
the boys takes one.*)

2nd Boy: Aren't they something . . . grand . . . like at the
cathedral . . .

1st Boy: That's what he said. . . .

2nd Boy: Who said?

1st Boy: Father Prado . . . he said Josefa was like a
cathedral . . .

2nd Boy: 'Cause she makes all this grand stuff?

1st Boy: I guess so . . . 'cause she's different . . . don'
you think?

2nd Boy: Ah . . . ha! She made all the altar linen. . . .

1st Boy: Yeah . . . Father Prado said she was like the
silence of the cathedral . . . and you know those glass
stained windows?

2nd Boy: Yeah. . . .

1st Boy: That's her soul. . . .

2nd Boy: You think something is wrong with Father
Prado?

*They laugh in jest; shove each other around in horse
play, then stop when the church bells ring again.*

1st Boy: Hey, come on . . . the procession is going t
start. . . .

*The room is empty again; this time the voices of the
choir beginning the procession hymns are heard . .
They are as ethereal as the room. Combined, the room
and the voices have a cathedral-like awesomeness
Clemencia breaks the atmosphere. She is in her Sunda
best.*

Clemencia: Josefa! . . . Where are you? (*She looks
the bedroom; then she peeks through the kitchen door
Mnnnn . . . where could she be? Everybody's waitin
Josefa! Oh, dear, oh, dear! They've started without h
. . . . (*She goes to the window.*) Look at those bird
Every year! . . . they come straight to this tree. Ah .
God's morning . . . the lake . . . the green pines . .
(*Suddenly something out in the lake catches her eye
What is that . . . floating in the lake? Mmmmmmm .

looks like a girl dressed in white . . . That's foolish! It is too early for the Bathing of the Virgins, yet . . . yes . . . wearing clothes?

As she hears the choir, she loses interest and goes to the mirror and straightens her hat.

CLEMENCIA (*with a sigh*): Why do we all end up looking like scarecrows? (*She turns to leave and catches sight of the open window.*) I better close the window . . . the room will be covered with birds!

She goes to the window again; as she starts to close it, she gazes out into the lake again fascinated by what she saw before.

CLEMENCIA: Yes . . . it is a body! A body floating in the lake . . . I'm sure of it!

She gasps, but at this moment the church bells ring again. Out of habit, she starts to hurry off, shrugging off what she has seen.

CLEMENCIA: The sun is too bright . . . it is my imagination! I better hurry . . . what a day this will be. . . .

She leaves the room. The voices of the choir, the church bell, the birds on the tree in full life, and the almost unearthly light streaming through the windows gives the essence of a presence in the room . . . of something beautiful.

7 • FICTION

Like poetry, fiction has been an important medium c
expression for the Mexican-American. Here too the tradi
tion of fiction for Mexican-Americans stems from th
Spanish and Mexican traditions of that genre, fiction whic
includes such masterpieces as *Lazarillo de Tormes* an
Don Quixote from the Spanish tradition; *Los de Abaj*
and *El Aguila y el Serpiente* from the Mexican traditior
both a distinctly Hispanic fiction.

Much of the early kind of fiction by Mexican-Americar
was cast in the form of the traditional *cuentos,* storie
which drew heavily from the elements of a folk existenc
Considering the remoteness of the northern Spanish, the
Mexican, borderlands from the center of the intellectu:
world in Mexico City, there were few creative writers i
the early periods save for those who chronicled accoun
of their journeys or adventures into the immense an
still largely unexplored regions *al norte.* An occasion
poet or balladeer made his way north from Mexico
Texas or Nuevo Mexico or Alta Pimeria (Arizona) (
Alta California, but for the most part those who ventur
north were encouraged in their pursuits less by the litera:
impulse than the drive for material gain and personal reco
nition for their exploits and prowess. Only in the period
settlement and colonization do we see any literary activi
flourishing in the northern borderlands. By 1848 the
were a fair number of creative writers per capita.
significant number of newspapers and journals publish
a variety of creative works, including poetry, fiction, ar
actos.

This was thus the literary setting for Mexicans of t

northern borderlands in their transition to becoming American. It was therefore perfectly natural that the Hispanic literary tradition would carry over for as many generations as necessary to produce Mexican-American writers literate in English. In most cases, within a generation such writers appear, writers like Napoleón Vallejo, Andrew García, Miguel Antonio Otero, and others. By the turn of the century, more and more Mexican-American writers were producing works in English.

The shift of emphasis in Mexican-American fiction from the *cuento,* rooted in the folklore tradition of the people, to what may properly be called the modern tradition—and in English—did not take place until after the First World War. Although against the backdrop of the sociological, economic, and political problems Mexican-Americans were experiencing, there was little fiction being produced. Some of the early Mexican-American writers of fiction of the modern period are Arthur L. Campa, Juan A. A. Sedillo, Jovita González, and Fray Angélico Chávez. While their works still demonstrate a concern for themes that are part of the past, they nevertheless reveal the artistry of the modern Mexican-American writer of fiction who draws his themes from his Hispanic heritage while employing the language of the political context he is a part of.

There was no question that after World War II change was in the air, for Mexican-Americans had gone looking for America and had not found it. The most significant change in Mexican-American fiction occurred after 1960, with the realization by Mexican-American writers that the pastoral themes of Mexican-Americans were only adding to the debilitating portrait of Mexican-Americans already to be found in American literature in the works of such writers as Bret Harte, Jack London, John Steinbeck, and others. Daniel Garza's story is an early effort of the contemporary Mexican-American-Chicano writer to draw his themes from the realities of his present existence. The year 1963 saw the publication of John Rechy's illuminating work, *City of Night,* fiction by a Mexican-American which did not deal with a Mexican-American theme. The

Mexican-American writer was breaking out of his traditional bonds.

The Chicano novel is a post-World War II phenomenon José Antonio Villarreal's novel, *Pocho,* was published in 1959. At that time it received scant attention and quickly went out of print. Although it appeared a decade too early it stands in the vanguard of the Chicano novel for depicting the Chicano experience in the United States. Villarreal's style was influenced by the American "pop" novel of the 1950s, and his portrayal of the linguistic characteristics of Chicanos was influenced perhaps by the works of Ernest Hemingway and John Steinbeck. The novel's strength however, is in the author's skillful presentation of the Mexican background of the Chicano migration to the United States.

Two recent novels by Chicanos represent the nexus between the Chicano and Anglo worlds at this time and indicate the direction the Chicano novel will probably take. Richard Vásquez' novel, *Chicano,* is a novel similar to *Pocho* and deals essentially with the same background theme of exodus, exile, and existence. The *Plum Plum Pickers* by Raymond Barrio (from which *Lupe's Dream* is extracted) focuses on the proletarian view of life. Lupe is drawn as a significant figure in the novel, not as a female trifle caught at the edges of that fictive *machismo* dominant in other works about the Mexican-American experience.

The list of Mexican-American writers of fiction is now growing, and more and more young Chicanos are turning their hands to that genre. The additional selections of fiction in this section are all by young Mexican-American writers, and indicate the variety of themes and points of view relevant to Mexican-American fiction.

Arthur L. Campa

Arthur L. Campa is chairman of the Department of Modern Languages at the University of Denver. His works have appeared in the leading national and international journals and magazines.

THE CELL OF HEAVENLY JUSTICE

I

"*¡Alto!*" shouted the Mexican captain. The firing squad halted solemnly before the prison door and waited for the next command. In the dim light of dawn the outline of a sturdy adobe prison was almost indistinguishable. This *calabozo* had been designed in Spanish days after the colonial fashion of the times, with four-foot walls, no windows, and only one opening in front. That opening, now firmly closed, was a massive, rough pine door reinforced with heavy iron clasps and locked with a Moorish contrivance edged in jagged design. Over the door, carved on a weatherbeaten crossbeam, was an inscription that the Mexican inhabitants knew by heart and respected almost religiously: *La Celda del Justo Juez,* "The Cell of Heavenly Justice." The squad standing at attention waited for the man that in a few moments their muskets would send to eternity. These soldiers too knew the significance of the inscription on the crossbeam. Five similar ceremonies had ended at this very prison door; an unseen hand had reached through the locked dungeon and robbed the law from the execution of justice. Five culprits had been found dead in the morning. This mysterious fate that overcame the guilty caused the *comandante* to have the inscription

275

carved on the crossbeam, and for fully two years it had
served as a warning to the villagers that heavenly justice
was meted in the village of Encinal.

"*El reo,*" ordered the captain in a low tone to the jailer.
Raising his lantern to the Moorish lock, the jailer in-
troduced a heavy iron key and set his light on the ground.
Then, taking the key in both hands, he slowly turned it.
Simultaneously a sudden force from within threw open the
door, sending jailer and lantern sprawling on the ground.

"*Ave María Purísima!*" exclaimed the old *carcelero,*
and before anyone knew or could realize what was happening, a crazed maniac with bulging eyes and disheveled
hair had thrown himself against the soldiers, panting and
gesticulating wildly.

The soldiers pinned the condemned man by the arms
lest he should become dangerous, and looked to the
equally surprised captain for orders. The frenzied man was
still wriggling and trying to say something that no one
could understand. Only a fragment of a torn shirt and the
upper portion of his cotton trousers clothed him. It seemed
that his clothing had been torn from his body.

"*Agua!*" he managed to say. One of the soldiers, at
the nod of the captain, opened his canteen and placed it
to the madman's lips. In the safety of armed men and
with a breath of cool, morning air, the man's feeling
subsided enough to talk, though still very incoherently and
with visible traces of mental anguish. His bloodshot eyes
had partly gone back into their sockets, but still maintained the wild look of a man who has just suffered the
tortures of third degree. The soldiers relaxed and waited
eagerly to hear the verdict of this unusual cell, while
from the open door emanated the strong odor of charred
cotton tinged with a peculiar stench of scorched flesh.

II

José Pacheco was an industrious youth in the village
of Encinal in the state of Durango, situated in the
northern part of Mexico. José lived peacefully, anticipating

his marriage to Alicia Mondragón, an equally pleasant and industrious peasant girl in the hacienda of Don Joaquín López Logroño. It was well known to the *rancheros* that José's wedding would take place as soon as the last load of corn had been gathered and placed in the cribs of Don Joaquín. The young eligibles constantly chided and bantered José with allusive and meaningful remarks that, though said in jest, were too piquant for a groom-to-be, so José blushed and tried to change the subject of conversation.

"Have you noticed how slowly the corn ripens this year, José?" someone would remark, and others followed with: "Cold weather should warm things up for you, *mi amigo!*" "Yes, first the corn, then the rice, and then what, José?" With such talk, a bit brusque and yet quite innocent, the ranchers burst into hearty laughter at the expense of a prospective groom.

Today the young fellows were in higher spirits than usual. There was to be a big fiesta and *baile* on Saturday; one of those social affairs that Don Joaquín, in spite of his *mal genio,* sponsored to keep up the prestige of a wealthy *hacendado.*

All the village participated in these fiestas and the charming señoritas were afforded an opportunity to cast devastating smiles at the promising young *muchachos.* A trovador or two would be there to sing and compose *trovas* and *décimas* at the whim of some lovelorn youth or admiring suitor. But best of all, José would dance all night with Alicia. Now that he was engaged to her there would be no objection, and perhaps he would press her hand as they joined hands in a *cuna* or some other folk dance. After the fiesta he would see her home, though in the presence of her aunt, that omnipresent *dueña,* always in the way.

III

Few weeks had ever dragged on so slowly for José. But even so it was already Thursday, two days before the fiesta. Instead of going to the fields he had volunteered to prepare the thrashing floors. Every year the wheat was stacked in four round stacks around which was built a corral where the year's crop of colts trampled the grain out with their sharp, unshod hoofs.

José had been repairing the corral around the stacks, but neither his eyes nor his thoughts were with his work. His mind was dwelling on Saturday night and his eyes were fastened on the door of a small adobe house on the hill above. For the last half hour he had been watching the doorway with an occasional glimpse at the sun to see if he had judged the time correctly. At last a lithe-bodied servant girl skipped from the doorway with a large earthen jar, going in the direction of the spring. It was Alicia on her way to get the day's supply of water. At such times José managed to be within sight, and Alicia very conveniently chose the same hour for drawing water. Once they had met at the spring and had been surprised by other less fortunate girls who had no fixed hour for drawing water.

José, upon seeing his sweetheart, decided that he was very thirsty and would go to the spring for a drink, but just as he dropped his tools he heard the sound of hoofs. It was Don Enrique, the young son of Señor López Logroño, riding by. *"Qué suerte!"* José would be content with the usual wave of the hand and a radiant smile from the distance. Being engaged to Alicia, he had the privilege of calling on her, but he was tired of carrying on a conversation in the presence of a *dueña;* he wanted to talk in the open, and alone by the spring as he had done once before. He went on working mechanically and soon lost himself in imaginative anticipation of the fiesta and of his forthcoming union with Alicia.

A few minutes later José was suddenly taken from his vagaries by what seemed to be the cry of a woman. He listened for the sound again, but apparently he had mistaken the neigh of a horse or the barking of a dog while lost in his musings. Then he remembered that Alicia had not returned from the spring, but his fears abated as quickly as they had arisen when he saw the familiar form carrying the earthen *olla,* like a Greek maiden he had once seen in a picture hanging in the *sala de recibo* of Don Joaquín. His heart went out to his beloved as he waved back and watched her disappear into her home. "Some day," thought José, "she will draw the water from the spring for me."

The sun had run its course that day and with a fiery glow was slowly sinking in the horizon, thus ending the day's work for the farmers of Encinal, who, in the absence of a factory whistle to mark their working time, clocked themselves with nature's timepiece—the sun. Throwing his leather jerkin over his shoulders, José tilted a broad-brimmed Spanish hat over his right temple and started in the direction of the spring. Instead of following the usual path worn deep by years of use, he went directly to a hollow pine and searched it with his hand. Not finding anything, he smiled and went further below to a large rock by an overhanging ledge. Alicia was fond of playing tricks upon her sweetheart; she would hide her messages in different places just to increase José's joy upon finding them. Tonight he searched every possible place until dark and found no message, for Alicia had not left the message she had carried with her.

After a hasty supper, José called at the home of Doña Dolores, Alicia's widowed mother. They sat in the parlor with the rest of the family and talked about the year's crops, the early frost, and other subjects equally uninteresting to both lovers. José tried to catch Alicia's eye, but she purposely avoided his gaze. After a two-hour visit he bade the family good night. Alicia's usual firm grip was gone—it was a limp hand she offered her lover.

All night long José tossed nervously in bed. Had Alicia changed her mind? Had some other man won her affection, or had he done something he should not have? Numerous questions arose rhetorically in his mind, and Alicia's cold handshake and evading look hovered over him until dawn when he was able to doze off for an hour before daybreak. José was glad that the night was over, and with the day's work before him he could occupy his mind and forget the night's affair.

IV

Today as the men attempted to jest, they were met with no response from the usually jovial José. One of his closer friends came near to him as they pitched bundles of wheat upon the ox-cart and ventured: "What's the matter, *compañero?* Something wrong?"

"Oh, no!" answered José, forcing a smile.

It was impossible to see Alicia on her way to the spring this afternoon, for all hands were busy bringing in the wheat. If only he could see her now! José looked at the sun and judged by its height that Alicia would be on her way to the spring just now. Was someone else there to wave at her? *"Maldita suerte!"*

At last the *mayordomo* ended the day's work with a longed for *"Vámonos!"* and the drivers started their teams with a vigorous "Arree buey!" The carts began creaking their homeward journey, bringing to a close another day. José threw a wooden-pronged pitchfork over his shoulder and left the field workers with a gay *"Hasta mañana, muchachos."*

He quickened his step as he approached the hollow pine, and reached it almost at a trot. With hand outstretched he reached into the bosom of the tree and felt the message that he had missed the day before. Not waiting until he should get home to read it, he unfolded it and began to read avidly. Hardly had he read half of it when he turned pale, exclaiming in a loud whisper: *"Dios mío!"* He crumpled the message in his fist and released it as he looked toward the closed door of Alicia's home. When he tried to read again his eyes had filled with tears of anger.

Then clenching a powerful fist, he said between his teeth with all the determination of justly aroused ire: "You damned *gachupín,* I'll make you pay for this!" The woman's cry of the preceding afternoon had been Alicia's futile call for help, and José had failed to heed it.

V

The carefree, happy atmosphere of Encinal had assumed a gloomy air. It was the day before the fiesta, but now the big *baile* was out of the question. All the village had turned out for a different purpose. Court was being held in one of the large halls in the home of Don Joaquín. The judge, a bald-headed, blue-eyed Castilian, peered over his glasses at the crowd that overflowed the room, requesting silence before passing sentence. Then, looking down at José, he repeated the words that the defendant fully anticipated:

"I condemn you to die at sunrise!"

In another room of the enormous home of López Logroño lay the only son and heir of the family, with a knife thrust dealt by the hand of an irate lover who sought to avenge the shame brought upon his sweetheart. In twenty-four hours a rejoicing, carefree girl had been robbed of the only possession she cherished, her honor; a jovial, happy lover had turned assassin, and the name of a noble Spanish family had run out in Durango.

Now José was to spend the night before his execution in that awful Cell of Heavenly Justice. Would the cell live up to its tradition? Would he be found guilty in the eyes of that unknown judge? That was the question in the minds of all his friends, as the crowd dispersed at the end of the trial.

VI

It was dark when the jailer returned. He swung the massive *portón* on its rusty hinges and placed a lighted candle in the center of a rough, colonial pine table; then turning to the prostrate form sitting on the earthen floor, the old man said in a half entreating tone, "There, *amigo*, a candle for your prayers tonight. *Buenas noches.*"

What a sudden turn all of José's plans had taken!

Soon he, too, would be gone from this world; gone from the life of his loved Alicia. He was not remorseful in the least for what he had done. If he had it to do over he would do no different. José's eyes wandered around the empty room. He shuddered at the utter barrenness of the cell. A wooden table and a candle were all the company he had. Soon that candle would melt away like the hopes of a happiness he had once entertained.

In the stillness of the night he heard the baying of Don Joaquín's hounds. He strained his ears eagerly to catch any sounds about him; even that would be company! He heard a footfall; someone was moving outside! His heart began to pound excitedly in his chest. A messenger of death! Again, it might be Alicia coming to say a last good-bye. But no, it was merely a hallucination.

José was getting nervous. As he walked around the cell, his shadow, large and imperfect, followed him along the wall. He thought of saying his prayers and glanced at the candle; it could burn for an hour more yet. Once more he sat down and watched his bare feet. Such disgrace!

For a moment José forgot Alicia and began to speculate on the mysterious death that had taken such a heavy toll. Would he, too, lie outstretched with a cadaverous grimace on his face or would he live to face the firing squad? He could see the barrels ominously pointing at him and waiting for the command of execution. *FUEGO!* José started as the word "fire" went through his mind, and remembered that he had not said his prayers. He would try. He got on his knees determined to prepare for his last. Impossible to start! A bit of dirt sliding along the wall caused him to jump to his feet expecting to find a ghost or an apparition ready to take his life. José had heard so many stories about how condemned men had died in this cell. A second and heavier stream of dirt rolled along the wall and called his attention to a crack in the wall close to the ceiling. From that crack the dirt continued to roll as though pushed by some moving object.

In a moment more, José's skin had tightened about him with a cold chill that covered his body with gooseflesh. An enormous scorpion was trying to come down the crack, but could not gain a foothold. Six inches of its enormous hairy body were fully in view as it clung to the fissure in the wall. Finally it ventured completely out along the uneven mud plaster, and continued to crawl. José looked about the room for a rock or a stick to hurl at this venomous spider, but the cell had been carefully cleared out of every loose particle.

Halfway down the wall the scorpion lost its hold and fell the remaining distance to the earthen floor with a dull thud. Its menacing pincers went up immediately like the horns on a Texas longhorn, as it raised its grayish belly on four pairs of bony legs. José kept his eyes riveted on it and watched every move. Twelve inches of the most vicious spider known lay before him! The scorpion charged. José ran around the table. Again and again the spider raised its lance to deal the fatal blow, but the elusive prey jumped over it. More determined than ever, the scorpion tried to approach José by moving cautiously toward him. More than once José had thought of stepping on the ugly monster, but the thought of touching such a dangerous hardshelled creature with his bare foot was too revolting. The nocturnal spider snapped its pincers in defiance and made for its prey poised on the tips of its stout legs. José backed slowly, watching his chance for a spring. Step by step he kept retreating until inadvertently he ran against the wall and stumbled. The scorpion saw its chance and charged, but José resorted to a *machicueta,* turning over his head with a handspring that cleared him fully six feet across the room. *"Caramba!"* he exclaimed. "That was too close a call!"

José began to realize that he could not overcome his enemy without a weapon. Ah, the table! He would pick it up and drop it on the spider. But like a flash it struck him that the candle was good for only a few minutes more. To move the table was to extinguish the candle, and that was suicide just now. He could already feel the scorpion's pincers closing upon his flesh and the sharp sting of the poisonous lance. To be left in utter darkness with this spider was fatal. Something had to be done immediately. José became desperate. He began to shout. *"Socorro! So-*

corro!" But the village was asleep and too far to hear his cries of agony. In a moment he would go mad. The spider would have him at its mercy. His body would be numb with the deadly poison and he too would be found stretched upon the floor like his predecessors.

José tore at his shirt trying to find something to hurl at the stubborn scorpion and brought a piece of cloth that fell limply at his feet as he threw it at the creature. He looked once more at the candle that, like a clock of old, seemed to measure the span of his existence. Only an inch of it was left. Then a happy idea came to him. He would try it as a last resort. His hand went over his shoulder and tore a large piece of shirt from his back. To the farthest corner of the room José taunted the spider and then, jumping over it, ran to the table. Before the spider could get to him he had placed a piece of his torn shirt over the flame, and in his nervous hurry had almost smothered the flame. He dodged another pass, and, running by the table once more, he picked up the burning rag.

Now José was armed with a weapon. Scorpions succumb easily to heat, even to the heat of the sun, and José knew it. Like a *matador* holding out his *muleta* to a furious bull, the young peasant waited for his adversary to charge. The scorpion was met every time with the suffocating breath of burning cotton. It charged no more. Now José was on the offensive. He taunted and followed the spider's retreat, singeing it with the burning cloth. More cloth was needed now that his shirt was gone, so he tore part of his trousers. At last the spider moved no longer and José threw the remaining cloth over it, watching its wriggling as it cooked in the slow fire of his own clothes.

The suffocating smoke dried José's throat. The combat had completely covered him with perspiration and the sting of charred cotton was burning his eyes. A flickering flame hardly discernible through the thick smoke sputtered and went out, leaving the cell in total darkness with the stench of a cooked scorpion.

A feeble glow in the middle of the room showed the funeral pyre of what once had been a menacing spider. The last bit of cloth had been consumed, leaving the strong fumes without an outlet in that almost airtight dungeon. José, hardly aware that the battle was over, kept his eyes riveted where he had seen the last of his adversary, expecting it to rise once more in the darkness and renew the attack. What if the scorpion had been only temporarily overcome with the heat and smoke! Instinctively, he felt in his shirt pocket for a match but his hand touched naked flesh—his shirt lay scattered in ashes around the room. His only hope for light was the crevice under the door, but it was hardly daylight.

Like a man whose avenues of escape have been completely cut off, José began to feel the oppression of being hemmed in. He was loath to feel along the wall for a loosely set adobe lest he should place his hand upon a squirming spider. Scorpions had become an obsession to him. In the dark he would become an easy prey to a scorpion's lance. He imagined he saw hosts of them coming down the walls to attack him. For, thought he, where there is one, surely there must be another, and another, and another. Good God! If he could only run out of this fatal dungeon; it reeked with smoke and hungry, bloodthirsty scorpions! The bitter fumes had dried José's throat and now he could hardly swallow. A drink of cool, fresh water from the spring out of the gourd from which he used to drink on a hot summer's day when returning from the fields! Oh, how he craved such a drink! But no, he bit his tongue in desperation and not even the flow of saliva would respond.

The suffocating air added to the discomfort of the poor prisoner. He approached the door with a mind to tear it down, but the massive prison *portón* remained impassive to the lunges that José made against it. The heavy bolts outside would not yield to such light weight. In the moments that preceded the dawn José would lose his mind and die from sheer exhaustion and mental agony. His eyes, red and swollen, were smarting and watery. His hair, disheveled and wet with perspiration, completed the picture of a madman.

At last the first signs of dawn began to show in the east, though unseen to the prisoner in the cell. The crowing of a cock, too, made no impression on him now, for José felt a ringing in his head and drunken dizziness as he still clung to the door, his only hope. Panting for breath he stood, moving his feet mechanically up and down to warn approaching scorpions that he would trample upon them with his bare feet.

A dog barked. Someone was moving about in the village. José listened and his ears caught the sound of marching feet. Thump, thump, thump. The firing squad! Anything for a breath of fresh air. The marching was clearer and nearer. The condemned man heard the command that stopped the march abruptly. Then the sound of a key finding the keyhole gave him a ray of hope, though his throat was parched and his eyes bulging out of their sockets.

José waited crouched at the door. At the first sign o

Another Heaven, another Earth (Arturo Franco, courtesy of *Nosotros* Magazine)

movement he lunged against it, bounding into the open air and into the arms of the firing squad. Like the knights of the preceding century the soldiers received the verdict of trial by combat and all the village abided by the decision of the Cell of Heavenly Justice.

Juan A. A. Sedillo

Juan A. A. Sedillo was a New Mexico writer whose stories have appeared in various publications.

GENTLEMAN OF RÍO EN MEDIO

It took months of negotiation to come to an understanding with the old man. He was in no hurry. What he had the most of was time. He lived up in Río en Medio, where his people had been for hundreds of years. He tilled the same and they had tilled. His house was small and wretched, but quaint. The little creek ran through his land. His orchard was gnarled and beautiful.

The day of the sale he came into the office. His coat was old, green and faded. I thought of Senator Catron, who had been such a power with these people up there in the mountains. Perhaps it was one of his old Prince Alberts. He also wore gloves. They were old and torn and his fingertips showed through them. He carried a cane, but it was only the skeleton of a worn-out umbrella. Behind him walked one of his innumerable kin—a dark young man with eyes like a gazelle.

The old man bowed to all of us in the room. Then he removed his hat and gloves, slowly and carefully. Chaplin

once did that in a picture, in a bank—he was the janitor
Then he handed his things to the boy, who stood obedient
ly behind the old man's chair.

There was a great deal of conversation, about rain and
about his family. He was very proud of his large family
Finally we got down to business. Yes, he would sell, as he
had agreed, for twelve hundred dollars, in cash. We would
buy, and the money was ready. "Don Anselmo," I said to
him in Spanish, "we have made a discovery. You re
member that we sent that surveyor, that engineer, up there
to survey your land so as to make the deed. Well, he finds
that you own more than eight acres. He tells us that your
land extends across the river and that you own almost
twice as much as you thought." He didn't know that. "And

Chicano senior citizen at his trade (Salvador Valdez,
courtesy of *Nosotros* Magazine)

now, Don Anselmo," I added, "these Americans are *buena gente,* they are good people, and they are willing to pay you for the additional land as well, at the same rate per acre, so that instead of twelve hundred dollars you will get almost twice as much, and the money is here for you."

The old man hung his head for a moment in thought. Then he stood up and stared at me. "Friend," he said, "I do not like to have you speak to me in that manner." I kept still and let him have his say. "I know these Americans are good people, and that is why I have agreed to sell to them. But I do not care to be insulted. I have agreed to sell my house and land for twelve hundred dollars and that is the price."

I argued with him but it was useless. Finally he signed the deed and took the money but refused to take more than the amount agreed upon. Then he shook hands all around, put on his ragged gloves, took his stick and walked out with the boy behind him.

A month later my friends had moved into Río en Medio. They had replastered the old adobe house, pruned the trees, patched the fence, and moved in for the summer. One day they came back to the office to complain. The children of the village were overrunning their property. They came every day and played under the trees, built little play fences around them, and took blossoms. When they were spoken to they only laughed and talked back good-naturedly in Spanish.

I sent a messenger up to the mountains for Don Anselmo. It took a week to arrange another meeting. When he arrived he repeated his previous preliminary performance. He wore the same faded cutaway, carried the same stick and was accompanied by the boy again. He shook hands all around, sat down with the boy behind his chair, and talked about the weather. Finally I broached the subject. "Don Anselmo, about the ranch you sold to these people. They are good people and want to be your friends and neighbors always. When you sold to them you signed a document, a deed, and in that deed you agreed to several things. One thing was that they were to have the complete possession of the property. Now, Don Anselmo, it seems that every day the children of the village overrun the orchard and spend most of their time there. We would like to know if you, as the most respected man in the village, could not stop them from doing so in order that these people may enjoy their new home more in peace."

Don Anselmo stood up. "We have all learned to love these Americans," he said, "because they are good people and good neighbors. I sold them my property because I knew they were good people, but I did not sell them the trees in the orchard."

This was bad. "Don Anselmo," I pleaded, "when one signs a deed and sells real property one sells also everything that grows on the land, and those trees, every one of them, are on the land and inside the boundaries of what you sold."

"Yes, I admit that," he said. "You know," he added, "I am the oldest man in the village. Almost everyone there is my relative and all the children of Río en Medio are my *sobrinos* and *nietos,* my descendants. Every time a child has been born in Río en Medio since I took possession of that house from my mother I have planted a tree for that child. The trees in that orchard are not mine, *Señor,* they belong to the children of the village. Every person in Río en Medio born since the railroad came to Santa Fe owns a tree in that orchard. I did not sell the trees because I could not. They are not mine."

There was nothing we could do. Legally we owned the trees but the old man had been so generous, refusing what amounted to a fortune for him. It took most of the following winter to buy the trees, individually, from the descendants of Don Anselmo in the valley of Río en Medio.

Fray Angélico Chávez

Fray Angélico Chávez is a Catholic cleric whose prose, poetry, and fiction have appeared in numerous national and international publications.

HUNCHBACK MADONNA

Old and crumbling, the squat-built adobe mission of El Tordo sits in a hollow high up near the snow-capped Truchas. A few clay houses huddle close to it like tawny chicks about a ruffled old hen. On one of the steep slopes, which has the peaks for a background, sleeps the ancient graveyard with all its inhabitants, or what little is left of them. The town itself is quite as lifeless during the winter months, when the few folks that live there move down to warmer levels by the Rio Grande; but when the snows have gone, except for the white crusts on the peaks, they return to herd their sheep and goats, and with them comes a stream of pious pilgrims and curious sightseers which lasts throughout the spring and summer weather.

They come to see and pray before the stoop-shouldered Virgin, people from as far south as Belén who from some accident or some spinal or heart affliction are shoulder-bent and want to walk straight again. Others, whose faith is not so simple or who have no faith at all, have come from many parts of the country and asked the way to El Tordo, not only to see the curiously painted Madonna in which the natives put so much faith, but to visit a single grave in a corner of the *campo santo* which, they have heard, is covered in spring with a profusion of wild flowers, whereas the other sunken ones are bare altogether, or at the most sprinkled only with sagebrush and tumbleweed.

And, of course, they want to hear from the lips of some old inhabitant the history of the town and the church, the painting and the grave, and particularly of Mana Seda.

No one knows, or cares to know, when the village was born. It is more thrilling to say, with the natives, that the first settlers came up from the Santa Clara valley long before the railroad came to New Mexico, when the Indians of Nambé and Taos still used bows and arrows and obsidian clubs; when it took a week to go to Santa Fe, which looked no different from the other northern towns at the time, only somewhat bigger. After the men had allotted the scant farming land among themselves, and each family raised its adobe hut of one or two rooms to begin with, they set to making adobes for a church that would shoulder above their homes as a guardian parent. On a high, untillable slope they marked out as their God's acre a plot which was to be surrounded by an adobe wall. It was not long before large pines from the forest nearby had been carved into beams and corbels and hoisted into their places on the thick walls. The women themselves mud-plastered the tall walls outside with their bare hands; within they made them a soft white with a lime mixture applied with the woolly side of sheepskins.

The padre, whose name the people do not remember, was so pleased with the building, and with the crudely wrought reredos behind the altar, that he promised to get at his own expense a large hand-painted *Nuestra Señora de Guadalupe* to hang in the middle of the *retablo*. But this had to wait until the next traders' ox-drawn caravan left Santa Fe for Chihuahua in Old Mexico and came back again. It would take years, perhaps, if there was no such painting ready and it must be made to order.

With these first settlers of El Tordo had come an old woman who had no relatives in the place they had left. For no apparent reason she had chosen to cast her lot with the emigrants, and they had willingly brought her along in one of their wooden-wheeled *carretas,* had even built her a room in the protective shadow of the new church. For that had been her work before, sweeping the house of God, ringing the Angelus morning, noon and night, adorning the

Little girls practiced ancient customs (Salvador Valdez, courtesy of *Nosotros* Magazine)

altar with lace cloths and flowers, when there were flowers. She even persuaded the padre, when the first of May came around, to start an ancient custom prevalent in her place of origin: that of having little girls dressed as queens and their maids-in-waiting present bunches of flowers to the Virgin Mary every evening in May. She could not wait for the day when the Guadalupe picture would arrive.

They called her *Mana Seda*, "Sister Silk." Nobody knew why; they had known her by no other name. The women thought she had got it long ago for being always so neat, or maybe because she embroidered so many altar cloths. But the men said it was because she looked so much like a silk-spinning spider; for she was very much humpbacked —so bent forward that she could look up only sideways and with effort. She always wore black, a black shiny dress and black shawl with long leglike fringes and, despite her age and deformity, she walked about quite swiftly and noiselessly. "Yes," they said, "like the black widow spider."

Being the cause of the May devotions at El Tordo, she took it upon herself to provide the happy girls with flowers for the purpose. The geraniums which she grew in her window were used up the first day, as also those that other women had tended in their own homes. So she scoured the slopes around the village for wild daisies and Indian paintbrush, usually returning in the late afternoon with a shawlful to spill at the eager children's feet. Toward the end of May she had to push deeper into the forest, whence she came back with her tireless, short-stepped spider-run, her arms and shawl laden with wild iris and cosmos, verbenas and mariposa lilies from the pine shadows.

This she did year after year, even after the little "queens" of former Mays got married and new tots grew up to wear their veils. Mana Seda's one regret was that the image of the Virgin of Guadalupe had not come, had been lost on the way when the Comanches or Apaches attacked and destroyed the Chihuahua–Santa Fe ox-train.

One year in May (it was two days before the close of the month), when the people were already whispering among themselves that Mana Seda was so old she must die soon, or else last forever, she was seen hurrying into the forest early in the morning, to avail herself of all the daylight possible, for she had to go far into the wooded canyons this time. At the closing services of May there was to be not one queen but a number of them with their attendants. Many more flowers were needed for this, and the year had been a bad one for flowers, since little snow had fallen the winter before.

Mana Seda found few blooms in her old haunts, here and there an aster with half of its petals missing or drought-toasted, or a faded columbine fast wilting in the cool but moistureless shade. But she must find enough flowers; otherwise the good heavenly Mother would have a sad and colorless farewell this May. On and on she shuttled in between the trunks of spruce and fir, which grew thicker and taller and closer-set as the canyon grew narrower. Farther up she heard the sound of trickling water; surely the purple iris and freckled lily flames would be rioting there, fresh and without number. She was not disappointed, and without pausing to recover her breath, began lustily to snap off the long, luscious stems and lay them on her shawl, spread out on the little meadow. Her haste was prompted by the darkness closing in through the evergreens, now turning blacker and blacker, not with approaching dusk, but with the smoky pall of thunderheads that had swallowed up the patches of blue among the tops of the forest giants.

Far away arose rumblings that grew swiftly louder and nearer. The great trees, which always whispered to her even on quiet, sunny days, began to hiss and whine angrily at the unseen wind that swayed them and swung their arms like maidens unwilling to be kissed or danced with. And then a deafening sound exploded nearby with a blinding bluish light. Others followed, now on the right or on the left, now before or behind, as Mana Seda, who had thrown her flower-weighted mantle on her arched back, started to run—in which direction she knew not, for the rain was slashing down in sheets that blurred the dark boles and boulders all around her.

At last she fell, whimpering prayers to the holy Virgin with a water-filled mouth that choked her. Of a sudden, sunlight began to fall instead between the towering trees, now quiet and dripping with emeralds and sapphires. The storm had passed by, the way spring rains in the Truchas Mountains do, as suddenly as it had come. In a clearing not far ahead, Mana Seda saw a little adobe hut. On its one chimney stood a wisp of smoke, like a white feather. Still clutching her heavy, rain-soaked shawl, she ran to it and knocked at the door, which was opened by an astonished young man with a short, sharp knife in his hand.

"I thought the mountain's bowels where the springs come from had burst," she was telling the youth, who meanwhile stirred a pot of brown beans that hung with a pail of coffee over the flames in the corner fireplace. "But our most holy Lady saved me when I prayed to her, *gracias a Dios*. The lightning and the water stopped, and I saw her flying above me. She had a piece of sky for a veil, and her skirt was like the beautiful red roses at her feet. She showed me your house."

Her host tried to hide his amusement by taking up his work again, a head he had been carving on the end of a small log. She saw that he was no different from the grown boys of El Tordo, dark and somewhat lean-bodied in his plain homespun. All about, against the wall and in niches, could be seen several other images, wooden and gaily colored *bultos,* and more *santos* painted on pieces of wood or hide. Mana Seda guessed that this must be the young stranger's trade, and grew more confident because of it. As she spread out her shawl to dry before the open fire, her load of flowers rolled out soggily on the bare earth floor. Catching his questioning stare, she told him what they were for, and about the church and the people of El Tordo.

"But that makes me think of the apparition of Our Lady of Guadalupe," he said. "Remember how the Indian Juan Diego filled his blanket with roses, as Mary most holy told him to do? And how, when he let down his *tilma* before the bishop, out fell the roses, and on it was the miraculous picture of the Mother of God?"

Yes, she knew the story well; and she told him about the painting of the Guadalupe which the priest of El Tordo had ordered brought from Mexico and which was lost on the way. Perhaps, if the padre knew of this young man's ability, he would pay him for making one. Did he ever do work for churches? And what was his name?

"My name is Esquipula," he replied. *"Si,* I have done work for the Church. I made the *retablo* of 'San Francisco' for his church in Ranchos de Taos, and also the 'Cristo' for Santa Cruz. The 'Guadalupe' at San Juan, I painted it. I will gladly paint another for your chapel." He stopped all of a sudden, shut his eyes tight, and then quickly leaned toward the bent old figure who was helping herself to some coffee. "Why do you not let me paint one right now—on your shawl!"

She could not answer at first. Such a thing was unheard of. Besides, she had no other *tápalo* to wear. And what would the people back home say when she returned wearing the Virgin on her back? What would She say?

"You can wear the picture turned inside where nobody can see it. Look! You will always have holy Mary with you, hovering over you, hugging your shoulders and your breast! Come," he continued, seeing her ready to yield, "it is too late for you to go back to El Tordo. I will paint it now, and tomorrow I and Mariquita will take you home."

"And who is Mariquita?" she wanted to know.

"Mariquita is my little donkey," was the reply.

Mana Seda's black shawl was duly hung and spread tight against a bare stretch of wall, and Esquipula lost no time in tracing with white chalk the outlines of the small wood-print which he held in his left hand as a model. The actual laying of the colors, however, went much slower because of the shawl's rough and unsized texture. Darkness came, and Esquipula lit an oil lamp, which he held in one hand as he applied the pigments with the other. He even declined joining his aged guest at her evening meal of beans and stale *tortillas,* because he was not hungry, he explained, and the picture must be done.

Once in a while the painter would turn from his work to look at Mana Seda, who had become quite talkative, something the people back at El Tordo would have marveled at greatly. She was recounting experiences of her girlhood which, she explained, were more vivid than many things that had happened recently.

Only once did he interrupt her, and that without thinking first. He said, almost too bluntly: "How did you become hunchbacked?"

Mana Seda hesitated, but did not seem to take the question amiss. Patting her shoulder as far as she could reach to her bulging back, she answered, "The woman who was nursing me dropped me on the hard dirt floor when I was a baby, and I grew up like a ball. But I do not remember, of course. My being bent out of shape did not hurt me until the time when other little girls of my age were chosen to be flowermaids in May. When I was older, and other big girls rejoiced at being chosen May queens, I was filled with bitter envy. God forgive me, I even cursed. I at last made up my mind never to go to the May devotions, nor to mass either. In the place of my birth, the shores of the Rio Grande are made up of wet sand which sucks in every living creature that goes in; I would go there and return no more. But something inside told me the Lord would be most pleased if I helped the other lucky girls with their flowers. That would make me a flower-bearer every day. Esquipula, my son, I have been doing this for seventy-four Mays."

Mana Seda stopped and reflected in deep silence. The youth who had been painting absent-mindedly and looking at her, now noticed for the first time that he had made the Virgin's shoulders rather stooped, like Mana Seda's though not quite so much. His first impulse was to run the yellow sun-rays into them and cover up the mistake, but for no reason he decided to let things stand as they were. By and by he put the last touches to his *oeuvre de caprice,* offered the old lady his narrow cot in a corner, and went out to pass the night in Mariquita's humble shed.

The following morning saw a young man leading a gray burro through the forest, and on the patient animal's back swayed a round black shape, grasping her mantle with one hand while the other held tight to the small wooden saddle. Behind her, their bright heads bobbing from its wide mouth, rode a sack full of iris and tiger lilies from the meadow where the storm had caught Mana Seda the day before. Every once in a while, Esquipula had to stop the beast and go after some new flower which the rider had spied from her perch; sometimes she made him climb up a steep rock for a crannied blossom he would have passed unnoticed.

The sun was going down when they at last trudged into El Tordo and halted before the church, where the priest stood surrounded by a bevy of inquiring, disappointed girls. He rushed forth immediately to help Mana Seda off the donkey, while the children pounced upon the flowers with shouts of glee. Asking questions and not waiting for answers, he led the stranger and his still stranger charge into his house, meanwhile giving orders that the burro be taken to his barn and fed.

Mana Seda dared not sit with the padre at table and hied herself to the kitchen for her supper. Young Esquipula, however, felt very much at ease, answering all his host's questions intelligently, at which the pastor was agreeably surprised, but not quite so astonished as when he heard for the first time of Mana Seda's childhood disappointments.

"Young man," he said, hurriedly finishing his meal, "there is little time to lose. Tonight is closing of May— and it will be done, although we are unworthy." Dragging his chair closer to the youth, he plotted out his plan in excited whispers which fired Esquipula with an equal enthusiasm.

The last bell was calling the folk of El Tordo in the cool of the evening. Six queens with their many white-veiled maids stood in a nervous, noisy line at the church door, a garden of flowers in their arms. The priest and the stranger stood on guard facing them, begging them to be quiet, looking anxiously at the people who streamed past them into the edifice. Mana Seda finally appeared and tried to slide quietly by, but the padre barred her way and pressed a big basket filled with flowers and lighted candles into her brown, dry hands. At the same time Esquipula took off her black shawl and dropped over her gray head and hunched form a precious veil of Spanish lace.

In her amazement she could not protest, could not even move a step, until the padre urged her on, whispering into her ear that it was the holy Virgin's express wish. And so Mana Seda led all the queens that evening, slowly and smoothly, not like a black widow now, folks observed, but like one of those little white moths moving over alfalfa fields in the moonlight. It was the happiest moment of her long life. She felt that she must die from pure joy, and many others observing her thought so too.

She did not die then; for some years afterward, she wore the new black *tápalo* the padre gave her in exchange for the old one, which Esquipula installed in the *retablo* above the altar. But toward the last she could not gather any more flowers on the slopes, much less in the forest. They buried her in a corner of the *campo santo,* and the following May disks of daisies and bunches of verbenas came up on her grave. It is said they have been doing it ever since, for curious travelers to ask about, while pious pilgrims come to pray before the hunchback Madonna.

Daniel Garza

Daniel Garza lives in Seguin, Texas, where he continues to write stories about the Mexican-American migrant workers. His stories have appeared in leading magazines, including *Harper's*.

EVERYBODY KNOWS TOBIE

When I was thirteen years old my older brother, Tobie, had the town newspaper route. Everyone in the town knew him well because he had been delivering their papers for a year and a half. Tobie used to tell me that he had the best route of all because his customers would pay promptly each month, and sometimes, he used to brag that the nice people of the town would tip him a quarter or maybe fifty cents at the end of the month because he would trudge up many stairs to deliver the paper personally.

The other newspaper boys were not as lucky as Tobie because sometimes their customers would not be at home when they went by to collect payment for that month's newspapers, or maybe at the end of the month the customers would just try to avoid the paper boys to keep from paying.

Yes, Tobie had it good. The biggest advantage, I thought, that Tobie had over all the newspaper boys was that he knew the Gringos of the town so well that he could go into a Gringo barbershop and get a haircut without having the barber tell him to go to the Mexican barber in our town or maybe just embarrassing him in front of all the Gringo customers in the shop as they often did when Chicano cotton pickers came into their places during the fall months.

The Gringo barbers of my town were careful whom they

allowed in their shops during the cotton harvest season in the fall. September and October and cotton brought Chicanos from the south to the north of Texas where I lived, and where the cotton was sometimes plentiful and sometimes scarce. Chicanos is what we say in our language, and it is slang among our people. It means the Mexicans of Texas. These Chicano cotton pickers came from the Rio Grande Valley in South Texas, and sometimes, even people from Mexico made the trip to the north of Texas. All these Chicanos came to my little town in which many Gringos lived, and a few of us who spoke both English and Spanish.

When the Chicanos came to my town on Saturdays after working frightfully in the cotton fields all week, they would go to the town market for food, and the fathers would buy candy and ice cream for their flocks of little black-headed ones. The younger ones, the *jovenes,* would go to the local movie house. And then maybe those who had never been to the north of Texas before would go to the Gringos' barbershops for haircuts, not knowing that they would be refused. The Gringo barbers would be very careful not to let them come too close to their shops because the regular Gringo customers would get mad, and sometimes they would curse the Chicanos.

"Hell, it's them damn pepper bellies again. Can't seem to get rid of 'em in the fall," the prejudiced Gringos of my town would say. Some of the nicer people would only become uneasy at seeing so many Chicanos with long, black, greasy hair wanting haircuts.

The barbers of the town liked Tobie, and they invited him to their shops for haircuts. Tobie said that the barbers told him that they would cut his hair because he did not belong to that group of people who came from the south of Texas. Tobie understood. And he did not argue with the barbers because he knew how Chicanos from South Texas were, and how maybe Gringo scissors would get all greasy from cutting their hair.

During that fall Tobie encouraged me to go to the Gringo's place for a haircut. "Joey, when are you going to get rid of that mop of hair?" he asked.

"I guess I'll get rid of it when Mr. López learns how to cut flat-tops."

"Golly, Joey, Mr. López is a good ole guy and all that, but if he doesn't know how to give flat-tops then you should go to some other barber for flat-tops. Really, kid-brother, that hair looks awful."

"Yeah, but I'm afraid."

"Afraid of what?" Tobie asked.

"I'm afraid the barber will mistake me for one of those guys from South Texas and run me out of his shop."

"Oh, piddle," Tobie said. "Mr. Brewer . . . you know, the barber who cuts my hair . . . is a nice man, and he'll cut your hair. Just tell him you're my kid-brother."

I thought about this new adventure for several days, and then on a Saturday, when there was no school, I decided on the haircut at Mr. Brewer's. I hurriedly rode my bike to town and parked it in the alley close to the babershop. As I walked into the shop, I noticed that all of a sudden the Gringos inside stopped their conversation and looked at me. The shop was silent for a moment. I thought then that maybe this was not too good and that I should leave. I remembered what Tobie had told me about being his brother, and about Mr. Brewer being a nice man. I was convinced that I belonged in the Gringo barbershop.

I found an empty chair and sat down to wait my turn for a haircut. One Gringo customer sitting next to me rose and explained to the barber that he had to go to the court-house for something. Another customer left without saying anything. And then one, who was dressed in dirty coveralls and a faded khaki shirt, got up from Mr. Brewer's chair and said to him, "Say, Tom, looks like you got yourself a little tamale to clip."

Mr. Brewer smiled only.

My turn was next, and I was afraid. But I remembered again that this was all right because I was Tobie's brother, and everybody liked Tobie. I went to Mr. Brewer's chair. As I started to sit down, he looked at me and smiled a nice smile.

He said, "I'm sorry, sonny, but I can't cut your hair. You go to Mr. López's. He'll cut your hair."

Mr. Brewer took me to the door and pointed the way to López's barbershop. He pointed with his finger and said, "See, over there behind that service station. That's his place. You go there. He'll clip your hair."

Tears were welling in my eyes. I felt a lump in my throat. I was too choked up to tell him I was Tobie's brother, and that it was all right to cut my hair. I only looked at him as he finished giving directions. He smiled again and patted me on the back. As I left, Mr. Brewer said, "Say hello to Mr. López for me, will you, sonny?"

I did not turn back to look at Mr. Brewer. I kept my head bowed as I walked to Mr. López's because tears filled my eyes, and these tears were tears of hurt to the pride and confidence which I had slowly gained in my Gringo town.

I thought of many things as I walked slowly. Maybe this was a foolish thing which I had done. There were too many Gringos in the town, and too few of us who lived there all the year long. This was a bad thing because the Gringos had the right to say yes or no, and we could only follow what they said. It was useless to go against them. It was foolish. But I was different from the Chicanos who came from the south, not much different. I did live in the town the ten months of the year when the other Chicanos were in the south or in Mexico. Then I remembered what the barber had told my brother about the South Texas people, and why the Gringo customers had left while I was in Mr. Brewer's shop. I began to understand. But it was very hard for me to realize that even though I had lived among Gringos all of my life I still had to go to my own people for such things as haircuts. Why wouldn't Gringos cut my hair? I was clean. My hair was not long and greasy.

I walked into Mr. López's shop. There were many Chicanos sitting in the chairs and even on the floor waiting their turn for a haircut. Mr. López paused from his work as he saw me enter and said, "Sorry, Joey, full up. Come back in a couple of hours."

I shrugged my shoulders and said O.K. As I started to leave I remembered what Mr. Brewer had told me to say to Mr. López. "Mr. López," I said, and all the Chicanos, the ones who were waiting, turned and looked at me with curious eyes. "Mr. Brewer told me to tell you hello."

Mr. López shook his head approvingly, not digesting the content of my statement. The Chicanos looked at me again and began to whisper among themselves. I did not hear, but I understood.

I told Mr. López that I would return later in the day, but I did not because there would be other Chicanos wanting haircuts on Saturday. I could come during the week when he had more time, and when all the Chicanos would be in the fields working.

I went away feeling rejected both by the Gringos and even my people, the entire world I knew.

Back in the alley where my bike was parked I sat on the curb for a long while thinking how maybe I did not fit into this town. Maybe my place was in the south of Texas where there were many of my kind of people, and where there were more Chicano barbershops and less Gringo barbers. Yes, I thought, I needed a land where I could belong to one race. I was so concerned with myself that I did not notice a Chicano, a middle-aged man dressed in a new chambray shirt and faded denim pants, studying me.

He asked, *"Qué pasó, Chamaco?"*

"Nada," I answered.

"Maybe the cotton has not been good for you this year."

"No, *señor*. I live here in the town."

And then the Chicano said, "Chico, I mistook you for one of us."

Suddenly the Chicano became less interested in me and walked away unconcerned.

I could not have told him that I had tried for a haircut at the Gringo's because he would have laughed at me, and called me a *pocho,* a Chicano who prefers Gringo ways. These experienced Chicanos knew the ways of the Gringos in the north of Texas.

After the Chicano had left me, I thought that maybe these things which were happening to me in the town would all pass in a short time. The entire cotton crop would soon be harvested, and the farmers around my town would have it baled and sold. Then the Chicanos would leave the north of Texas and journey back to their homes in the valley in the south and to Mexico.

My town would be left alone for ten more months of the year, and in this time everything and everybody would be all right again. The Gringo barbers would maybe think twice before sending me to Mr. López's.

Early in November the last of the cotton around my town had been harvested. The people of South Texas climbed aboard their big trucks with tall sideboards and canvas on the top to shield the sun, and they began their long journey to their homes in the border country.

The streets of the little town were now empty on Saturday. A few farmers came to town on Saturday and brought their families to do their shopping; still the streets were quiet and empty.

In my home there was new excitement for me. Tobie considered leaving his newspaper route for another job, one that would pay more money. And I thought that maybe he would let me take over his route. This was something very good. By taking his route I would know all the Gringos of the town, and maybe . . . maybe then the barbers would invite me to their shops as they had invited Tobie.

At supper that night I asked Tobie if he would take me on his delivery for a few days, and then let me deliver the newspaper on my own.

Tobie said, "No, Joey. You're too young to handle money. Besides, the newspaper bag would be too heavy for you to carry on your shoulder all over town. No, I think I'll turn the route over to Red."

My father was quiet during this time, but soon he spoke, "Tobie, you give the route to Joey. He knows about money. And he needs to put a little muscle on his shoulders."

The issue was settled.

The next day Tobie took me to the newspaper office. Tobie's boss, a nice elderly man wearing glasses, studied me carefully, scratched his white head, and then asked Tobie, "Well, what do you think?"

"Tobie's boss looked at me. . . ." (Héctor Melgoza)

"Oh," Tobie said, "I told him he was too young to handle this job, but he says he can do it."

"Yes, sir," I butted in enthusiastically.

Tobie's boss looked at me and chuckled, "Well, he's got enough spunk."

He thought some more.

Tobie spoke, "I think he'll make you a good delivery boy, sir."

A short silence followed while Tobie's boss put his thoughts down on a scratch pad on his desk.

Finally, the boss said, "We'll give him a try, Tobie." He looked at me. "But, young 'un, you'd better be careful with that money. It's your responsibility."

"Yes, sir," I gulped.

"O.K., that's settled," the boss said.

Tobie smiled and said, "Sir, I'm taking him on my delivery for a few days so he can get the hang of it, and then I'll let him take it over."

The boss agreed. I took his hand and shook it and promised him that I would do my extra best. Then Tobie left, and I followed behind.

In a few days I was delivering the *Daily News* to all the Gringos of the town, and also to Mr. Brewer.

Each afternoon, during my delivery, I was careful not to go into Mr. Brewer's with the newspaper. I would carefully open the door and drop the paper in. I did this because I thought that maybe Mr. Brewer would remember me, and this might cause an embarrassing incident. But I did this a very few times because one afternoon Mr. Brewer was standing at the door. He saw me. I opened the door and quickly handed him the newspaper, but before I could shut the door he said, "Say, sonny, aren't you the one I sent to Mr. López's a while back?"

"Yes, sir," I said.

"Why'd you stay around here? Didn't your people go back home last week? You do belong to 'em, don't you?"

"No, sir," I said. "I live here in the town."

"You mean to say you're not one of those . . . ?"

"No, sir."

"Well, I'll be durned." He paused and thought. "You know, sonny, I have a young Meskin boy who lives here in town come to this here shop for haircuts every other Saturday. His name is . . . durn, can't think of his name to save my soul . . ."

"Tobie?"

"Yeah, yeah, that's his name. Fine boy. You know him?"

"Yes, sir. He's my older brother."

Then Mr. Brewer's eyes got bigger in astonishment, "Well, I'll be doubly durned." He paused and shook his head unbelievingly. "And I told you to go to Mr. López's. Why didn't you speak up and tell me you was Tobie's brother? I woulda put you in that there chair and clipped you a pretty head of hair."

"Oh, I guess I forgot to tell you," I said.

"Well, from now on, sonny, you come to this here shop, and I'll cut your hair."

"But what about your customers? Won't they get mad?"

"Naw. I'll tell 'em you're Tobie's brother, and everything will be all right. Everybody in town knows Tobie, and everybody likes him."

Then a customer walked into the barbershop. He looked at Mr. Brewer, and then at me, and then at my newspaper bag. And then the Gringo customer smiled a nice smile at me.

"Well, excuse me, sonny, got a customer waitin'. Remember now, come Saturday, and I'll clip your hair."

"O.K., Mr. Brewer. Bye."

Mr. Brewer turned and said good-bye.

As I continued my delivery I began to chuckle small bits of contentment to myself because Mr. Brewer had invited me to his shop for haircuts, and because the Gringo customer had smiled at me, and because now all the Gringos of the town would know me and maybe accept me.

Those incidents which had happened to me during the cotton harvest in my town: Mr. Brewer sending me to Mr. López's for the haircut, and the Chicano cotton picker avoiding me after discovering that I was not one of his people, and the Gringo customers leaving Mr. Brewer's barbershop because of me; all seemed so insignificant. And now I felt that delivering the *Daily News* to the businessmen had given me a place among them, and all because of the fact that everybody in my town knew Tobie.

Raymond Barrio

Raymond Barrio is a novelist who makes his home in Ventura, California, where he is presently finishing a novel about Mexico. His novel *The Plum Plum Pickers* has been identified as one of the most significant of the '70s.

LUPE'S DREAM

When Lupe Gutiérrez heard the crashing glass, her first wish was that they were breaking up the Golden Cork bar again. Good God, she prayed—*ay Dios, Dios.*

She stumbled sleepily to the window, shaking the cobwebs from her mind, unable to make anything out at first. A dark shadow sped through the compound yard. She had to hold herself together. Manuel, Manuel, she whispered; he had to get up anyway. She hated to wake him. Who was that running like that for? And where were they running to? Or from?

She saw a dark hulk standing in Mr. Quill's doorway, and then another. She recognized Pepe Delgado talking to Mr. Quill. They were probably discussing plans to tear down the shacks after all. Their homes. That was it. They were already starting. She was ready to start crying. After all this time. Moving, always moving. From Guadalajara to Monterrey to Reynosa, then across the border to Laredo and then that *hijo* of a *maldito malcriado hijo de la gran puta* Texas Ranger in Rio Grande City—and now here, Santa Clara. Moving, moving, always moving. A big jump. She'd heard that that's what gypsies were like, and she didn't like it, not one bit. She? A gypsy?

An invisible motorcycle made a tremendous burst across the compound yard, cutting into her dark thoughts, and disappeared into the orchard behind the big hangman's oak, followed a few minutes later, in the growing daylight, by a perfect stick of six soldiers, no, wait, they were police, wearing crash helmets with night sticks, waving in unison as in a night frieze, as in a stark Greek tragedy.

The baby cried.

Lupe sighed. Crazy world. She shrugged her tired shoulders, and turned the ghastly overhead bulb on. Manuel, *pobre hombre,* poor man, was still profoundly asleep. She would have to wake him. What news she had to tell him. What a jolt that was going to be. A Hell's Angel—and she crossed herself hard, for she was sure that was what it was, or whatever it was, it had to be the devil himself at play— could have roared right through their shack and Manuel would not even have awakened.

> *Ando borracho*
> *ando tomando*
> *el destino cambió mi suerte....*

—for when I'm drunk, moaned the girl on the radio singing softly, I go around drinking, and fate has changed my luck. . . . The coffee pot bubbled merrily, joining contrapunta to the singer's romantic warbling.

> *Yo—yo, que tanto*
> *llore por tus besos....*

I—I, who cried so much for your kisses—

> *Yo—yo, que siempre*
> *te hablé sin mentiras....*

I—I, who always spoke to you without lying, humming

along, Lupe pushed some strands of her hair back, holding
Cati in the crook of her arm, frying chile with eggs, pun-
gent and strong and good and healthy and noisily filling the
air. Turning around, looking back behind her, the one
light globe piercing her eye, she saw her little Manuelito
wake up and climb upon his father's sleepy head. Then
little Mariquita followed suit. Lupe smiled. A silent struggle ensued. Soon Manuel sat up, roughing their two little
heads. *"Que—ah, que pasó, corazón?"* He wanted to know
what the matter was, my heart.

What was the matter?

Nothing.

Lupe, almost in tears, and the day not yet begun, held
her tongue. This rickety stove was what was the matter.
This stupid bare splintered wooden floor was what was the
matter. This one simple room was the matter. This lack of
privacy was also the matter. This having to walk down to
the public bathroom, sharing it with fifteen other families,
was the matter. Those skimpy curtains were the matter
too. And no hot water was the matter. The children—

"Nada." No, nothing, my heart. . . .

He heard some commotion outside. "Probably Ramiro
and his hot motorcycle," he chuckled.

"Ramiro has a motorcycle?"

"Well, he says he was going to get one."

"He says, he says. You and your cousin."

"Aghhh," sighed Manuel, as though explaining everything. "Anyway, does it make much difference? He has no
family at least. Let him have his fun. He should enjoy himself."

And we shouldn't. Lupe thought it but did not say it.
Manuel stood barewaisted and shaved at the tin basin next
to the stove, with the water brought in from the night before and heated on the stove, the noise of his splashing
mingling with the frying chile. The children pulled his
trouser legs, imitating his shaving motions, as Lupe
changed Cati's diaper on the cot. Cati screamed out in
rage, kicking her tiny legs furiously.

They ate their breakfast on the narrow, crowded, un-
painted wooden table in silence. Manuel, silent most of

the time anyway, was by nature of a quiet disposition, which was just fine for Lupe as she liked so to rant on and on. Except now. Now she wanted to be quiet too. So many things were bothering her all at once. The time the Texas Rangers arrested Manuel for walking with the pickets, when she was too speechless to talk, when the Ranger threatened to arrest her and take her children from her, still frightened her, like a living nightmare. Afterwards, Manuel planned their move away from Texas, any-where, when he saw the children hungry. To try to find a little better way, a less bitter way to live and to work and to find a little joy. Lupe didn't want that to ever happen again. She prayed it would never happen again. She would be good, she would be quiet, please, dear *Dios,* she would complain no more; at least she didn't have the police to worry about here in Santa Clara; she felt confident with them, and was confident they were at least impartial, and for that alone she was grateful.

Serafina Delgado could make all the fun of her Pepe she wanted to; half her children were already grown tall. She could laugh and relax. But right now, with Manuel gone off to the apricots or wherever Roberto Morales' gang was taking him, that vicious Roberto, to pick the Della Sierra apricots in Sunnyvale, Lupe just didn't feel like talking to anyone. She felt in fact a little dizzy. A little? A lot. *Ay Dios,* she hoped she wasn't pregnant. That would be all she needed. She had not been drinking, so that wasn't the cause. She leaned over the cracked, chipped, badly mot-tled, mildewed sink and pushed a loose hair back, looking into the raw new herringbone sky, and she found the only thing she really felt like doing was kicking their only broken chair. A thick, shiny, dark brown cockroach the size of a small mouse scudded past her toe with great con-fidence. She almost threw up. She had to get a good grip on herself. What in God's name was one more cockroach? It looked so much like a big ambulating red kidney bean. She couldn't help herself. She couldn't be pregnant. She just couldn't be. No, no, dear God, *Dios mío.* She looked up through the smudge in the window at the gray sky, at all those gaunt, silent plum trees outside, and prayed silently herself. She couldn't help pitying herself. The world seemed like a fury and all the Gringos therein intent on lying and stealing and having their special fun and everything they wanted in huge carload lots, wholesale, special. And here she couldn't even get herself a new dress. Not even a cheap dress. She wouldn't even be able to make one, with baby Cati taking all her time. She was trapped. Would she rob a stage? She didn't know what she'd do. Maybe they wanted her to become a cheap prostitute, like Phyllis Ferguson, who seemed so happy at her profession, making so many men happy, and so much easy money. Well, if she did it, she'd be a good one. She knew how.

But—she couldn't.

She kept on dressing. Would any of her dreams ever come true? No? Would she get a new dress? No? Ever? Never? When hair grew on trees, perhaps. When would that be, Manuel, dear God, *ay Dios mío,* Manuel out there, *Dios, Dios, Dios,* picking all those tender cots, everybody and Roberto's crew, picking like filching idiots in the hot maniacal sun to the limit all summer long, storing away like squirrels for the hungry fall hunger and the starveling winter, those long cold days, and for the nice rich people like the Turners, picking apricots, picking berries, picking pickles, picking luscious pears, picking prickly pears too, picking prunes, picking peaches, picking poison, picking grapes, stooping over to pick ripe tomatoes too, Ponderosa and those meaty tomatoes. Maybe they really did want her to become a prostitute. Maybe that was all there was to it. Mother, prostitute, and wife. *Ay Dios.*

Into all those thrice-blessed crops poured the intense rays of God's own California golden sun, which should have pleased her some, and the fine sugary fragrances, which should have given her some small delight. Instead little creases of strain worried and pinched her, registering their annoyance on her usually calm, plump face.

She sat pensive for a long time, studying her little brown ceramic statuette of la Virgen de Guadalupe, her namesake, and Mexico's greatest mother, a young, loving, smiling, peaceful, warm, life-loving madonna, so sweet and serene, so lost, so unperturbed, half in dim yellow light,

"She sat pensive for a long time. . . ." (José Medina)

half lost to subdued shadows, next to the torn window curtain casting its shadow against the rugged textured grain of the wall planks.

Hanging the diapers cold in the nippy morning air. The sun glinting gold in her face. Screeching bands of urchins from neighboring shacks in the compound. Flipping about like loose little Indian gods inside the Western Grande's enclosure. Yelling, hooting, hog calling. Hey, you pig! Manuelito, already a wise traveler at six, couldn't be enticed outdoors. Baby Cati at last lay asleep. Relieved, Lupe realized she'd awakened too early that morning. Baby Cati, that wiggly fat Mayan statuette, that entrancing beauty in miniature, lay comfortable and warm in her own private world, her orange-crate crib, cuddled in, breathing sweetly, beneath the lace-like shredded curtains, guarded over by her virgin. Manuelito lay back on the lumpy sofa, his little eyes closed, sniveling, shivering, moaning with a slight fever. Could it be the devil's own fever? Devil Mountains, and summertide, *Dios mío,* what might not a summery fever bring. Mariquita, four and a half, sniffled and pulled her mother's thin dress. Lupe dried her hands on her apron and stuffed a radish in the child's mouth to quiet her, hardly listening to the radio's tinny blurb from San Jose:

> ah, summer is heah at last!
> warm lush fragrant beautiful
> summer!
> have you done your
> summer shopping yet?

The summer that was so full of idiotic impulses thrust itself forcefully upon Lupe's gentle fellow farm folk. She could almost taste it. She could forgive almost everything that could be forgiven, even the sin of extravagance. All around Drawbridge, up and down Santa Clara County's unflappable peninsular towns, Sunnyvale and Mountain View, Palo Alto and Los Altos, Santa Clara and San Jose, practically anything that could be disgorged by the summer gods was disgorged. The sun beamed proudly down with its incredibly potent rays, fully meriting worship as man's most powerful god, from across incredible distances already being spanned by intrepid spacemen, stirring the seeds, pulling up the sap, energizing the green chlorophyll of countless billions of leaves. The whole trick, which Lupe hadn't yet been able to figure out, was how first to get ahold of some magic money, and then hire somebody to do all the stupid work. The springtime cornucopia of plenty was bursting and aching once again right on schedule, to turn anything out, anything anyone wanted or could ever want. Delightful riches everywhere in stores were for everybody, for ordinary orchard owners, for simple farm folk, for common growers, for truck drivers, for pleasant professors, for sincere citizens, for efficient processors, for supermarketeers, charge checkers, inspectors, generals, governmental agricultural bureaucrats, cockroaches, rats, not to mention forty million thrifty American housewives. For everybody, fortunately, forever, thanks be to God, except—for the fruit pickers.

Lupe listened.

She listened to the cicadas and to the worshiping branches, praying that her Manuel, lost out there somewhere in those lush, vast, early morning orchards, picking fruit, wouldn't dare get into another fight.

At times she indulged in lush dreams of Guadalajara.

At times her inner tensions were unbearable.

At times she relieved her formless yearnings by visions of enormous mansions and sweeping close-cropped green lawns.

Her strange inner mirages had a nasty tendency of twisting, changing shapes, and finally disappearing.

She couldn't have a clean dream.

Mr. Quill, no mirage, sat there, plump and contented, the general manager of the Western Grande, out in front of his country store, living it up, nibbling on goose liver, munching popped corn, draining beer cans, dispensing ice cream, dreaming he was alive. Not much help there. What was Miami like? Should they have gambled on Florida instead? She'd heard it was even worse. So here they were, stuck in California. Forever. Manuel, having to hitch a ride again with Alberto's crew, causing Silvestre to grumble, to get to the tomato paste patch in time, or to the apricot line, or whatever it was they had to pick that day. Manuel's own used car refused even to cough. And he had no money for repairs. Troubles always came doubles. Manuel had no license either. Another trouble. She could have smashed the window into flying shards in that insolent sun. She could have knocked the wind out of her dreams to let the evening breezes in, the sweet air she remembered painfully from her yesterday's girlhood in Salpinango, near Guadalajara. It had been so sweet; now life was so complicated. She didn't go back because—because they couldn't. How could they? She could easily knock the dirty grease-stained window out with a cup, and build at least half a cathedral of dreams with memories. But they didn't have even half a brick to call their own.

Four of Manuel's *compañeros,* Alberto, Silvestre, Jesus and Santiago—four galloping fruit pickers from Rio Grande City in South Texas—traveled all over the country summers together, picking oranges down south, the lemons, melons, squash, the beans and walnuts for the Gringo *güeros chingados* sponging off humanity in this permanent disease called California, the newest of most modern tortures, offering many fineries before your dangling tongue and never, never letting you sip. Those four traveling *caballeros* shared cottage No. 12, jestingly christened the Bar-Noon Saloon by Mr. Quill. Two of them unmarried, the other two with families back in their Texas home. They traveled all over the western world picking crops together, from Texas to Idaho, Arizona to Fresno, to Oregon and back, high roads and low roads made no difference, 99 or 101, laughing, pushing on. Lupe didn't really mind them, they were so funny, making her laugh, making Manuel laugh, she liked that, Manuel was so serious, and they were countrymen. The one thing they did which as a woman she did not like she could do little about: she didn't like their dragging Manuel to the Golden Cork cantina across the boulevard on El Camino Real for their Saturday night hijinks. To dine on beer

Manuel could drink up a whole day's pay in one night. Though most of their big debts were once again nearly paid up, they were still in debt to Mr. Quill and Mr. Turner for the unpaid part of last winter's food and lodging.

Manuel, he worked very hard and he could find work where others gave up. He certainly did work hard. Certainly he had a right to a little distraction. But didn't she also? Of course she did. Fighting to keep a tear from spurting out, Lupe squashed the sponge in her dripping fist. The dishes took an unmerciful beating that morning.

Plump plum trees filled the fertile land for miles around. Hundreds, thousands of plump prune-making plum trees in neat rows all the same size and all the same height, all pruned exactly the same way. Her own hunger, the babies' food, their very survival depended on the well-being of those thousands of prune trees. Without them, without their fruit, they could . . . do worse. Fruit and vegetable picking and stooping over meant backbreaking, backstraining work, with only very little energy for laughter left over. Sweat and grime and flies and dirt and stink and latrines and pain and endless aches and fear and tired nights were always the most certain pay of all. Mr. Turner owned many of the cherry orchards too. Was here nothing he did not own? The cherries were already ripe. They went fast. The apricots would soon be under way. The prunes would be next, and the walnuts would come in later in the fall, all marching endlessly down the rows, picking, plucking, gathering, filling, boxing, crating. How could there be so much cultivated fruit? How could one single man own so much? The honied huns, at little yellow-glow Ping-Pong apricots had to be gathered before they too fell splat, before they puddled into apricot mud on the ground for ants and earwigs to reincarnate themselves into still more useless ants and earwigs, varmints of the earth, something just a little lower than the fruit pickers themselves.

Lupe dipped her head forward, hunched, leaning on the sink. She studied her scuffed shoes . . . her worn, misshapen, and Scotch-taped shoes. She thought of her only other pair, the high heels that hurt so when she walked in them, as she was not used to them, and she thought of how some ladies owned as many as three and even four pairs of shoes. What would it feel like to own her own home? Or just a little square plot of earth just to plant her tiny avocado tree in? A dream. Yes. A fool. *Tonta. Si.* A crazy dream. *Un sueño loco. Ay Dios, Dios.* Just looking at the hundreds of boxy new houses hedging in all the flat land of the valley all the way up to San Francisco, fifty teeming miles of rich, happy growth, knocking down the orchards, made her sick.

This was paradise, they all said.

GLOSSARY

SUGGESTED FURTHER READING

GLOSSARY

Abuelita: Granny
Abuelos: Grandparents
Actos: Acts
Agringado: Americanized
Agua: Water
Al norte: Northern
Al principio: At the beginning
¡Alto!: Halt!
Amigo: Friend
¡Arree buey!: Giddyap!
Atole: Flavored thin corn mush or beverage
¡Ave María Purísima!: Good Lord! (equivalent)
Aztlán: Poetic name for Northern Mexico, now the South-
    west U.S., mythical land of the Aztecs; symbolic home-
    land of Chicanos
Baile: Dance, ball
Barrios: rural neighborhoods in Mexico; in U.S. ghettos
Bayo potro: Bay colt
Bizcochitos: wafers, biscuits or small bread
Bruja: Witch
Brujo: Sorcerer, witch doctor
Buena gente: Good people
Buenas noches: Good evening (greeting); good night (fare-
    well)
Bultos: Statues, images
Calabozo: Calaboose, jail
Caliche: Flaking wall plaster
Califas: Caliphs, people with pull or influence
Camarada: Comrade
Campesino: Peasant, farm worker
Campos: Fields

Campo santo: Cemetery

Cantina: Bar

¡Caramba!: An expression of surprise or emphasis

Carcelero: Jailer

Carga: Load

Carnalismo: Ethnic kinship

Carne adobada: Ragout of beef

Carreta: Horse-driven cart

Causa: Common cause

Cazuela: Earthenware pot, casserole

Centavos: Money; small change

Chicanismo: Chicano brotherhood

Chichi: Teat, breast

Chile con asadura: Chitterlings and peppers

Chorizo: Spanish sausage

Chueca y quemada: Games played with ball and pins

Cinco, seis, siete: Five, six, seven

Colonias: Residential sections

Comandante: Commandant, major

Compadres: Relationship between the godfather and the god-child's father; good friends, good neighbors

Compañero: Friend, companion

Con mucho gusto: With pleasure

Corrido: A romance or legend sung to a steady guitar rhythm

Cristóbal Colón: Christopher Columbus

Cuarta: Whip, riding crop

Cuentos: Short stories

Cuero: Hide, leather

Curandero: Healer

Curato: Parochial church

De todos nosotros: Ours

Dignidad y unidad: Dignity and unity

Dios me perdone: May God forgive me

Dios que la perdone: May God forgive her; leave her to heaven

Don(s): Spanish title used before masculine Christian names, formerly given only to noblemen and now used to connote respect

Duelos: Hardships

Dueña: Chaperone; owner, landlady

Duende: Elf; ghost

El alma: The soul

El espíritu duende: The ghost, the elf spirit

El Movimiento: The Movement

Escuadra: Straight, square (person)

Eso es lo que es: That's what it is, that's it

Esta tierra es nuestra: This land is ours

Estado Unidense: North American, of the United States

Familias: Families

Fandango: Spanish folk dance

Fiesta: Party, ball

Fuego: Fire

Gabacho: Frenchman (derogatory)

Gachupín: Spaniard (derogatory)

Gracias: Thanks

Gracias a Dios: Thank God

Greña: Hair

Gringo: White North American male; Anglo; foreigner

Gringuita: White American child; affectionate name for adult

Gritos: Shouts

Güeros chingados: Fucking blonds, damned Gringos

Guitarreros: Street singers, strolling musicians

Guitarristas: Guitar players

Hacendado: Farm owner, rancher, gentleman farmer

Hacienda: Farmstead

Hasta el infierno: Till we meet in hell

Hasta la Victoria Siempre: Till Victory Forever (one of the slogans of the Cuban Revolution, adopted by Latin American youth)

Hasta mañana: Good night (equivalent)

Hermanos y hermanas: Brothers and sisters

Hijo: Son

Hijo de la gran puta: Son of a whore

Hijo [of a] maldito malcriado: Spoiled son of a damned bastard

Hombre: Man; please!

Huelga: Labor strike

Jacal: Shack

Jamaicas: Bazaars

Jesucristo, perdona a tu hija: Jesus, forgive your daughter

Jesús, María y José me favorezcan: Jesus, Mary and Joseph help me

Juventud: Youth, young people

La Causa: The struggle; the cause

La Corre: Slang for the School of Corrections (reformatory) at Gatesville, Texas

Laguna: Lagoon

Linda: Beautiful

Los jóvenes: The young fellows

Machicueta: Acrobatics

Machos: Males, braggarts

Madre patria: Motherland

Maguey: The agave plant

Maldita suerte: Damned luck

Mal genio: Bad temper

Manito: The humble Mexican, John Doe

Mañana: Tomorrow

Mariachi: Typical Mexican folk band

Marquesa: Marquise

Matador: Star bullfighter

Mayordomo: Foreman

Misa: Mass

Mitos: Myths

Monos: Voodoo dolls

Monte: Wilderness

Morral: Knapsack

Muchachos: Boys

Muleta: The matador's fighting cape (held on a staff)

Nada: Nothing

Nomás: Nothing else, that's all

No somos mexicanos: We are not Mexicans

Nuestra juventud: Our youth, our young people

Nuestra Señora de Guadalupe: Our Lady of Guadalupe (patron saint of Mexico)

Olla: Cooking vessel—in this context, meaning an urn

Olvídense: Forget it

Oye . . . ¿dónde están?: Listen . . . where are they?

Pachucos: Zoot-suiters

Padre: Father, priest
Picardía: Archness, roguishness
Pobrecita: Poor little one
Pocho: Americanized Mexican
Portal: Porch, doorway
Portón: Main door
Primero: First
¡Qué gacho!: What a drag! (How tragic!)
¡Qué horror!: How awful!
?Qué pasó, chamaco?: What happened, kid?
?Qué pasó, corazón?: What happened, sweetheart?
Querida: Dear
¡Qué suerte!: How lucky!
Rancheros: Cowboys, wranglers
Rancho: Ranch
Rascachi: Low, humble and ribald (Chicano humor)
Raza: Race, people
Reata: Rope, lariat
Reina del barrio: Queen of the neighborhood or ghetto
Reo: Accused, prisoner
Retablo: Altar piece
Sala de recibo: Living room
Salas: Salons, auditoriums
San Anto: San Antonio (city)
San Jo: San Jose (city)
Santo: Saint
Sarape: Mexican blanket used as a cloak
Sea por Dios: Be it as God wishes
Señor: Sir, mister
Señora: Lady
Señores: Gentlemen
Sobrinos y nietos: Nephews and grandchildren
Socorro: Help
Surcos: Furrows
Tacos, tamales, tortillas: Typical Mexican food
Teatro campesino: Rural theater group
Testigo: Witness
Texano: Texan
Tierra: Land, earth

Tilma: Small, rough poncho

Tonta: fool

Tricolor: The Mexican flag

Trovas y décimas: Romances and ballads

Vámonos: Let's go

Vaquero: Cowboy

Vendido: Sold-out, cop-out

Yesca: Marihuana (also, hallucinatory mushroom)

Zarape: Same as *sarape*

SUGGESTED FURTHER READING

ELIU CARRANZA, *Pensamientos on Los Chicanos: A Cultural Revolution* (Berkeley: California Book Co., 1969).

ABELARDO DELGADO, *The Chicano Movement: Some Not Too Objective Observations* (Denver: Totinem Press, 1971).

AURELIO M. ESPINOSA, "New Mexican Spanish Folk-Lore," *Journal of American Folk Lore* (October-December, 1910).

JOSÉ ANGEL GUTIÉRREZ and MARIO COMPEAN, *La Raza Unida Party in Texas* (New York: Pathfinder Press, 1970).

W. STORRS LEE (ed.), "At Six Dollars an Ounce," *California: A Literary Chronicle* (New York, 1968).

GILBERTO LOPEZ Y RIVAS, *Los Chicanos: Una Minoría Nacional Explotada*, Editorial, *Nuestro Tiempo:* Mexico, 1971.

CAREY McWILLIAMS, *North from Mexico* (New York: Greenwood Press, 1968).

NATIONAL EDUCATION ASSOCIATION, *The Invisible Minority: Report of the NEA-Tucson Survey on the Teaching of Spanish to the Spanish-Speaking* (Washington, D.C.: NEA, Department of Rural Education, 1966).

PHILIP D. ORTEGO, "The Education of Mexican-Americans," *The New Mexico Review* (Part I, September, 1969; Part II, October, 1969); "Mexican-Americans and the Schools," *Idea* (Winter 1971–1972); "Schools for Mexican-Americans: Between Two Cultures," *Saturday Review* (April 17, 1971); and "Which Southwestern Literature and Culture in the English Classroom?" *Arizona English Bulletin* (April, 1971).

PHILIP D. ORTEGO and JOSÉ A. CARRASCO, "Chicanos and American Literature," *Searching for America* (Champaign, Ill.: NCTE, 1972).

THOMAS M. PEARCE, "American Traditions and Our Histories of Literature," *American Literature* XIV, 3 (November, 1942).

FRANCISCO RÍOS, "The Mexican in Fact, Fiction, and Folklore," *El Grito: A Journal of Contemporary Mexican-American Thought* (Summer 1969).

RUBÉN SALAZAR, *Strangers in One's Land* (Washington, D.C.: U.S. Commission on Civil Rights, U.S. Government Printing Office, 1970).

GEORGE I. SÁNCHEZ, *Forgotten People: A Study of New Mexicans* (University of New Mexico Press, 1940).

EDWARD SIMMEN (ed.), "Preface," *The Chicano: From Caricature to Self-Portrait* (New York: New American Library, 1971).